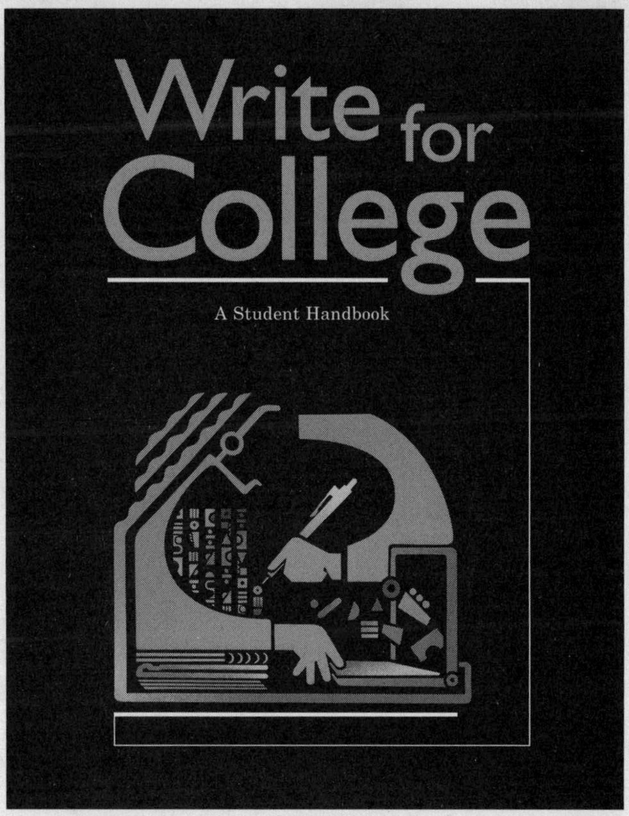

. . . a teacher's guide to accompany

Write for College

WRITE SOURCE®

GREAT SOURCE EDUCATION GROUP
a division of Houghton Mifflin Company
Wilmington, Massachusetts
www.greatsource.com

A few words about the *Teacher's Guide*

The *Write for College Teacher's Guide* reflects the latest thinking on a number of writing-related issues. It will . . .

- introduce you to the handbook,
- discuss approaches for using *Write for College* as a writing and learning resource,
- review current trends in language instruction, and
- provide you with a series of writing workshops.

We are genuinely enthused about this *Teacher's Guide,* just as we are about the handbook itself. We hope that after you've seen our materials, you'll share our enthusiasm. If you have any questions, suggestions, or observations, please let us know. We'd love to hear from you at contact@thewritesource.com.

Written and Compiled by

Patrick Sebranek, Dave Kemper, and Verne Meyer

Contributors and consultants: Laura Bachman, Ron Bachman, Gary Baughn, Mark Bazata, Bev Jessen, Rob King, Lester Smith, Vicki Spandel, Connie Stephens, John Van Rys, Claire Ziffer

Printed in the United States of America

International Standard Book Number: 978-0-669-00042-9

3 4 5 6 7 8 9 10 -BNM- 12 11 10 09

Contents

A **Quick Tour** of *Write for College*

Write for College serves as the perfect writing and learning handbook for advanced-placement high school students. It will help students improve their abilities to write (prewriting through publishing), to think (creatively and analytically), and to learn (in the classroom, in small groups, and independently). This quick tour highlights the nine main sections of the handbook.

Overview of the Handbook

What are the key sections of *Write for College*?

The *Write for College* handbook is divided into nine major sections, each dealing with a key area of writing and language learning:

The Process of Writing emphasizes techniques that help writers move through the steps of generating and selecting material, drafting and revising, and, finally, polishing, editing, and proofreading. The traits of effective writing are stressed throughout the process of writing.

The Basic Elements of Writing deals with specific challenges in the writing process—crafting and expanding sentences, developing strong paragraphs, and learning the basics of the academic essay.

The **Writer's Resource** explains the rhetoric (style) of writing; covers common writing problems and the use of clear, fair language; and offers a glossary of writing terms and techniques.

The Forms of Writing offers help for composing 23 forms (personal, report, analytical, and persuasive) of writing. There's also a section on writing about literature. Each form is introduced by a one-page set of guidelines followed by both a student model and a professional model.

The Research Center clearly and thoroughly describes the steps in the research process. Sample parenthetical references and bibliographic entries are given for MLA and APA research styles. Information is included on using and citing electronic sources along with models of each type of paper.

The Tools of Learning includes information about improving reading and note-taking skills, critical listening, and test-taking skills. Special emphasis is also given to formal speaking and multimedia presentations.

The Testing Center features guidelines for on-demand writing situations, responding to document-based questions, preparing for AP exams, and approaching college-entrance exams.

The **Proofreader's Guide** is a handbook within a handbook, answering any questions a writer might have concerning punctuation, grammar, usage, and mechanics.

The **Almanac** includes useful lists to make *Write for College* an across-the-curriculum reference.

How does *Write for College* teach writing?

The *Write for College* handbook presents brief guidelines that lead writers through the writing process, "Quick Guides" that offer helpful tips, and numerous models of how students and professionals write.

For writers trying to solve simple, immediate problems, *Write for College* presents short sections of information easily accessed with the index. For writers trying to solve more complex, extensive problems, *Write for College* presents entire chapters and in-depth information on the writing process—from prewriting and drafting to editing and publishing.

The handbook presents language and learning concepts for all high school students. The (ELL) English Language Learner Considerations in the chapter notes provide additional language acquisition support for ELL students.

How should you use the *Write for College Teacher's Guide*?

In addition to the chapter notes and objectives, numerous other instructional suggestions provide the basis for planning a writing syllabus. The trait-based writing workshops can be used as suggested in the teacher's notes, with writing groups, or independently as needed. The cross-curricular writing assignments provide starting points for making writing a vital part of learning in any discipline.

1 The Process of Writing

This section helps students understand that writing is a process of exploring and shaping meaning. Checklists for using the traits of effective writing during the writing process give students a foundation for developing and assessing their own writing.

20

Checklist for Effective Writing

If a piece of writing meets the following standards, it exhibits the traits of effective writing. Check your work using these standards.

Ideas

The writing . . .

____ maintains a clear, specific focus or purpose.
____ presents information that elaborates on the focus.
____ holds the reader's attention and answers questions about the topic.

Organization

____ includes a clear beginning, middle, and ending.
____ contains specific details—arranged in the best order—to support the main ideas.

Voice

____ speaks to the intended audience.
____ shows that the writer cares about the topic.

Word Choice

____ contains specific nouns, active verbs, and colorful modifiers.
____ presents an appropriate level of formality or informality.

Sentence Fluency

____ flows smoothly from sentence to sentence.
____ displays varied sentence beginnings and lengths.

Conventions and Presentation

____ adheres to the rules of grammar, capitalization, spelling, and punctuation.
____ follows established guidelines for presentation.

1

One Writer's Process

How do you get from the start ("My sociology instructor gave me this writing assignment.") to the finish ("This may be my best essay yet.")? You may know the answer already: You use the writing process. This important process can help you . . .

- collect and focus your thoughts (*prewriting*),
- generate an initial version of your writing *(drafting)*,
- improve upon your writing *(revising)*, and
- prepare it for submission *(editing/proofreading)*.

You should also remember that (1) the writing process is personal—different writers follow different routes; (2) it's reciprocal—you may, for example, go from *revising* back to *prewriting* and then to *revising* again; and (3) it's adaptable to any writing task—from research papers to responding to prompts.

WHAT'S AHEAD

In this chapter, you will see firsthand how a writer uses the writing process to shape an initial writing idea into an effective personal essay.

2 The Basic Elements of Writing

This section provides students with information about writing effective sentences and developing strong paragraphs. It also discusses and models the basic academic essay.

75

Developing Strong Paragraphs

When it comes to writing well, you must remember these two words: support and organization. You need to select details that support your main point, and you need to organize those details effectively. That's where one basic form of writing, the paragraph, comes into play. Paragraphs help you organize your thoughts and make it easier for the reader to follow your line of thinking.

During the sometimes messy revising process, it is the paragraph that enables you to rearrange your details into logical units that deliver a strong, clear message from start to finish. You'll know your writing succeeds when each paragraph works by itself and with the others that come before and after it.

WHAT'S AHEAD

This chapter reviews the parts and types of paragraphs and includes information about understanding and arranging details. You'll find a helpful chart of transitional words and phrases.

3 Writer's Resource

This section addresses matters of style, from how to develop a sense of style to how to avoid common writing problems that hamper a writer's style. It also covers designing writing and common writing terms and techniques.

Developing a Sense of Style

How can you best develop your writing style, your special way of saying something? You can begin by reading the information below, which explains how accomplished writers learn about and practice stylistic writing. The two pages after that discuss the style matrix as well as specific qualities of effective style.

Becoming a Student of Writing

- **Read widely.** William Faulkner was once asked what advice he would give to young writers. He said, "Read everything—trash, classics, good and bad, and see how they do it. . . . Read! You'll absorb it. Then write." Follow Faulkner's advice, and gain an appreciation for the written word in all of its different forms.
- **Be on the lookout** for those unique slices of life that can add so much to your writing. You may enjoy this "slice" recorded in Ken Macrorie's book *Uptaught*:

  An elderly, sparse man who makes a career out of auditing classes is sitting next to me taking notes on both sides of a paper. Now he turns it upside down and writes over his own notes.
- **Keep track of your reading and observing.** Get into the habit of recording and reflecting upon your experiences. Some of these ideas may later serve as inspiration or models for your own writing.
- **Experiment with a variety of writing forms.** In the process, sharpen your writing abilities: Journaling promotes writing fluency. Corresponding helps you develop your writing voice. Writing articles gives you a sense of form and structure. Crafting poems helps you gain an appreciation for word choice.
- **Write to learn.** Writing helps you examine ideas and feelings more thoughtfully. As Ray Bradbury once said, writing "lets the world burn through you." The more experiences you have as a writer (exploring your personal thoughts), the better able you will be to express yourself intelligently, meaningfully, and stylistically.
- **Understand the basics.** Gain an understanding of the core traits of writing: *ideas, organization, voice, word choice, sentence fluency,* and *conventions.* (Your handbook will help you in all of these areas.) Also begin to build your writing vocabulary. Learn, for example, what it means *to narrate* or *to analyze.* Know the difference between terms like *active* and *passive, abstract* and *concrete.*

Analytical Writing

The word *analysis* means "to break apart" or "to loosen." An effective analysis explores a topic, examines the parts, compares them, and puts them back together again. This cerebral process of breaking down and rebuilding happens everywhere in the world—from the Senate floor to a lecture hall to Al's garage.

Analyses use a variety of mental "muscles." You might break a process into steps, compare and contrast objects, classify strategies or practices, define a complex term, trace the causes and effects of a phenomenon, explain a problem and advocate a solution, or evaluate the merits of a new trend. Whatever strategy you choose for your analysis, in the end, you must demonstrate that you have rigorously worked through the topic and understand it fully.

WHAT'S AHEAD

In this section, you will find guidelines and models for many types of analytical writing: process, comparison, classification, definition, cause and effect, problem and solution, and evaluation.

"Writing is how we think our way into a subject and make it our own."
—William Zinsser

Guidelines

Writing an Essay of Argumentation

An essay of argumentation presents a sensible discussion of a topic based on thorough research and logical thinking. This type of essay centers on a debatable proposition and a carefully crafted argument featuring convincing supporting evidence and reasonable counters to opposing points of view. The essay should enlighten as well as persuade. Follow these guidelines.

PREWRITING

Select a topic. Review your texts or class notes for topics. Also consider issues you hear debated locally or nationally. Find a topic that is serious, specific, timely, and debatable.

Research the topic. Begin by writing down your first thoughts. Then collect as much information as necessary through reading, interviewing, observing, and so on.

Develop a proposition. Write down the proposition that you want to defend. Then list at least three solid arguments supporting it. Also write down arguments against it and ways to counter them.

WRITING

Write your first draft. Introduce your topic and lead to your proposition. In the middle paragraphs, argue by providing a variety of support and answering major objections. In the ending, summarize your argument and make a final case for your stand.

REVISING

Check your ideas. *Is my proposition clearly stated and debatable? Have I included a variety of compelling support? Have I countered significant objections?*

Review your organization. *Do I have a strong beginning, middle, and ending? Have I built my argument in the most logical, convincing way? Do I use transitions to connect the ideas in my sentences and paragraphs?*

Revise for voice, word choice, and sentence fluency. *Does my voice sound both knowledgeable and persuasive? Does my word choice demonstrate my thorough understanding of the topic? Have I created sentences that flow smoothly?*

EDITING

Check for conventions. *Have I used correct punctuation, capitalization, spelling, and grammar?*

PUBLISHING

Present your work. Read your essay to your class, or stage a debate between yourself and someone who holds an opposing view.

Persuasive

4 The Forms of Writing

This section provides students with information, guidelines, and student and professional samples of a wide variety of writing forms—from journal entries to the essay of argumentation, from a summary or a report to the business letter.

5 The Research Center

Students learn everything they need to know about conducting research, including writing responsibly and citing both print and electrontic sources using MLA and APA style. Complete sample MLA and APA research papers are also provided.

MLA Research Paper

Writer and teacher Ken Macrorie says, "Good writing is formed partly through plan and partly through accident." His words certainly apply to the process of writing a research paper. Producing an effective finished product requires a great deal of planning, from selecting and researching an intriguing topic to organizing your ideas for writing. But a truly memorable paper is also born of wrong turns, unexpected discoveries, and of your own thoughts and feelings developed during the research process.

As you read the sample MLA paper that follows, keep Macrorie's quotation in mind. Is Fidel Novielli's research paper the result of careful planning? Is it also an expression of the writer's thoughts and feelings about his topic?

WHAT'S AHEAD

Novielli's paper deals with an important social issue: the rise of private entrepreneurs who tackle public problems. As you will see, he refers to a variety of sources, including books, magazines, and Web sites, in his research. The sample paper also demonstrates MLA documentation style.

Title Page and Outline
Research Paper
Works-Cited Page

Avoiding Plagiarism

You owe it to your sources, your readers, and yourself to give credit for other people's words and ideas used in your writing. Not only is this the legal thing to do, it's also the smart thing to do. Citing sources adds authority to your writing. Using sources without giving credit is called *plagiarism*, the act of presenting someone else's ideas as your own. Don't plagiarize.

Forms of Plagiarism

- **Submitting another writer's paper:** The most blatant form of plagiarism is to put your name on someone else's work (another student's paper, an essay bought from a "paper mill," the text of an article from the Internet, and so on).
- **Using copy-and-paste:** It is unethical to copy phrases, sentences, or larger sections from a source and paste them into your paper without giving credit for the material. Even if you change a few words, this is still plagiarism.
- **Neglecting necessary quotation marks:** Whether you quote just a phrase or a larger section of text, you must put the exact words of the source in quotation marks and cite them.
- **Paraphrasing without citing a source:** Paraphrasing (rephrasing ideas in your own words) is an important research skill. However, paraphrased ideas must be credited to the source, even if you entirely reword the material.
- **Confusing borrowed material with your own ideas:** While taking research notes, it's important to identify the source of each idea you record. Then you will know whom to credit as you write your paper.

Other Source Abuses

- **Using sources inaccurately:** Make certain your quotation or paraphrase accurately reflects the meaning of the original. Don't twist someone else's words to support your own ideas.
- **Overusing source material:** Your paper should be primarily your thoughts and words, supported by outside sources. If you simply string together quotations and paraphrases, your own voice will be lost.
- **"Plunking" source material:** When you write, smoothly incorporate any outside material. Dropping in quotations or paraphrases with no introduction or comment creates choppy, disconnected writing.
- **Relying too heavily on one source:** If your writing is dominated by one source, readers may doubt the depth and integrity of your research.

Using a Note-Taking Guide

Note taking helps you listen in class, organize your teacher's ideas, and remember what was said. However, there are pitfalls. You can take so many notes that you are overwhelmed when it comes to reviewing them, or you can take notes in such a haphazard fashion that it's impossible to follow them. That's when a note-taking guide comes into play. The right guide can help you coordinate your textbook, lecture, and review notes into an efficient system.

Keeping Text and Presentation Notes Together

If the lecturer closely follows the textbook, try using your reading-assignment notes as a classroom note-taking guide. As you follow your reading notes, you will be prepared to answer your teacher's questions and take additional notes as well. Simply jot down anything that clarifies the material for you. Combining your reading and classroom notes in this way will give you one set of well-organized study notes.

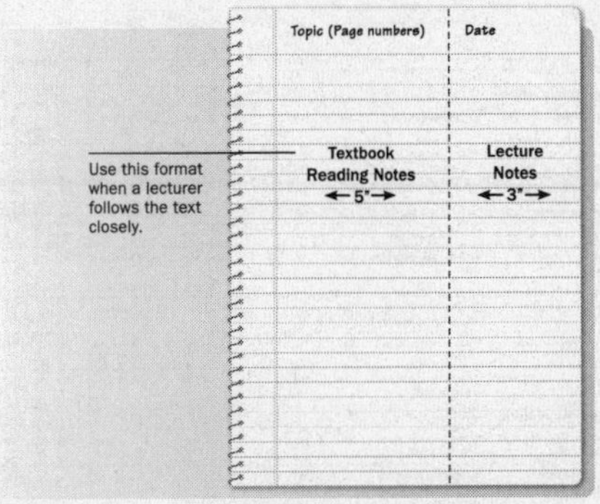

NOTE: Use the left two-thirds of your paper for reading notes; use the right one-third for class notes.

6 The Tools of Learning

Write for College provides up-to-date guidelines for searching for information. Learning skills such as critical reading, vocabulary building, speaking, and test taking are also covered. These study and learning tips give students an advantage across the curriculum as well as prepare them for AP tests and college-placement exams.

7 The Testing Center

This section covers a variety of testing situations—from general classroom and standardized tests to on-demand writing assignments, such as answering document-based questions and writing for AP and college-entrance exams.

473

Answering Document-Based Questions

In one of your classes, perhaps a history class, you may be asked to respond to a document-based question (DBQ), often as part of an exam. A DBQ requires that you analyze a series of related documents that may include excerpts from books, magazines, Web pages, diaries, or other text sources. Visual documents, such as photographs, maps, editorial cartoons, tables, graphs, or time lines, may also be included.

In most cases, a DBQ asks you to write an essay, drawing information from the documents as well as from material you have previously learned. Sometimes you may be asked to glean information from one or more documents and present it in a different form, perhaps as a graph or a table. In either situation, you must work quickly and accurately because time is not on your side: You may have no more than 60 minutes to form your response.

WHAT'S AHEAD

This chapter will help you respond to document-based questions. It offers responding tips plus a sample DBQ with corresponding documents and response essay.

Responding Tips
Sample Documents
Sample DBQ and Response

Marking Punctuation 509

"Cut out all those exclamation marks. An exclamation mark is like laughing at your own joke."
—F. Scott Fitzgerald

Marking Punctuation

Period

509.1 At the End of a Sentence

Use a **period** at the end of a sentence that makes a statement, requests something, or gives a mild command.

(Statement) **The man who does not read good books has no advantage over the man who can't read them.** —Mark Twain

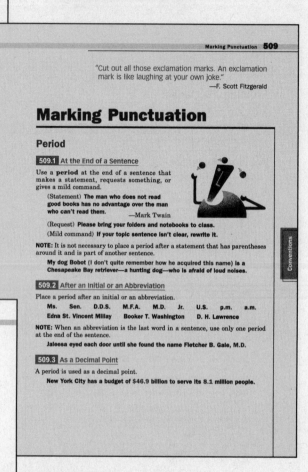

(Request) **Please bring your folders and notebooks to class.**

(Mild command) **If your topic sentence isn't clear, rewrite it.**

NOTE: It is not necessary to place a period after a statement that has parentheses around it and is part of another sentence.

My dog Bobot (I don't quite remember how he acquired this name) is a Chesapeake Bay retriever—a hunting dog—who is afraid of loud noises.

Conventions

509.2 After an Initial or an Abbreviation

Place a period after an initial or an abbreviation.

Ms. Sen. D.D.S. M.F.A. M.D. Jr. U.S. p.m. a.m.
Edna St. Vincent Millay Booker T. Washington D. H. Lawrence

NOTE: When an abbreviation is the last word in a sentence, use only one period at the end of the sentence.

Jaleesa eyed each door until she found the name Fletcher B. Gale, M.D.

509.3 As a Decimal Point

A period is used as a decimal point.

New York City has a budget of $46.9 billion to serve its 8.1 million people.

596

Common Parliamentary Procedures

Motion	Purpose	Needs Second	Debatable	Amend-able	Required Vote	May Interrupt Speaker	Subsidiary Motion Applied
I. ORIGINAL OR PRINCIPAL MOTION							
1. Main Motion (general) Main Motions (specific)	To introduce business	Yes	Yes	Yes	Majority	No	Yes
a. To take from the table	To consider tabled motion	Yes	No	No	Majority	No	No
b. To reconsider	To reconsider previous motion	Yes	When original motion is	No	Majority	Yes	No
c. To rescind	To nullify or wipe out previous action	Yes	Yes	Yes	Majority or two-thirds	No	No
II. SUBSIDIARY MOTIONS							
2. To lay on the table	To defer action	Yes	No	No	Majority	No	No
3. To call for previous question	To close debate and force vote	Yes	No	No	Two-thirds	No	Yes
4. To limit or extend limits of debate	To control time of debate	Yes	No	Yes	Two-thirds	No	Yes
5. To postpone to a certain time	To defer action	Yes	Yes	Yes	Majority	No	Yes
6. To refer to a committee	To provide for special study	Yes	Yes	Yes	Majority	No	Yes
7. To amend	To modify a motion	Yes	When original motion is	Yes (once only)	Majority	No	Yes
8. To postpone indefinitely	To suppress action	Yes	Yes	No	Majority	No	Yes
III. PRIVILEGED MOTIONS							
9. To raise a point of order	To correct error in procedure	No	No	No	Decision of chair	Yes	No
10. To appeal for a decision of chair	To change decision on procedure	Yes	If motion does not relate to indecorum	No	Majority or tie	Yes	No
11. To withdraw a motion	To remove a motion	No	No	No	Majority	No	No
12. To divide a motion	To modify a motion	No	No	Yes	Majority	No	Yes
13. To object to consideration	To suppress action	No	No	No	Two-thirds	Yes	No
14. To call for division of house	To secure a countable vote	No	No	No	Majority if chair desires	Yes	Yes
15. To suspend rules	To alter existing rules and order of business	Yes	No	No	Two-thirds	No	No
16. To close nominations	To stop nomination of officers	Yes	No	Yes	Two-thirds	No	Yes
17. To reopen nominations	To permit additional nominations	Yes	No	Yes	Majority	No	Yes
IV. INCIDENTAL MOTIONS							
18. To call for orders of the day	To keep assembly to order of business	No	No	No	None unless objection	Yes	No
19. To raise question of privilege	To make a request concerning rights of assembly	No	No	No	Decision of chair	Yes	No
20. To take a recess	To dismiss meeting for specific time	Yes	No, if made when another question is before the assembly	Yes	Majority	No	Yes
21. To adjourn	To dismiss meeting	Yes	No	Yes	Majority	No	No
22. To fix time at which to adjourn	To set time for the continuation of this meeting	Yes	No, if made when another question is before the assembly	Yes	Majority	No	Yes

8 Proofreader's Guide

The Proofreader's Guide, or the "Yellow Pages," provides students with answers to their questions about punctuation, mechanics, using the right word, parts of speech, and using the language. Explanations and examples illustrate the basic conventions.

9 Student Almanac

This information makes *Write for College* a valuable resource in any class.

Teacher's Notes

Chapter-by-Chapter Notes

Standards-Based Instruction

Today, teachers are expected to use standards to inform instruction. Standards are the tools used to justify and document what is being taught and what students are achieving. As you will see on the next five pages, *Write for College* can serve as an important resource for planning instruction that meets the essential *writing standards* developed at the national, state, or local level. (The performance standards that follow reflect the writing skills and forms that students should understand and employ.)

The Process of Writing

Understanding How Writing Works

The student is expected to . . .	*Write for College*
■ **use** prewriting strategies, such as freewriting and clustering, to generate and collect ideas for writing.	21–30
■ **use** appropriate reference materials and resources as needed during the writing process.	29, 322–323, 383–392, 393–399
■ **review** a collection of her or his own writing to determine its strengths and weaknesses and to set goals as a writer.	20, 59
■ **establish** a central idea *(topic sentence, focus or thesis statement)*, collect details, and organize supporting information for writing.	30, 76, 320–321
■ **apply** different methods of support, including statistics, quotations, anecdotes, definitions, sensory details, and so on.	34–35, 80–83, 136–138, 332
■ **revise** selected drafts by adding, deleting, and rearranging copy—striving for effective content, logical organization, and appropriate voice.	8–11, 14, 39–52
■ **edit** drafts to ensure smooth-reading sentences, effective word choice, and clear and accurate copy.	12–13, 14, 53–56
■ **use** available technology to support aspects of prewriting, drafting, revising, editing, and publishing texts.	57–61

Evaluating Written Work

The student is expected to . . .	*Write for College*
■ **assess** writing according to the traits of effective writing.	15–20, 44–45
■ **respond** in constructive ways to others' writing.	49–52
■ **use** published examples as models for writing.	15–20, 73, 240–243, 268
■ **consider** his or her purpose and audience when developing writing.	29, 41, 46, 51, 134–135

The Forms of Writing

Writing to Share

The student is expected to develop . . .	*Write for College*
■ **personal narratives** that . . . • focus on specific experiences. • develop three key elements: characterization, setting, and action. • begin in the middle of the action, focus on the essential details, and end right after the most important narrative moment. • reveal the significance of, or the writer's attitude about, the subject.	81, 85, 145
■ **expository compositions** that . . . • engage the interest of the reader and state a clear focus. • elaborate on the focus with supportive details. • follow an organizational pattern appropriate to the form. • conclude with a summary linked to the purpose of the composition.	80, 84–87, 161–185
■ **persuasive compositions** that . . . • state a clear position or focus. • include relevant and organized support. • differentiate between fact and opinion. • anticipate and address the reader's significant concerns and counterarguments.	81, 229–253
■ **reflective compositions** that . . . • examine the importance of personal experiences and events. • establish an effective balance between the description of the experience or event and the reflective details. • reveal significant insight and a greater understanding of the experience, position, event, or life in general.	146–155
■ **research reports and papers** that . . . • originate with an important, relevant subject. • focus on a specific part or main idea about the subject. • present a clear and organized discussion or argument. • use a variety of primary and secondary sources. • support the focus or thesis with facts, specific details, and examples from multiple sources. • provide clear and accurate documentation.	317–326, 394–395

Writing to Share (continued)

The student is expected to develop . . .	*Write for College*
■ **summaries** that . . . • highlight the main idea and significant details in a reading selection. • reflect a clear understanding of the selection.	424–426
■ **responses to literature** that . . . • develop interpretations exhibiting a careful reading and understanding of the literary work. • take a point of view and support it with textual references. • display a personal connection with the literary work.	280–297
■ **business and workplace forms** that . . . • are purposeful and address a specific audience. • follow the conventions and style for the respective form.	299–309, 310–315
■ **multimedia presentations** that . . . • combine text, images, and sound from a number of different media. • use each medium effectively.	459–461

Writing to Learn

The student is expected to . . .	*Write for College*
■ **write to learn** in all subjects by . . . • keeping dialogue journals. • using learning logs. • writing response journals. • making lists. • summarizing or paraphrasing what is heard or read. • connecting knowledge within and across the disciplines. • synthesizing information.	23, 143, 422–423

The Mechanics of Writing

Research

The student is expected to . . .	*Write for College*
■ **organize** prior knowledge about a topic using graphic organizers or other prewriting strategies.	24–28
■ **generate** questions to direct research.	28
■ **use** various reference materials such as the dictionary, encyclopedia, almanac, thesaurus, atlas, and online information as aids to writing.	383–399
■ **use** print and electronic sources to locate books and articles.	383–392, 393–399
■ **take** notes from sources such as guest speakers, periodicals, books, online sites, and so on.	322, 413–420
■ **summarize** and organize ideas taken from multiple sources.	163, 323, 330–331
■ **evaluate** the research and frame new questions for further investigation.	318, 322
■ **follow** accepted formats for writing research papers, including documenting sources.	324–326, 333–350, 361–370
■ **give** credit for quotations and information in a bibliography (*works-cited page*).	339–350, 360, 365–370

Grammar and Usage

The student is expected to . . .	*Write for College*
■ **employ** standard English—including correct subject-verb agreement, pronoun-antecedent agreement, verb forms, and so on—to communicate clearly and effectively in writing.	567–572, 588–590
■ **understand** the different parts of speech.	561–579
■ **write** in complete sentences (and eliminate sentence errors in writing).	63–65, 576–579
■ **vary** the types of sentences in writing (*simple, compound, complex*).	576
■ **use** conjunctions to connect ideas meaningfully.	72, 88–89, 578

Grammar and Usage (continued)

The student is expected to . . .	*Write for College*
■ **make** writing precise and vivid using action verbs, specific nouns, and colorful modifiers.	118–119
■ **learn** vocabulary-building strategies.	429–444
■ **correctly use** commonly misused words.	551–556

Punctuation, Capitalization, and Spelling

The student is expected to . . .	*Write for College*
■ **use** correct punctuation and capitalization in writing.	509–528, 529–544
■ **spell** accurately in final drafts, including frequently misspelled words, contractions, plurals, and homophones.	520–522, 532–533, 538–543, 551–560
■ **spell** derivatives correctly.	434–444, 538
■ **use** syllable constructions and syllable boundary patterns to spell correctly.	390–391

The Process of Writing Teacher's Notes

One Writer's Process

Write for College, 1–14

Novelist John Steinbeck called writing a "strange and mystic business" because crafting a text is full of so many uncertainties: *What should I write about? How should I start? How can I keep the reader interested?* And on and on. Thinking of writing as a process or series of steps helps demystify writing. This chapter shows how one student uses the writing process to develop a personal essay. Each step in the process is modeled, from prewriting to publishing. Along the way, some of the complexity and "messiness" of the process is demonstrated, with ideas and words cut or moved and new material added as the writer improves and refines his work.

Of Special Interest

- "Prewriting" demonstrates different ways students can gather information, including freewriting, clustering, questioning, and researching. (pages 2–5)
- "Revising" shows how effective writing takes shape—by making a variety of changes to improve the ideas, organization, voice, sentence fluency, and word choice in the piece. (pages 8–11)
- "Editing" demonstrates the types of changes that are necessary to ensure that a piece of writing is accurate. (pages 12–14)
- The writing process is recursive, so writers are encouraged not to think of it as a linear process. (page 14)

Rationale

- Taking students through one writer's process helps them to understand how the writing process can work for them.

Major Concepts

- Student writers should approach writing as a process rather than an end product. (page 1)
- Planning before writing is essential. (pages 2–5)
- The goal of a first draft is to get all the ideas on paper, without worrying about every word and comma being correct. (pages 6–7)
- Revising and editing are two separate steps. Revising focuses on improving the content of the writing; editing focuses on accuracy. (pages 8–14)

Performance Standards

Students are expected to . . .

- follow the steps necessary to produce an effective piece of writing.

One Writer's Process

Start-Up Activity

Before you review the chapter with students, list the steps of the writing process on the board. Ask students to explain the type of work typically involved in each step. Also discuss the value of the writing process. (During this discussion, stress the significance of prewriting and revising.) You may also want to discuss with students one or more of the following writing-related quotations. Ask students to "place" the quotation within the writing process.

> **"Writing comes more easily if you have something to say."**
> —Sholem Asch

> **"By the time I reach the fifth version, my writing begins to have its own voice."**
> —Ashley Bryan

> **"I believe in impulse and naturalness, but followed by discipline in the cutting."**
> —Anaïs Nin

> **"I think one is constantly startled by the things that appear before you on the page while you write."**
> —Shirley Hazzard

ELL Consideration

Students may be reluctant to cross out words, add ideas, and otherwise change a developing text. Whenever students need a reminder concerning this point, direct them to pages 8–11, which show how the student writer revised his first draft. Remind students that the primary key to improving a text is to address the ideas, organization, and voice in the writing.

Extension Activity

After reviewing the chapter, have students freewrite for 8 to 10 minutes in order to explore their own process of writing. During their freewriting, students should compare their own process of writing with the process demonstrated in the chapter. Afterward, ask for volunteers to share parts of their writing with the class for discussion.

Minilessons

Any Questions, TG 226

Traits of Writing

Write for College, 15–20

Ernest Hemingway stated, "Prose is architecture, not interior decoration," meaning that effective writing is grounded in the essentials, the key traits of writing—*ideas, organization, voice, word choice,* and so on. This chapter introduces students to the six traits of writing. Each trait is defined and modeled to show quality writing in action.

NOTE: The traits are also addressed in the process and forms chapters in *Write for College.*

Of Special Interest

- The "Quick Guide" defines each trait clearly and concisely, showing why it is important to good writing. (page 16)
- The "Checklist for Effective Writing" gives students a quick way to assess the overall effectiveness of any piece of writing. (page 20)

Rationale

- Defining the traits and showing them in action will help students understand the elements of good writing.
- Working with the traits will help students become better writers.

Major Concepts

- Effective writing has specific features, or traits, that can be identified and described. (page 16)
- Students who know about the traits can use them to assess the strengths and weaknesses in their own writing and in their classmates' writing. (pages 17–19)

Performance Standards

Students are expected to . . .

- assess writing according to specific standards.
- analyze writing samples.
- review collections of their own written work to determine strengths and weaknesses and to set writing goals.

Traits of Writing

Start-Up Activity

Share a professional or student writing sample with the class. Ask students to assess the quality of the writing. List their comments on the board; then ask students what criteria they used to make their assessment. Next, list the traits of writing on the board and inform students that these qualities serve as an effective assessment guide. Demonstrate how the traits can be used to evaluate the writing sample.

ELL Considerations

Two traits of effective writing—voice and word choice—will be difficult for students to assess in their own work. Until they become more fluent in English, have your students focus more attention on the other traits, especially ideas and organization. To help students with word choice, display word charts around the room, including ones that provide synonyms for overused words.

Extension Activity

On a regular basis, have students assess writing, using the traits of writing as a guide. The "Checklist for Effective Writing" (page 20) serves as an efficient guide for these assessments. Make sure students practice both *formative* assessments (evaluating writing in progress) and *summative* assessments (evaluating completed pieces).

Minilessons

Sizing Up the Situation, TG 226
Great-Ideas Exchange, TG 226
Work the System, TG 227
Making Connections, TG 227
A Deal for You, TG 227
Bigger Not Always Better, TG 227

A Guide to Prewriting

Write for College, 21–30

Writer Georgia Heard states, "Writing is not easy. We all have scars." To ease the "pain," it's critical that student writers pay proper attention to prewriting, the first step in the writing process. Prewriting refers to all of those things a writer should do before beginning a first draft—selecting an effective topic, gathering details about it, forming a thesis or focus for writing, and organizing the appropriate details. This chapter will help students begin an essay assignment, offering a variety of selecting and shaping strategies, easy-to-use graphic organizers, and tips for forming a thesis statement.

Of Special Interest

- "Selecting a Topic" and "Shaping a Topic" help writers select specific topics and gather details about them. (pages 22–25)
- "Using Graphic Organizers" offers 10 forms to help writers gather and organize details. (pages 27–28)

Rationale

- Students need strategies to help them choose appropriate writing topics and collect and organize details for writing.

Major Concepts

- Prewriting involves selecting and developing a topic. (page 22)
- Strategies such as freewriting, clustering, and listing help students identify specific writing topics. (pages 24–25)
- After some initial prewriting, students should take inventory of their progress. (page 29)
- A student must develop a specific thesis or focus for a topic before beginning a first draft. (page 30)

Performance Standards

Students are expected to . . .

- use prewriting strategies, such as freewriting and clustering, to generate and collect ideas for writing.
- use appropriate reference materials and resources during prewriting.
- consider purpose and audience when planning writing.
- collect details, establish a central idea (thesis or focus statement), and organize supporting information for writing.

A Guide to Prewriting

Start-Up Activity

Write on the board this quotation by Joyce Carol Oates: " . . . as soon as you connect with your true subject, you will write." Ask students to react to the quotation, focusing on what it means to "connect with a subject." Then read the opening page in the chapter (page 21). Point out that "connecting with a subject" is only part of prewriting; shaping and focusing a subject is another critical part of this step. Afterward, review the contents of the chapter.

ELL Considerations

Some students will be unfamiliar with the selecting strategies in the chapter. As a result, you will need to model them before asking students to use them. Students may also need guided instruction to form thesis or focus statements. Model this process as needed. Also refer to page 94 in *Write for College* for additional examples.

Extension Activity

Have small groups of students work with the "Basics of Life Checklist" (page 23). Each group should select one of the categories and list four or five potential writing ideas related to that topic. Then each group member should explore one of the ideas in a freewriting. (See page 24 for guidelines.) Students should review their writings, underline ideas they like, and consider how they could further develop one of these ideas. After students share their discoveries within the groups, conduct an all-class discussion of their work. (Focus on the value of freewriting as a starting point for writing.)

Minilessons

One Red Pen, TG 227
What I Found, TG 228
Shaping a Topic, TG 228
Tracking Down the Thesis, TG 228
The Shape of Things to Come, TG 228

A Guide to Drafting

Write for College, 31–38

This chapter explains how to complete a first draft. Writer Ann Lamont calls the first draft "the down draft—you just get it down." Writer and teacher Donald Murray calls it "the discover draft—a vision of what might be." These quotations identify the role that drafting plays in the writing process: It is the step in which the writer connects his or her ideas on paper. The guidelines and examples in this chapter will help students develop the beginning, middle, and ending parts of their draft.

Of Special Interest

- "Writing the Opening," "Developing the Middle," and "Bringing Your Writing to a Close" serve as guidelines for each part of a first draft. (pages 32–37)
- "Integrating Quotations" helps students incorporate quotations into their writing. (page 38)

Rationale

- During the first draft, writers should focus on the development of the ideas, organization, and voice in their writing.
- The beginning, middle, and ending parts all must work together in a piece of writing.

Major Concepts

- Drafting is the process of connecting the ideas the writer has collected during prewriting. (pages 31–32)
- The beginning in a piece of writing should introduce the topic, interest the reader, and identify the thesis (focus); the middle should explain and support the thesis; and the ending should bring the writing to a satisfying close. (pages 32–37)
- Quotations should support a writer's own ideas, not replace them. (page 38)

Performance Standards

Students are expected to . . .

- connect their thoughts after collecting details.
- apply different methods to support their thesis.

A Guide to Drafting

Start-Up Activity

Discuss the following questions about the drafting process: (Important points to consider are provided after each question.)

- **How important is prewriting when it comes to writing a first draft?**
  Whenever students are working on analytical or persuasive writing, extensive prewriting is essential. Students need to establish a thesis (focus) and gather and organize support before they attempt a first draft. When students are developing a personal piece of writing, they can complete a first draft with minimal prewriting.
- **What traits are important during the drafting process?**
  Three traits are critical during drafting—ideas, organization, and voice. Students should stay focused on their thesis and purpose (ideas), follow their prewriting plan (organization), and speak confidently and sincerely (voice).
- **What is the best way to complete this step?**
  Students should follow the direction established by their prewriting, but they should also entertain new ideas as they come to mind. Students should try to write as freely and naturally as possible to allow a free flow of ideas.
- **What should students do if they have trouble getting started?**
  Students can talk about their topic with a classmate; afterward, the words may flow more freely. Another idea is to approach drafting as a freewriting, recording ideas nonstop without being judgmental. Students can also write a first draft as a letter or an e-mail message to a friend or family member.

ELL Considerations

Many students mistakenly believe they must produce perfect drafts in one sitting, as on an exam. They need to know that the purpose of a first draft is to get their ideas on paper. Assure them that they will be able to make improvements and corrections during the revising and editing steps.

Extension Activity

Using the information in this chapter, analyze the opening and closing paragraphs of some of the essays in *Write for College*. Challenge students to write different openings and closings for a number of these essays.

Minilessons

For Example, TG 228
Sparking Interest, TG 228

A Guide to Revising

Write for College, 39–52

In his book *On Writing Well,* William Zinsser eloquently discusses the craft of writing. According to Zinsser, writers must learn to "simplify, prune, and strive for order." These basic tools are especially important during the revising process, when a writer shapes an initial draft into a more finished piece of writing. This chapter covers all aspects of the revising process—from using basic revising guidelines to observing revising in action, from revising for the traits to peer reviewing.

Of Special Interest

- "Revising on the Run" provides guidelines for situations when students have little time for revising. (page 40)
- "A Closer Look at Revising" helps students focus on purpose and audience. (page 41)
- "Revising for the Traits" helps students revise their writing for ideas, organization, voice, word choice, and sentence fluency. (pages 44–48)
- "Peer Reviewing" provides information to help students respond to each other's writing. (pages 49–51)

Rationale

- Revising is the all-important third step in the writing process, the step in which a writer shapes a first draft into an effective piece of writing.
- The goal of revising is to improve the content of a draft.
- Students can learn revising strategies to improve their writing.

Major Concepts

- Revising is the process of adding, cutting, reordering, and rewriting parts of a draft. (page 40)
- During the final stages of revising, writers should try to improve any stretches of uninspired writing. (page 41)
- Students who understand the traits of effective writing are more likely to improve their writing. (pages 44–48)
- Peer feedback is especially helpful during the revising process. (pages 49–51)

Performance Standards

Students are expected to . . .

- revise their writing by adding, cutting, deleting, and rearranging copy, striving for effective content, logical organization, and appropriate voice.

A Guide to Revising

Start-Up Activity

Write this Jane Yolen quotation on the board: *"[My writing] is never perfect when I write it down the first time, or the second time, or the fifth time. But it always gets better as I go over it and over it."* Ask students which part or parts of the writing process Yolen is referring to. Then find out if any students have ever reworked an essay or a story five or more times. If some students have, ask them to share these experiences with the class. (Students will stay with a piece of writing longer if they have a strong personal attachment to the work.) Afterward, review the opening three pages in the chapter.

ELL Considerations

Revising is a sophisticated process that takes time to learn, especially for many ELL students. Some researchers have noted that when students begin to use the revising process, their writing may seem less effective than before. But it is important to encourage students to continue to take risks and to make significant changes in their writing. Eventually, their writing will become more completely and thoughtfully developed.

NOTE: Students should learn to see the strengths in their writing as well as the weaknesses. A strength can be anything from expressing sincere feelings to including realistic dialogue.

Extension Activity

Throughout the school year, provide sample essays for your students to critique as a class, using "Escaping the 'Badlands'" (page 41) as a guide. List their suggestions on the board. Encourage students to use this page when they are revising their writing.

Minilessons

Best Foot Forward, TG 229
Field Trip, TG 229
Mock Trial, TG 229

A Guide to Editing

Write for College, 53–56

Editing is a critical step in the writing process, the step in which writers make sure that their writing follows the conventions of the language. But it only becomes important *after* the key changes in the content are made. If writers focus too much attention on the correctness of their writing too early in the process, they will not pay enough attention to the development of their ideas. Students can use the guidelines and list in this chapter to edit their revised writing and to proofread the finished product before publishing it.

Of Special Interest

- "Guidelines" serves as a handy editing and proofreading checklist. (page 54)
- "Common Writing Errors" lists the 12 most common errors for students to watch for. (page 56)

Rationale

- A writer's message is best conveyed in writing that is carefully edited and proofread.

Major Concepts

- Editing deals with the "surface errors," or problems with conventions (spelling, punctuation, capitalization, and grammar). (page 54)
- Student writers should take a systematic approach to editing and proofreading. (page 54)

Performance Standards

Students are expected to . . .

- edit and proofread their writing for correctness.
- apply the convention rules to their writing.

A Guide to Editing

Start-Up Activity

Post the following sentences on the board. Ask students to identify the error in each one and suggest how to correct it. Then refer students to page 56 for a list of the 12 most common errors to watch for when editing and proofreading.

- When Bob talked with Mr. Wilson, he offered him a scholarship.
  (confusing pronoun reference)
- I made the varsity baseball team, I will be a pitcher.
  (comma splice)
- A list of new band members have been posted in the band room.
  (subject-verb agreement error)
- Either Sally or Maria dropped their books in the puddle.
  (pronoun-antecedent agreement error)
- Because of the terrible thunderstorm our school bus was late.
  (missing comma after longer introductory phrase)
- Carry that carton out to the coachs car.
  (missing apostrophe to show ownership)

ELL Considerations

Many researchers note that students' errors are often made because they mistakenly apply the rules of their first language. Making errors is part of the learning process—as is the discussion and correction of those errors. To prevent students from becoming overwhelmed, ask them to edit for only two or three types of errors at a time, and mark only those items on their papers.

Extension Activity

Throughout the school year, have students edit writing samples (from previous years), using the guidelines on page 54. Remind students to use this page whenever they edit their own work.

Minilessons

Delete, TG 229
Stand-Ins, TG 229

A Guide to Publishing

Write for College, 57-61

Publishing makes all of the writing and rewriting of an essay worth the effort. Publishing is to a writer what a live performance is to a musician or an exhibit is to an artist. Writer and teacher Tom Liner says, "Writing becomes real when it has an audience." Students always do their best work when they know they are writing for an authentic audience. This chapter provides students with publishing ideas, guidelines for preparing a portfolio, and tips for sending writing out and publishing online.

Of Special Interest

- "Publishing Ideas" shares many different ways for student writers to share their texts with an audience. (page 58)
- "Preparing a Portfolio" lists the key components for a well-constructed showcase portfolio. (page 59)
- "Submitting Writing to a Publisher" and "Publishing Online" serve as starting points for students interested in submitting their writing. (pages 60–61)

Rationale

- Publishing is sharing a piece of writing that effectively expresses a writer's thoughts and feelings.
- If students publish their own work, the importance of careful and thorough writing becomes more apparent.

Major Concepts

- Publishing takes many forms. (page 58)
- A portfolio is a collection of a student's writing that showcases her or his skills and progress. (page 59)
- Sending out writing can be an exciting, and frustrating, form of publishing. (pages 60–61)
- The Internet offers many publishing opportunities. (page 61)

Performance Standards

Students are expected to . . .

- design and publish documents by using publishing software and graphics programs.

A Guide to Publishing

Start-Up Activity

Ask students to list their publishing experiences—other than sharing their writing with their peers. Discuss some of these experiences as a class. Then refer to "Publishing Ideas" (page 58) so students can see all of the publishing options open to them. Ask students to list two or three new forms of publishing that they would like to try during the year. Compile and post a master list, showing each student and his or her publishing goals. Throughout the school year, remind students about their publishing plans.

ELL Consideration

Some students may not be aware that "publishing" means more than turning in a paper to the instructor. To change this perception, require students to try at least one new form of publishing per quarter. These publishing experiences will help students gain a better appreciation of the entire writing process.

Extension Activity

Have students create an electronic or print publication (literary magazine). Provide plenty of class time for students to develop the publication. Encourage every one of your students to contribute to the project.

Minilesson

Ready to Launch, TG 229

The Basic Elements of Writing Teacher's Notes

Making Sentences Work

Write for College, 63–74

Literary critic and philosopher Roland Barthes stated that a writer is "someone who thinks sentences." This extensive chapter in *Write for College* helps student writers do just that. It covers everything from writing complete and clear sentences to combining and expanding sentences.

Of Special Interest

- "Writing Complete Sentences" serves as a basic guide when students are checking their writing for sentence errors. (page 64)
- "Combining Sentences," "Modeling Sentences," and "Expanding Sentences" help students write sentences that are more stylistic. (pages 72–74)

Rationale

- To become effective writers, students must immerse themselves in the language, which includes experiencing sentences in all of their glory through reading, writing, oral presentations, and so on.

Major Concepts

- The most common sentence errors are fragments, comma splices, run-on sentences, and rambling sentences. (pages 64–65)
- Incomplete comparisons, ambiguous wording and pronoun reference, and problems with modifiers must be corrected. (pages 66–67)
- In academic writing, sentences should be written using standard English. (pages 68–71)
- There are many ways to combine sentences. (page 72)
- Modeling sentences and expanding sentences help students develop their writing style. (pages 73–74)

Performance Standards

Students are expected to . . .

- understand sentence construction (parallel structure, subordination, and so on) and standard English usage.
- write regularly in a variety of forms.
- use published examples as models for critiquing writing.

Making Sentences Work

Start-Up Activity

Ask for a volunteer to explain the meaning of *fragments, comma splices,* and *run-ons*. Then present the following examples of sentence errors on the board or on an overhead. Have someone identify the type of error in each one and correct the problem. (Corrections will vary.)

- Countless writers and artists believe that creativity and madness are linked, experts today say that isn't quite the case. *(comma splice) Change the comma to a semicolon.*
- A creative mind-set and bipolar disorder share certain characteristics both lead to thinking "outside the box." *(run-on) Place a semicolon after "characteristics."*
- When Aneko opened the box. Spaghetti rolled all over the table. *(fragment) Change the period after "box" to a comma and lowercase the "S" in spaghetti.*
- Commuters had been bottlenecked on the freeway, some of them had a crazed look in their eyes. *(comma splice) Add the conjunction "and" following the comma.*
- I thought the test would never end I had a classic case of writer's cramp. *(run-on) Add a period after "end."*
- I tripped over a root the color of the ground. Spikes of pain up my left arm as I tried to stand. *(fragment) Add the verb "shot" after the word "pain" in the second sentence.*

ELL Considerations

Some ELL students may repeat the same basic sentence structure in their writing. Demonstrate how clauses can be combined with coordinating and subordinating conjunctions. Provide plenty of sentence-combining practice for these students.

Extension Activity

Throughout the year, have students regularly practice sentence modeling (page 73). Perhaps once a week you could ask for volunteers to provide one or two well-made sentences for the class to use as models. Afterward, ask students to write their own versions of each sentence on the board for class discussion.

Minilessons

Sincere Flattery, TG 230
All Arranged, TG 230
Going in Style, TG 230
Complex Authors, TG 230
Like They Always Say, TG 231

Developing Strong Paragraphs

Write for College, 75–90

Most student writers find paragraphs uninteresting, perhaps even unimportant. They don't, for example, head to the bookstore to buy a book of paragraphs. Nor do they want to pursue a writing career to write award-winning paragraphs. However, as this chapter illustrates, paragraphs are very important building blocks for other kinds of writing. These pages cover the basic parts of paragraphs, the primary paragraph types, and the kinds and arrangement of details.

Of Special Interest

- Sample expository, descriptive, narrative, and persuasive paragraphs are provided. (pages 80–81)
- "Understanding Details" shows students different ways to support their main ideas. (pages 82–83)
- "Using Transitions" offers a helpful list of transitions and linking phrases. (pages 88–89)

Rationale

- The paragraph is the structural and conceptual basis for all writing.
- Learning to write effective paragraphs helps students focus and organize their thoughts and equips them to write longer, more complex pieces.
- Understanding the different types and arrangements of paragraphs helps students match their writing to their purpose.

Major Concepts

- There are three parts to a paragraph: the topic sentence, the body, and the closing. (page 76)
- There are four basic types of paragraphs: expository, descriptive, narrative, and persuasive. (pages 80–81)
- Paragraph unity helps deliver a clear message. (page 79)
- There are many types of details that can be used to support main ideas. (pages 82–83)
- The details in paragraphs can be organized in a number of ways. (pages 84–87)

Performance Standards

Students are expected to . . .

- establish a central idea (focus or topic sentence), collect details, and organize supporting information for writing.
- apply different methods of support, including facts, anecdotes, quotations, explanations, comparisons, and so on.

Developing Strong Paragraphs

Start-Up Activity

Read and discuss the first part of the chapter (pages 75–79). Pay special attention to the formula for writing effective topic sentences. This formula will also help students write effective thesis statements. After discussing the four basic types of paragraphs (pages 80–81), list the following topics on the board. Ask students to determine which type of paragraph they would write for each topic (answers are shown in parentheses).

- How cheese is made *(expository)*
- The teacher who challenged me most *(narrative)*
- Art classes should be required in high school. *(persuasive)*
- The crowd, stage, and performers at a high-powered concert *(descriptive)*
- All textbooks should be available as e-books. *(persuasive)*
- First job-related memory *(narrative)*
- The costs of making a Hollywood film *(expository)*
- The appearance of a unique individual *(descriptive)*

ELL Consideration

Point out to students that transition words help organize the details in each type of paragraph, especially expository and persuasive, the two forms most used for academic writing. Advise students to refer to the chart of transitions (pages 88–89) whenever they write paragraphs or essays.

Extension Activity

Review with students the types of details on pages 82–83. Point out how these different details are necessary to support students' main ideas. Then have students create their own example of each type of detail. Afterward, ask them to share their work with the class.

Minilessons

On Topic, TG 231
Too Many Pets, TG 231
Paragraph Roundup, TG 231

Mastering the Academic Essay

Write for College, 91–109

According to writer and teacher James Burke, writing in an academic setting is "a tool, a means of seeing what students know and how well they understand it. [Writing] is a performance that makes visible what kids think, what they learn." This chapter provides students with a solid foundation for their academic writing, helping them develop all types of expository and persuasive essays. Once students understand the basics of essay writing, they will be able to concentrate more fully on making meaning, on sharing what they have learned.

Of Special Interest

- "Quick Guide" provides an overview of the essay-writing process. (page 92)
- "Forming a Thesis Statement" helps students establish a central idea for their essays. (page 94)
- "Planning and Organizing Your Essay" identifies different patterns of organization. (pages 95–97)
- "Two Sample Essays" provides a traditional and an original essay, both focusing on the same topic. (pages 103–109)

Rationale

- Writing academic essays helps students to think clearly and logically.
- Academic writing assignments provide students with an opportunity to show what they have learned.

Major Concepts

- For academic writing, the key is starting out in the right way—understanding the assignment and selecting a topic. (page 93)
- A thesis statement identifies the specific part of a topic that will be the focus of the essay. (page 94)
- An organizational pattern for an essay often evolves during the initial planning and organizing. (page 95)
- Academic essays develop in a fairly predictable fashion. (page 96)
- The level of originality in an essay depends on the nature of the assignment. (page 93)

Performance Standards

Students are expected to . . .

- demonstrate a clear understanding of a topic.
- state a central idea (thesis statement) in the opening paragraph.
- develop supporting details in the middle paragraphs.
- write a closing that connects with the essay's central idea.

Mastering the Academic Essay

Start-Up Activity

To get started, have students answer the following questions on their own paper. Use their responses as part of an opening discussion of the chapter.

1. **What is an essay?** *(A piece of prose in which ideas on a simple topic are presented, explained, argued, or described in an interesting way)*
2. **What types of essays have you written?** *(Personal essays, persuasive essays, literary analyses, research papers, articles, and so on)*
3. **Why do teachers assign essays?** *(Essays help teachers assess a student's understanding of topics related to the course work. Essays also help teachers assess a student's ability to think logically and coherently.)*
4. **What makes essay writing challenging?** *(Selecting an engaging topic, gathering enough information about a topic, presenting a compelling explanation or argument, and so on)*

ELL Consideration

While planning academic essays, students will find it helpful to discuss their topics with the teacher or a classmate. This discussion helps students tap into prior knowledge of a topic and determine where additional information can be found. Peers can also help one another gather supporting details and organize these ideas for writing.

Extension Activity

As a class, plan a number of expository or persuasive essays using the guidelines presented in the chapter. As part of the planning, ask students how they would approach each topic in a traditional way and in an original way.

Minilesson

While You Were Out, TG 231

Writer's Resource Teacher's Notes

Understanding Style in Writing

Designing Your Writing

Writing Terms and Techniques

Understanding Style in Writing

Write for College, 111–124

Impress upon students that stylistic writing begins and ends with commitment. Students must feel strongly about their writing in order to give it the proper care and attention. Also impress upon them William Zinsser's golden rule about writing with style: Students must "be themselves." No rule, however, is harder to follow. As Zinsser states, "It requires writers to do two things which by their metabolism are impossible. They must relax and they must have confidence." As you probably know, it *is* possible for student writers to feel comfortable with writing, but only if they are willing to write on a regular basis, as in every day, for a number of different purposes.

Of course, in academic assignments, the expectations of the teacher impact style considerations. Students must learn to balance their individual style with an awareness of audience expectations.

As time permits, review the various stylistic reminders and techniques discussed in this chapter. Also make sure that students are aware of common ailments of style and that they check for these problems whenever they revise their work.

Of Special Interest

- "Key Stylistic Reminders" identifies three simple rules of style. (page 112)

Rationale

- Writers can develop their style by reading avidly, by writing regularly, and by avoiding the "ailments of style."
- Style is personal; it develops naturally as a writer practices and gains experience.

Major Concepts

- There are three simple rules of style: Be purposeful. Be clear. Be sincere. (page 112)
- Anecdotes, metaphors, and repetition can add style to writing. (pages 117–121)
- Specific nouns, vivid verbs, and effective modifiers add style to writing. (pages 118–119)
- Avoid short, choppy sentences, passive voice, and the overuse of qualifiers in writing. (page 118)

Performance Standards

Students are expected to . . .

- use precise language, action verbs, sensory details, appropriate modifiers, and active rather than passive voice.

Understanding Style in Writing

Start-Up Activity

Have students respond on paper to the following question: *What is meant by writing style?* Then ask for volunteers to share their responses with the class. Afterward, read and discuss the opening three pages in the chapter. When you analyze the writing samples on page 113, consider these questions:

1. Is the writing purposeful? Said in another way, does the writer seem to care about the topic?
2. Are the ideas clearly stated and easy to follow?
3. Does the writer sound sincere and knowledgeable about the topic?
4. Are the sentences smooth-reading?
5. What else might the writer have done to enhance the style of the piece?

Also share other writing samples for stylistic discussion, including passages from the writing of Kurt Vonnegut, Mark Twain, and Rachel Carson. You may also want to consider some writing samples that are clearly "out there" stylistically, starting, perhaps, with a passage or two from something written by Tom Wolfe.

ELL Consideration

Model for students the use of the style matrix on page 115 when planning a piece of writing. Then require students to answer the matrix questions before they begin their work on a writing assignment. Completing this task will help students write with style.

Extension Activity

Discuss "Writing Metaphorically" on page 117. Stress that metaphors can create powerful images but also remind students that metaphors should be used selectively. Writing that contains too many metaphors will sound forced. As a class, turn each of these statements into a metaphor.

- The sunset changed the color of our rivers. *(At sunset, our rivers were ribbons of purple and red.)*
- His performance was disappointing. *(His performance was a real choke sandwich, all peanut butter and no jelly.)*

Then have students extend a metaphor within a passage or brief paragraph. Afterward, share some of the examples with the class for discussion. During this discussion, students should consider how their own notion of writing style compares with the information presented on pages 116–117.

Minilessons

Time for a Makeover, TG 232
A Slice of Life, TG 232
Take Action!, TG 232
Getting a Kick out of This, TG 232

Designing Your Writing

Write for College, 125–132

Students must recognize that presentation is an important part of the writing process. Their choice of layout and typestyle makes an immediate impression on the reader before she or he reads a single word. Taking care of the document design shows that students value their writing and respect the reader. Through effective use of headings, graphics, and white space, students can help the reader follow their ideas. This chapter helps students understand the elements of effective document design.

NOTE: The design elements in this chapter differ slightly from MLA design guidelines. For example, MLA style does not use any boldfaced type.

Of Special Interest

- "Design Overview" and "Effective Design in Action" present tips and a model for page layout and typography choices. (pages 126–128)
- "Document Design Checklist" provides students with a way to assess the design of their finished work. (page 132)

Rationale

- A computer is a valuable writing tool, providing innumerable design options for all types of documents: essays, pamphlets, brochures, and so on.

Major Concepts

- Quality page design makes a text clear and easy to follow. (pages 130–131)
- Adding visuals or graphics depends on the audience and the purpose of the writing. (page 129)
- Color enhances page design if it is used selectively and tastefully. (page 131)
- Evaluating page design requires an understanding of layout, headings, graphics, and so on. (page 132)

Performance Standards

Students are expected to . . .

- use available technology to prepare their writing for publication.

Designing Your Writing

Start-Up Activity

After reviewing the chapter, have students compare the design elements (good and bad) used in a history-text chapter with those in a newsmagazine article. Identify elements that are the same and different. Also consider how the design of each piece does or does not fit the intended audience.

ELL Consideration

An acceptable format for essays may need to be taught directly. Different cultures may consider different format features acceptable. Also, depending on students' previous educational experiences, some may have limited computer skills or knowledge of word-processing applications. If this is the case, give students extra time for a computer skills tutorial.

Extension Activity

Have students redesign one of their existing essays using the information in this chapter as a guide. Upon completion, students should share their work in small groups. Consider the effectiveness (or ineffectiveness) of the new design elements in each piece.

Minilesson

Looking Good, TG 232

Writing Terms and Techniques

Write for College, 133–141

The vocabulary of writing is rich and diverse. It's important that you use this vocabulary in the daily discourse with your student writers. By the time students are juniors and seniors, they should be "speaking the language." This chapter serves as a handy reference to the vocabulary of writing, including common terms, techniques, and forms. Also included is a quick guide to foreign words and phrases. Students should turn to this chapter whenever they have a question about a particular writing-related word or phrase.

Of Special Interest

- "Writing Techniques" provides explanations and examples of common rhetorical devices. (pages 136–138)
- "Survey of Writing Forms" classifies the common forms of writing. (page 141)

Rationale

- Students should become familiar with common writing terms and techniques.
- Students should experiment with a number of different forms of writing.

Major Concepts

- Writing terms are words used to discuss the writing process. (pages 134–135)
- Writing techniques are methods used to achieve particular effects in writing. (pages 136–138)
- Foreign words and phrases are commonly used in classroom texts. (pages 139–140)

Performance Standards

Students are expected to . . .

- use writing terms, techniques, and resources during the writing process.

Writing Terms and Techniques

Start-Up Activity

List on the board a few of the writing terms, writing techniques, and foreign words or phrases included in this chapter. Ask for volunteers to explain each one. Compare their explanations with the information provided in the chapter. Then refer students to the "Survey of Writing Forms" (page 141). Note the forms that students have worked with in the past and identify any additional forms they will work with this year.

ELL Considerations

This chapter will be helpful when students have questions about words or phrases related to writing instruction. For that reason, be sure that your students are aware of this information early in the school year. Note the terms and techniques that you will refer to often during the school year.

Extension Activity

Ask students to write original examples for five writing techniques (pages 136–138). Upon completion, students should share their examples in small groups; group members should guess which techniques the examples demonstrate. Afterward, ask for volunteers to share examples during a class discussion.

Minilessons

Making Connections, TG 233
Categories of Forms, TG 233
A Young Audience, TG 233
Inductive Reasoning, TG 233
Cést La Vie, TG 233

The Forms of Writing Teacher's Notes

Personal Writing

Report (Expository) Writing

Analytical Writing

Persuasive Writing

Writing About Literature

Business Writing

Implementing the Forms of Writing

The notes that follow will help teachers carry out the writing activities as classwide projects. (In a writing workshop, teachers can assign the forms of writing on an individual basis, allowing students to use the writing guidelines and models on their own.)

Planning

1. Gain a clear understanding of the writing activities by previewing the "Teacher's Notes" in this guide and the writing guidelines and the related models in the handbook.
2. Review the "Related Activities" listed in the "Teacher's Notes" for possible inclusion in the activity.

Introducing the Activity

3. Introduce the activity by implementing any combination of the following:
   - Begin with the discussion points.
   - Ask students to review the writing guidelines and read and react to one or more of the writing models in the handbook.
   - Discuss and display the "Framing Questions" to help students establish a focus for their work.
   - Implement one or more of the "Selecting Activities."
   - Offer a related writing prompt for an introductory exploratory writing.

Facilitating the Students' Work

4. Help students carry out their work by doing the following:
   - Guide them in their searching, selecting, generating, and writing as outlined in the writing guidelines.
   - Provide opportunities for them to write, read, and share in class.
   - Consider implementing one of the activities listed under "Related Activities."
   - Identify relevant *Write for College* handbook pages.

Closing Out the Activity

5. Bring the writing activity to an effective close in one or more of these ways:
   - Ask students to conduct peer revising and editing sessions.
   - Have them share (and evaluate) finished products.
   - Encourage students to submit their work for publication.
   - Challenge them to write additional pieces related to this form of writing.

Personal Writing

Write for College, 143–159

Personal writing is writing that comes from within, carried out because the writer has a personal need to explore or share an experience. Common forms of personal writing for juniors and seniors include personal reminiscences (narratives), personal essays, and college-entrance essays. As students get into personal writing, they'll soon realize that their thoughts and experiences are no more than starting points. They will begin to turn these initial ideas inside out and see them in new ways. This might sound like heady stuff, but it really isn't. Personal writing is simply an effective way to make sense out of life's highs and lows.

Of Special Interest

- Guidelines for writing personal reminiscences, personal essays, and college-entrance essays are provided. (pages 145, 151, and 156–157)
- Samples of the above forms of personal writing are included. (pages 146–148, 149–150, 152–155, and 159)

Rationale

- All students have experiences that are important to them and worth sharing with others.
- Students can learn to shape their experiences into stories that have compelling beginnings, middles, and endings.

Major Concepts

- In a personal reminiscence, students explore a defining moment in their lives. (pages 145–150)
- In a personal essay, students analyze and reflect upon an important experience. (pages 151–155)
- In a college-entrance essay, students respond to a prompt exploring who they are or why a particular college might be right for them. (pages 156–159)

Performance Standards

Students are expected to . . .

- use chronological order to organize ideas.
- create an engaging story line by employing dialogue, sensory details, specific action, and personal feelings.
- revise and edit their writing using the traits of effective writing as a guide.

Writing a Reminiscence (145–150)

DISCUSSION Writing a reminiscence involves reawakening and re-creating a memory, connecting it with the present, and reflecting on its meaning. Such autobiographical writing asks, "How did this experience help define who I am?" and shares the answer with the reader. Help your students by emphasizing four things about a reminiscence:

1. **Dig deeply into the memory rather than scratching the surface.** Bring a particular incident alive with details that let the reader see, hear, feel, and basically relive the experience.
2. **Choose a life-changing or an ordinary memory.** One of the sample essays—"Coming Home"—recalls a life-changing experience; the other essay—"The Pond in Ralph's Swamp" recalls more of an everyday experience.
3. **Avoid oversimplifying the memory.** Relate the ambivalence or inner conflict of an experience.
4. **Focus on a memory and bring it to life for the reader.**

Framing Questions

- What memories would I be willing to share? Which ones would be of interest to others?

> "The version we dare to write is the only truth, the only relationship we can have with the past. Refuse to write your life and you have no life."
>
> —Patricia Hampl

- Why was this experience important to me? How has it fit into the big picture of my life? How might my life have been different if I hadn't had this experience?
- What should my focus be? What insights do I want my reader to gain? How do I want him or her to react?
- Should I use a chronological approach or another method? What details should I include to make the memory vivid and meaningful for my reader?

Selecting Activities

Collaborative Activity Have students list experiences under these headings: events, places, people, and objects. Encourage them to share their lists and memories either in pairs or in small groups.

Freewriting Allow students time to freewrite about a particular memory in order to remember details and explore possible meanings.

Focused Assignment For students having trouble generating a subject, suggest a memory related to their ethnic identity, a cross-generational relationship, or an experience that increased or hindered their self-confidence.

In-Process Activities

1. Have students examine the techniques used by the writers in the sample essays (sensory details and narrative techniques).
2. Help students focus their essays by . . .
   - "spotlighting" specific elements of their memory, and by
   - implying rather than stating their essay's thesis or theme.

Related Activities:

- Minilesson, What a Day, TG 234
- Ideas: Searching and Selecting, TG 181
- Ideas: Discovering Interesting Subjects, TG 182

Write for College References

22 Selecting a Topic
24 Freewriting Guidelines
30 Focusing Your Efforts
34 Developing the Middle
112 Evaluating Your Style
118 Using Strong, Colorful Words

Writing a Personal Essay (151–155)

DISCUSSION A personal essay takes a reminiscence one step further. Instead of attempting to capture a moment that is past, the personal essay analyzes a longer period of time and relates the events to the larger context of the writer's life. When writing a personal essay, students should keep the following tips in mind.

1. **Show a change in the writer.** Each individual event in the experience should move the writer toward a new way of thinking, feeling, or behaving.
2. **Include only significant events.** The essay should focus on the events that were most important in prompting the change during this period of time.
3. **Reflect higher-level thinking.** The essay should demonstrate a mature perspective through analysis, synthesis, and so on.
4. **Aim for a universal appeal.** Alice Walker once described a personal essay as "a personal account that is yet shared, in its theme and its meaning, by all of us."

Framing Questions

> "There are many truths of which the full meaning cannot be realized until personal experience has brought it home."
>
> —John Stuart Mill

- Who am I now? Who was I before? What period of time brought about the transformation?
- What specific events during the time period contributed most strongly to the change? How do those events relate to form a whole narrative?
- What main point do I want to make?
- How could I best introduce the ideas in the essay? How can I capture the reader's interest and introduce my main point?
- How do I feel about this time period? What adjective would best describe my feeling (and the tone I should use)?

Selecting Activities

Collaborative Activity Have students list what they consider to be strong feelings. Then have them connect different periods of time or extended experiences (events, people, places, objects) with these feelings. Finally, ask these questions: (1) What caused these feelings and what are their effects? (2) Have these feelings changed or remained the same?

Freewriting Get students to explore intense feelings through a writing prompt in this format: "I've been frustrated (or angry, joyful, and so on) because . . . . "

Focused Assignment Suggest one of the following subjects: styles or fashions, gender relationships, work and play, an experience of injustice.

In-Process Activities

Help students add depth, honesty, and energy to their writing by interacting with the model essays in the following ways:

1. Have students study how the writers blend the narrative with the analysis. Where do the writers narrate and describe? Where do they explain and analyze? Where do they evaluate and synthesize?
2. Ask students to explore the depth of the experience. Have them identify the overall tone of the piece as well as separate emotions expressed in different spots.
3. Ask students to find the universal component of the essays. What is the essay about on the surface? What does it describe on a deeper level?

Related Activities:

- Minilesson, Going Through a Phase, TG 234
- Voice: Finding a Voice, TG 192
- Conventions: Pronoun References, TG 211

Write for College References

44 Selecting Supporting Details
84 Arranging Your Details
111 Writing with Style
114 Developing a Sense of Style
122 Using an Alternative Style
124 Avoiding Cliches

Writing a College-Entrance Essay (156–159)

DISCUSSION Writing a college-entrance essay involves responding to a prompt as part of a college application. This type of writing helps an admissions officer determine whether or not the applicant is a good match for the institution. In college-entrance essays, students should speak sincerely and honestly to the reader and remember these hints:

1. **Respond to the prompt.** An effective response essay answers the prompt and follows any specific guidelines, including word count.
2. **Put forth your best effort like an audition on paper.** The writer should work very hard to make a sincere, personal connection with the reader.
3. **Engage the reader.** Admissions officers read hundreds of application essays; the ones that grab their attention contain original ideas and interesting details.
4. **Reveal mastery of basic writing skills.** The essay should demonstrate that the writer has the skills to handle college-level writing.

"Be honest with yourself and your reader. Don't try to write only what you think the reader wants to hear."
—Verne Meyer

Framing Questions

- What does the prompt ask about me? What key words does the prompt use (*recall, describe, explain,* and so on)? What does the prompt ask about the school?
- What experience (*belief, goal,* or so on) could I write about? What does this experience really say about me? Can I write effectively about this experience given the specified word count?
- What should my focus be? What level of language should I use? How can I connect with my reader? How do I want the reader to react?
- How should I structure my response—as a chronological narrative or in another way? How can I work in sensory details, dialogue, personal reflection, and so on?

Selecting Activities

Collaborative Activity Have students cluster possible writing ideas around the nucleus words "great personal achievement."

Freewriting Give students time to freewrite about one of the ideas from their cluster. Encourage students to write for at least 10 minutes (nonstop).

Focused Assignment For students having trouble generating a writing idea, suggest a significant achievement related to an academic challenge, a work-related experience, or a holiday.

In-Process Activities

1. Have students examine the techniques used by the writer in the sample essay. Did the writer include sensory details, dialogue, personal reflection, an engaging voice, and so on? Also analyze sample college-entrance essays online.
2. Help students develop their responses by . . .
   - analyzing their focus or thesis statements. (Do these statements effectively address the prompt?)
   - discussing the structure of their responses. (Will they be organized chronologically or by some other order?)
   - considering different ways to conclude a response. (Will the closing sum up the experience or reflect on its importance?)
3. Have students react to sample responses as if they were admissions officers.

Related Activities:

- Minilesson, After high school, then what . . . , TG 234
- Ideas: Searching and Shaping Subjects, TG 183

Write for College References

Report (Expository) Writing

Write for College, 161–185

It's tempting to suggest that the contents of reports include "just the facts." Certainly reports that focus on scientific research, observations, or interviews should share with the reader the main points about the topic. However, a more careful reading of most reports shows that they do much more. For example, the writers of the samples in the handbook analyze, synthesize, and reflect upon the information in their reports. The types of reports included in *Write for College* are summary reports, compiled reports, interview reports, observation reports, and personal research reports.

Of Special Interest

- Guidelines for writing summary reports, compiled reports, interview reports, observation reports, and personal research reports are provided. (pages 163, 165, 170, 176, and 182)
- Samples of the above forms of report writing are included. (pages 164, 166–169, 171–175, 177–181, and 183–185)

Rationale

- All students need to summarize information for research projects.
- Students can improve their observational skills by developing observation reports.
- Students can learn firsthand about research by shaping personal research reports.

Major Concepts

- Summary and compiled reports highlight the main points in one or multiple sources. (pages 163–169)
- An interview report shares information about another person. (pages 170–175)
- An observation report saturates the reader with sights, sounds, and smells related to a specific setting. (pages 176–181)
- A personal research report shares the story of a writer's research into a topic of interest. (pages 182–185)

Performance Standards

Students are expected to . . .

- find primary and secondary sources of information.
- glean the main ideas from longer texts.
- summarize what they have learned from different sources.

Writing a Summary Report (163–164)

DISCUSSION A summary extracts main ideas from a piece of writing and then shapes that material clearly and coherently. Summarizing helps students (1) sharpen reading and thinking skills, (2) support ideas in essays, (3) write abstracts for research projects, and (4) prepare for workplace summaries of documents and meetings. Students need to see a summary as more than simply skimming an article and copying out some sentences. Have them consider these points:

1. **Annotate** photocopied material.
2. **Skim** material for its purpose, audience, main point, and structure.
3. **Locate key ideas** by looking at paragraphs' topic sentences, concluding sentences, and transitional words.
4. **Leave out secondary material,** such as background information, examples, and unnecessary descriptive details.

NOTE: Allow students to pursue their own interests, writing summaries aimed at informing each other about topics of mutual interest. **Consider connecting the summary with another writing project.** For example, have students summarize an article on the environment for a research paper in that subject area.

Framing Questions

- Why am I summarizing this material? How brief or detailed should my summary be? Who might use it and why?
- What is the writer's purpose? Who are the intended readers?
- What main point is the writer making?
- What secondary ideas and information support and develop the main idea?
- What is the piece's structure or organization?
- What ideas *don't* I understand in this piece of writing? How can I clarify them?
- How can I put these ideas together clearly and smoothly, in my own words?

Selecting Activities

Consider these options for making the assignment relevant and manageable:

Collaborative Activities Assign a single article or chapter for the whole class, connecting the piece with a project, a visiting speaker, and so on. Discuss with students the reason for the selection.

Divide the class into small groups. Assign each group an article or a chapter. Make the assignment collaborative.

Allow students to choose their articles or chapters for summarizing. Provide guidelines on length and types of material.

In-Process Activities

1. Share examples of summaries in newspaper and magazine articles, textbooks, research abstracts, business reports, meeting minutes. Have students discuss the purpose and usefulness of summaries.
2. Provide a copy (overhead) of Einstein's first letter to President Roosevelt summarized by Aleasha Jensen, on page 164 in the handbook. (The letter is available online.) Have students compare and contrast the original material to the summary.
3. Review "Writing a Summary Report" (pages 163–164) with students. Then give them the opportunity to freewrite a personal summary of the article they are reading.
4. Let students work on improving the coherence of their rough drafts by reviewing "Using Transitions" (pages 88–89).

Related Activities:

- Minilesson, The Key Elements, TG 234
- Fluency: Creating Connections, TG 205

Write for College References

84 Arranging Details
424 Writing a Summary
428 Writing an Abstract

Writing a Compiled Report (165–169)

DISCUSSION A compiled report presents the reader with carefully integrated and focused information from a number of sources. Compiling involves two tasks: (1) tapping a variety of sources, and (2) making sense out of them. Students should consider the following points:

1. **Choose a subject that is current, focused, and interesting to you.**
2. **Think of a compiled report as a summary of the available knowledge on a subject.** Therefore, seek out a rich variety of credible sources that complement and contrast each other.
3. **Focus the report around your conclusions about the material's meaning.**
4. **Remember that unlike the traditional research paper, the compiled report does not involve formulating an original thesis and developing a lengthy argument in its support.**

Framing Questions

- What current subject interests me?
- How can I narrow my subject so that it's manageable?
- What sources of information related to my subject are available? Where can I get a range of perspectives? How can I access the information I need?
- What can I expect to gain from investigating this subject? What do I hope to give my reader?
- To what conclusion about this subject does this information lead me?
- What strategies can I use for developing this focus, organizing the information, and weaving sources together smoothly?

Selecting Activities

Preliminary Reading Send students to newspapers, current events magazines, and textbooks in other courses to develop a list of topics they might be interested in researching.

Narrowing the Topic Encourage students to narrow their topic by using clustering.

Focusing the Research Direct students to brainstorm for questions they want to answer about their topic.

Checking for Sources Encourage students to consider a variety of information sources, both primary and secondary.

Focused Assignment For students who have problems selecting a subject, suggest a recent development in technology, popular culture, the environment, or the arts.

In-Process Activities

1. Review the handbook models to check out the writers' conclusions, variety of sources used, integration of sources, and methods of creating reader interest.
2. Help students work with sources by practicing on a newspaper or magazine article: Provide each student a copy of an article; read it aloud; let students reread it and pull out the main ideas and key concepts.
3. Assist students in coming to conclusions about the information they've gathered through focused freewriting on (a) the connections and (b) the contrasts between their sources.

Related Activities:

- Minilesson, The Right Source, TG 234
- Organization: Devising a Writing Plan, TG 189
- Conventions: Proofreading Review, TG 217

Write for College References

82 Understanding Details
319 Steps in the Process (research paper)
327 Writing Responsibly
333 MLA Documentation Style
383 Searching for Information
393 Using Electronic Sources
424 Writing a Summary
457 Conducting Interviews

Writing an Interview Report (170–175)

DISCUSSION When carefully planned and executed, the interview report allows students to conduct primary research and share another person's story. Help students by emphasizing the following:

1. **Choose an appropriate interview subject.** Interview subjects fall naturally into two categories: experts on a subject and people who have had a special experience.
2. **Develop effective interview questions.** Your questions imply a focus for your report.
3. **Follow the process—from exploring the subject's background to writing a follow-up thank-you note.**

NOTE: Integrate the interview into a larger project. If possible, connect the interview report with a research paper or more extensive group research project.

Framing Questions

- Do I know someone I want to interview? An expert? What person do I know who has had a unique experience?

> "The chief reward of [interviewing] is the joy of learning, of coming away from each person with a wider angle of vision on the time I live in."
> —Bill Moyers

- What do I know about the subject and the person? Where can I look up more information about him or her, or about the topic?
- What can and can't this person tell me?
- What questions do I want to ask?
- How should I plan the time and place for the interview?
- How do I want to shape and share the report?

Selecting Activities

Warm-Up Give students an opportunity to browse through magazines and newspapers for interviews or to look through books or other collections of interviews. Ask them to consider the types of people who are interviewed and the kinds of questions they are asked.

Collaborative Activity Let students brainstorm lists of people either who are experts in a subject or who have had special experiences. Students may also brainstorm lists of issues or topics they find interesting in the community. Give them time to match up topics with people to interview.

Focused Assignment Push students to step outside their comfort zones by focusing on "differences"—people coming from different ethnic groups, working in unusual careers, belonging to different socioeconomic groups.

In-Process Activities

1. Use "Conducting Interviews" (page 457) as a resource. Let students practice drafting questions for various people. Explore how the questions create a focus. Discuss the differences between open-ended, closed or slanted, and neutral questions.
2. Review the model interview reports in the handbook and discuss organization options: (a) combining background, paraphrase, summary, and quotation in a general report form; (b) reporting the interview in a straight transcript form. Have students consider which form will bring their interviewee's story to life.
3. Invite students to share first drafts of their interview reports. Have them complete this prompt: "This interview report taught me . . . "

Related Activities:

- Minilesson, Searching for Information, TG 234
- Organization: Logical Organization, TG 191
- Word Choice: Economy, TG 201

Write for College References

23 Selecting a Subject (Basics of Life List)
115 Writing with a Plan in Mind
458 Conducting Interviews

Writing an Observation Report (176–181)

DISCUSSION An observation report takes readers inside the writer's experience of a place or an event. Help your students develop their observation skills by stressing the following:

1. **Observe actively, not passively.** Work on employing all five of your senses in the act of observation.
2. **Avoid trying to be purely objective.** Observation activates the senses, mind, and heart—engaging emotions, reason, and imagination. Saturated with impressions, observers become filters for experiences.
3. **Aim to make the unfamiliar familiar or the familiar fresh.** Taking the reader inside the experience involves detailed and suggestive description, carefully chosen comparisons, and focused reflection on the experience's impact and meaning.
4. **Take both yourself and your reader out of your comfort zones.**

Framing Questions

- What place or event would be interesting to observe? Why?
- How can I go about recording sensory impressions (sights, sounds, smells, tastes, touches)? How will I position myself as an observer?
- How should I present my observations . . . as a continuous flow of impressions, or in a more structured format?
- How should I place myself in the writing?

Selecting Activities

Collaborative Activity Have students brainstorm two lists: (1) places and events that are familiar or comfortable and (2) places and events that are unfamiliar or uncomfortable. Let them share their lists. Then discuss the different observation strategies needed for comfortable and uncomfortable experiences.

Focused Assignment Suggest any public location that provides students with a slice of life—a mall, market, coffee shop, post office, library, sports event, and so on.

In-Process Activities

1. Give students a feel for recording sensory observations by playing a 10- to 15-minute videotape of a busy location, or by actually visiting such a place, recording the sights and sounds together. Discuss both the actual sensations and the broader impressions (thoughts, feelings). Remind students that a videotape leaves out taste, touch, and smell.
2. Explore the models in the handbook, pointing out the following:
   - The observations take both writers out of their comfort zones.
   - The writers keep the focus on the experience but also reveal their own presence as observers.
   - Both writers put the observation in context, provide rich sensory details, use comparisons, and reflect on the experience.

   Consider sharing bits of effective observation from your favorite writers (for example, Annie Dillard or Barry Lopez). Invite students to find well-made observations in books and magazines of their choice.

Related Activities:

- Minilesson, Eyewitness Accounts, TG 235
- Organization: Finding a Form, TG 188
- Fluency: Parallel Structure, TG 203

Write for College References

22 Selecting a Subject
115 Writing with a Plan in Mind
117 Special Features of Style
118 Using Strong, Colorful Words
122 Using an Alternative Style

Writing a Personal Research Report (182–185)

DISCUSSION As the name suggests, the personal research report combines elements of personal and report writing by presenting the writer's experience of researching a personally important topic. The skills students learned in exploring experiences, remembering, interviewing, and observing will be useful here. Note the following strategies for doing a personal research report:

1. **Approach it as a research quest.** The topic must be personally important, one rooted in a deep curiosity or concern.
2. **Strive to use primary sources for your research—experiences, memories, observations, interviews, surveys, even experiments.** Traditional library research may supplement this primary research.
3. **Focus on the research journey, pointing out discoveries made along the way.**

"Where there is curiosity, a mouse may be caught."
—Lu Po Hua

Framing Questions

- What have I always been curious or concerned about? What am I interested in right now? What knowledge would help me in the future?
- How is my chosen topic of personal relevance?
- What research strategy should I follow to explore this topic? Is researching this topic within my abilities, scope, and time frame?
- What do I already know about this topic?
- Can I do some firsthand research on this topic?
- What do I hope to find out?
- How should I present my research journey and share my discoveries?

Selecting Activities

Freewriting Use a prompt to get students thinking about what they find important:

"I always wanted to know . . . "

"I am concerned about . . . "

"In a few years, I will be . . . "

"I think that it's crazy (great, fascinating, foolish, and so on) that . . . "

Focused Assignment Follow the lead of the handbook model by suggesting the following topics:

(a) an illness, a fear, a disability, a social attitude, a weakness, a memory, or a loss that has affected the student's life or development

(b) an element of local history—the origins, development, and future of the student's neighborhood, city, or rural area

In-Process Activities

1. Explore differences between the personal research report and the traditional research paper. Help students see the value of a research journal—a place where they can keep notes on their investigative journeys and the questions, mysteries, and insights they are exploring.
2. Review the handbook model and discuss why the writer researched her topic, what she did, and what she discovered.

Related Activities:

- Minilesson, Learning About Yourself, TG 235
- Ideas: Improving Focus, TG 187
- Ideas: Improving Openings, TG 186

Write for College References

22 Selecting a Topic
25 Shaping a Topic
30 Focusing Your Efforts
319 Steps in the Process
322 Searching for Information
457 Conducting Interviews

Analytical Writing

Write for College, 187–227

Analytical writing is simply a type of writing that requires high-level thinking. In an analysis, students interpret information rather than report on it; they form new understandings rather than simply give the facts. Typically, analytical writing asks students to compare, contrast, classify, define, connect, evaluate, and so on. Writers should approach analytical writing with a genuine interest in the topic and with the patience to explore it carefully and thoroughly.

Of Special Interest

- Guidelines for writing process analyses and essays of comparison, classification, definition, cause and effect, problem and solution, and evaluation are provided. (pages 189–225)
- Sample essays of the above forms of analytical writing are included. (pages 189–225)

Rationale

- Students need to engage in writing projects that require higher levels of thinking.
- Analytical writing helps students explore information and make connections.

Major Concepts

- An analysis of a process explains how to do something or how something works. (pages 189–192)
- An essay of comparison demonstrates the similarities and differences between two topics. (pages 193–197)
- An essay of classification breaks a topic down into reasonable parts. (pages 199–202)
- An essay of definition clarifies a complex concept. (pages 203–206)
- A cause-effect essay carefully examines the relationship between events. (pages 207–211)
- A problem-solution essay examines a problem and one or more solutions. (pages 213–218)
- An essay of evaluation explores the worth of an event, trend, decision, etc. (pages 219–225)

Performance Standards

Students are expected to . . .

- establish a central idea (focus or thesis statement).
- select a topic's main points and connect ideas logically.
- show knowledge and interest in the topic.

Writing an Analysis of a Process (189–192)

DISCUSSION A process is a sequence of events that leads to a specific outcome—a drama, so to speak. Processes make up the fabric of daily life—from people buying groceries to leaves growing and dying to students developing research papers. Help students analyze processes effectively by using the following strategies:

1. **Focus on** how to do something (instructions), how something works (operation), or how something develops or happens (natural phenomena).
2. **Provide an overview** of the process and point to the outcome; break down the process and show links between the various stages.
3. **Carefully explore the process** and develop an expertise that you can share with the reader.

> "Writing has been for a long time my major tool for self-instruction and self-development."
> —Toni Cade Bambara

Framing Questions

- What processes am I an "expert" in? What processes am I curious about?
- What is the outcome or goal of the process I've chosen?
- What are the main steps and the substeps in the process?
- How do I want to shape my process analysis—as instructions for the reader or as a process to understand?
- How can I help the reader "see" the process?
- What tone would work best—formal or informal? Should I be present in the analysis, or should I remain in the background?

Selecting Activities

Collaborative Activities Have students turn to the "Basics of Life" list (page 23) and brainstorm processes related to a variety of the items. You may also choose to have students brainstorm lists of topics under these headings: (1) Subjects I Have Some Expertise In and (2) Subjects I'm Curious About but Don't Fully Understand.

In-Process Activities

1. Demonstrate an actual process (perhaps on videotape). Repeat the demonstration and have students map out the stages using the "Process Analysis" graphic organizer (page 226) as a guide.
2. Suggest the following mapping options:
   - Design a flowchart
   - Create a table with these headings: Step #, Action/Development, Relationship to Other Steps, Tools/Materials Needed
   - Outline dramatic concepts of plot (beginning, middle, climax, end)
3. Remind students to keep focused as they draft and revise their process analysis by (a) thinking about their reader and (b) getting at the heart of the process.
   - What would the reader already know? What questions would readers have about the process?
   - What is the outcome, goal, or climactic moment of the process? How can this moment be the focus of the analysis?
4. Help students write coherently by reviewing transitions that show time (pages 88–89).

Related Activities:

- Minilesson, The Way It Works, TG 235
- Voice: Evaluating Style, TG 196
- Voice: Unifying Tone, TG 193

Write for College References

Writing an Essay of Comparison (193–197)

DISCUSSION Comparing and contrasting means exploring the similarities and differences between two things—holding them up side by side, studying and balancing them in order to arrive at some insight into both. Have students consider these key points to perform an effective balancing act:

1. **Compare compatible topics**—have a logical connecting point, a basis for comparison. Avoid comparing two different types of things or one thing that is simply an example of the other.
2. **Develop a specific focus** for an in-depth comparison.
3. **Create a rich comparison** with insights that explore degrees of similarity and difference. Interpret as well as describe the similarities and differences.
4. **Develop the essay of comparison for a specific purpose** by carefully choosing points to compare, giving roughly equal weight to both topics and choosing whether to emphasize similarities or differences.

Framing Questions

- What two people, objects, places, experiences, events, or concepts would I like to compare and contrast? Why do I want to compare these topics?
- What's the link, the basis of comparison, between the two topics?
- What do I already know about each topic? What do I need to research?
- What elements or aspects of each can I compare? How are the topics similar and different with respect to each point of comparison?
- How should I develop and organize the comparison? Given my focus and purpose, how should I balance similarities and differences?

Selecting Activities

Collaborative Activities Have students brainstorm topics on blank paper, one sheet per heading: (1) ideas, concepts, and principles; (2) events and experiences; (3) objects; (4) places; (5) people; (6) works of art; (7) texts; etc. Then have students note items with obvious connections (similarities and differences); ask them to list the connections.

In groups, let students test their comparison choices: Can the two things actually be compared? Will a comparison of these things be fruitful? Is information available for the comparison?

Focused Assignment Have students compare two types of institutions (such as homes, schools, or places of worship) or ask them to compare two family sitcoms, one from the past and the other from the present.

In-Process Activities

1. Give students practice in making comparisons. For example, you could bring incandescent and compact fluorescent lightbulbs to class, let students explore similarities and differences, and then hand out *Consumer Reports* articles comparing the bulbs.
2. Examine the comparison models in *Write for College* for (a) the basis of comparison, (b) elements compared, (c) balance, (d) combination of description and interpretation, (e) purpose, and (f) insights gained.
3. As they draft, have students explore organization options: topic by topic, whole versus whole, or all similarities and all differences. They can experiment to discover which option suits their essay.
4. Point students to "Using Transitions" (pages 88–89) for words used to compare and contrast.

Related Activities:

- Minilesson, Apples and Oranges, TG 235
- Word Choice: Using Adverb Clauses, TG 198
- Conventions: Consistency, TG 209

Write for College References

Writing an Essay of Classification (198–202)

DISCUSSION Classifying organizes and clarifies knowledge by grouping things based on similarities and differences (for example, bookstore shelves, filing systems, literary genres). The essay of classification, then, takes what is scattered or all mixed together, discovers patterns or categories, and creates a framework for understanding. Here are some key features:

1. **Consider different principles of grouping** to create different understandings of the material. For example, different classification schemes for cars could include use, horsepower, weight, size, image.
2. **Create categories that are consistent and complete**—based on a careful analysis of the topic.
3. **Establish a purpose for the classification** to determine the kind of grouping needed. Whether giving the big picture or putting elements in a larger context, classification makes sense of information.
4. **Avoid isolating items within categories.** Show the connections between the example items (parts) and the whole.

Framing Questions

- What group of people, practices, ideas, and so on am I interested in classifying?
- Is my chosen topic focused enough for in-depth analysis?
- What's the point of my classification? What purpose does it serve?
- How can my goal help me develop consistent and complete categories?
- How can I make my essay insightful and interesting for my reader?

Selecting Activities

Collaborative Activities To begin generating topics, point students to the "Basics of Life" list (page 23), which is itself a classification scheme. After a brainstorming session, encourage them to use clustering (page 22) as a strategy for breaking a topic down into categories.

Review and discuss the Library of Congress or Dewey decimal classification system (page 387)—what it is, how it works, why it's useful. Then have students use the categories in one of the systems as a starting point for a topic search.

Freewriting Students might freewrite about a possible topic by completing this statement: "This topic can be classified by . . . "

Focused Assignment Students could focus on high school life—types of students, courses, tests, instructors, assignments, social activities.

In-Process Activities

1. Bring in objects for students to group according to similarities and differences. Discuss the various principles they come up with. Which groupings prove most useful and understandable?
2. Ask students to find classification schemes in different places, particularly in their textbooks. Have them share the logic of the schemes they've found.
3. Explore the handbook's classification essays by considering (a) personal purpose (value for writer), (b) public purpose (value for reader), (c) the classification principle at work, (d) strategies used to develop consistent and complete categories, (e) the rationale for the method of organization.
4. Point students to the "Classification" graphic organizer (page 226) as a tool for exploring options for their topics.

Related Activities:

- Minilessons, Classified Information, TG 235
- Ideas: Experimenting with Form, TG 184
- Voice: Improving Diction, TG 195

Write for College References

25 Shaping a Topic
84 Classification
91 Mastering the Academic Essay
115 Writing with a Plan in Mind
198 Selecting a Topic
226 Using Graphic Organizers

Writing an Essay of Definition (203–206)

DISCUSSION The essay of definition explores the significance of a difficult concept, idea, or ideal and shares that deeper understanding with the reader. Help students probe and clarify by stressing the following:

1. **Broaden the reader's comprehension of the term** using either of the following methods.
   - Be objective, seeking to get at a term's "essence."
   - Explore the term's relevance for the writer—a personal connection or fascination.
2. **Consider a two-part structure for an essay of definition.** An opening creates a focus, generates interest, and provides a sentence definition. The body develops and extends the definition by offering facts, examples, anecdotes, quotations, explanations, and comparisons; by tracing the word's origin; or by stating what the term is not.

" 'When I use a word,' Humpty Dumpty said, in rather a scornful tone, 'it means just what I choose it to mean—neither more nor less.' "
—Lewis Carroll, *Through the Looking Glass*

Framing Questions

- What concept or idea interests me or relates to my experience?
- What are my initial thoughts and feelings about the term? Do I need to go beyond my own knowledge and experience?
- Is the term complex enough for the assignment? What is the term's importance? What are the challenges of understanding this term?
- What larger class does it belong to? What are its distinguishing features?
- What approach—tone and attitude—should I take in the essay? What will the reader gain from this definition?

Selecting Activities

Collaborative Activities Pointing students to the "Basics of Life" list and the guidelines for freewriting and clustering (pages 22 and 23), have them list concepts important to their own lives and related to their own curiosity.

Have students share their choices with classmates, getting feedback on interest level, the term's complexity, possible ways of researching the term, and methods of developing the definition.

Focused Assignment Have students define a term at the heart of their high school experience or of another community they belong to.

In-Process Activities

1. Explore the handbook models for the connection between the concept and the writer's life, the way the term is used, and the strategies that develop the definition.
2. Challenge students to capture their term in a one-sentence definition using this equation: **term** = larger class + distinguishing features.
3. Encourage students to develop their definitions through personal and traditional research:
   - Reflect on the relationship between personal experiences and the term.
   - Have a peer freewrite about the term for other perspective.
   - Use the "Definition" graphic organizer (page 227).
   - Question the concept (page 26).
   - Consider what the reader would and would not know about the term.
   - Research dictionaries, thesauruses, and writings by experts.

Related Activities:

- Minilesson, Beyond Dictionary Meaning, TG 235
- Fluency: Adding Energy and Originality, TG 202
- Word Choice: Clarity, TG 199

Write for College References

22 Selecting a Topic
25 Shaping a Topic
26 Asking Questions (concepts)
91 Mastering the Academic Essay
115 Writing with a Plan in Mind
203 Definition
226 Using Graphic Organizers
429 Building a College-Sized Vocabulary

Writing a Cause-Effect Essay (207–211)

DISCUSSION The cause-effect essay explores causal links within a chain of events, developments, or conditions. Students probe their topics by asking "Why?" and testing out "because" answers. Here are some ideas for this challenging thinking and writing task:

1. **Trace the links in the cause-effect chain in either of two directions:**
   - forward from an initiating action to its various results
   - backward from an event or a condition to its possible causes
2. **Develop and support sound logical relationships by** detailing the causal connections and considering any outside forces at work in the situation.
3. **Address cause-effect complexities.** Causes can be immediate or remote, root or perpetuating, obvious or hidden. Effects can be specific or wide ranging, simple or complex, short term or long term, superficial or serious. Causes and effects can be easily confused; moreover, events can seem causally related without being so.

Framing Questions

- What event, development, or condition am I curious about? What causal connection or chain reaction would I like to explore? Why?
- Do I want to trace the range of effects from a specific cause or speculate on the possible causes of a specific effect?
- What are the actual causal connections at work? How can I discover them, research them, support them, clarify them?
- What do I want to gain from this analysis? What do I want the reader to understand?
- How should I organize and present the cause-effect chain reaction?

Selecting Activities

Collaborative Activity Have groups of students brainstorm a list of trends they've noticed, speculate on the causes behind and the effects of one such trend, and then decide which causes are most plausible and which effects most important.

Freewriting Let students explore their topics by writing out and exploring "Why?" questions. Begin by listing these broad topics on the board or overhead: workplace, high school, personal life, politics, the environment, products and services, life stages, the arts.

Clustering Have students choose a cause (an event, a development, or a condition) that they are familiar with or curious about. Then let them cluster all possible results of this cause.

Focused Assignment Have students focus on the popularity of an event, an activity, or a place in their school or community.

In-Process Activities

1. Explore the handbook essays for the (a) writer's motivation, (b) sources of information, and (c) method of organization. Have students map out the cause-effect chain reactions.
2. Encourage students to research cause-effect connections through a variety of sources: personal experience, analysis and experiment, observations and interviews, articles and books.
3. Challenge students to experiment with organizing and clarifying their cause-effect links: (a) Will they move from cause to effects or from effect to possible causes? (b) How will they introduce the topic? (c) How will they develop causal connections in a logical order and support their arguments with evidence?

Related Activities:

- Minilesson, Cause or Effect?, TG 235
- Fluency: Crafting Sentences, TG 206
- Conventions: Commas and Semicolons, TG 215

Write for College References

22 Selecting a Topic
25 Shaping a Topic
91 Mastering the Academic Essay
115 Writing with a Plan in Mind
207 Cause and Effect
226 Using Graphic Organizers

Writing a Problem-Solution Essay (212–218)

DISCUSSION Like a cause-effect essay, the problem-solution essay explores a causal chain reaction; however, it seeks to break a chain linked to a frustrating or harmful situation. This essay assignment helps students to identify problems and take responsibility for solutions. It prepares them to write proposals that lead to productive changes (in the workplace, government, and elsewhere). Here are some key points for developing sound problem-solution essays:

1. **Explore a real problem**—demonstrating a concrete, detailed, and personal understanding of it.
2. **Present a creative, reasonable, and well-supported solution**—attacking the problem's root causes. (No bandages allowed!)
3. **Develop a simple structure:** describe the problem, offer a solution (the thesis), and defend the solution. Deciding how to combine and balance these elements, however, is complex. Should the problem be simply described or carefully explicated? Should the reader be given a solution or called to action?
4. **Use a tone that fits the seriousness of the problem.**

"A problem well defined is a problem half solved."
—Proverb

Framing Questions

- What problem do I want to write about? Why?
- What is the nature of this problem—its parts, history, causes, effects, larger context? Do I know of any comparisons for it, examples of it?
- What do I know about the problem, and what do I need to research?
- Is this a solvable problem?
- What are some solutions that get at root causes or counter major effects of the problem?
- Should I, and how can I, encourage the reader's ownership of the problem and solution?
- What tone should I adopt?

Selecting Activities

Collaborative Activity Allow students to generate ideas with these prompts:

- List groups to which you belong and problems specific to each group.
- Consider situations with a gap between what should be and what is.
- Consider situations in which you see potential danger or injustice.

Focused Assignment Students may focus on problems related to gender relationships or money.

In-Process Activities

1. Students can explore problems and solutions in the following ways:
   - Use "Asking Questions" (page 26), the "5 W's of Writing" (page 25), and the "Problem and Solution" graphic organizer (page 227).
   - Create a dialogue between someone affected by the problem and someone who doesn't think the problem is serious or real.
   - Do primary research (observation, interview, survey) to gain insight.
   - Do secondary research (books, articles) to find background, facts, examples, authoritative opinions, and opposition.
2. Encourage feedback sessions during drafting and revising.
   - Offer "yes, but" responses to a peer's "problem" and "solution."
   - Draft two introductions and get feedback on which one works best. (See pages 50–51 in the handbook.)

Related Activities:

- Minilesson, One Solution to the Problem, TG 236
- Fluency: Complex Sentences, TG 204

Write for College References

25 Shaping a Topic
26 Asking Questions
91 Mastering the Academic Essay
115 Writing with a Plan in Mind
212 Selecting a Topic
226 Using Graphic Organizers

Writing an Essay of Evaluation (219–225)

DISCUSSION Evaluation builds on other analytical skills—cause-effect, comparison, definition, classification. Without such a foundation, an evaluation may be a shaky opinion rather than a solid judgment. As a thinking and writing skill used in school, work situations, and consumer purchases, evaluation is crucial to students' lives. By using standards to measure the significance of a topic, students sharpen their judgment skills. Here are some key points for writing an essay of evaluation:

1. **Become a limited expert on your topic** in order to discover the proper criteria for your evaluation process, arrive at a solid judgment, and support that judgment.
2. **Take a variety of approaches** (objective or personal, positive or negative), but the goal is to present a reasonable and fair evaluation of the topic.

Framing Questions

- What do I want to evaluate? Why?
- What are my initial thoughts, feelings, and attitudes toward this topic? How does this topic affect me and others?
- What criteria (standards) should I use to make my judgments? How can I weigh my criteria?
- What research should I do in order to become an expert on this topic—what rereading, reviewing, revisiting?
- What strategies could I use for developing and supporting my evaluation?
- What tone should I use—witty, serious, enthusiastic, objective, personal?

Selecting Activities

Warm-Up Have students watch or listen to a show, short film, one-act play, concert, or CD and evaluate the "performance." On what basis do they make their judgments? What evidence do they use to support their views? What's the difference between an opinion and an expert judgment?

Freewriting Use the following freewriting prompts:

"Participating in or witnessing ________ was important to me because . . . "

"We shouldn't ignore ________ because . . . "

Focused Assignment Focus the class's work on one subject—films, for example. Together, the class could develop expertise on that one subject, learn criteria used by professional critics, and evaluate specific films.

In-Process Activities

1. Ask students to study the handbook models and gather book, film, TV show, or product reviews from magazines. Then have them explore (a) the writer's connection with the topic, (b) the evaluation's usefulness to the reader, (c) the evaluative language used, (d) the basis of the judgment, and (e) the research strategies used.
2. Suggest these research strategies:
   - Primary research—personal reflection, rereading, reviewing, revisiting
   - Secondary research—where the topic comes from, what it's part of, what type of topic it is, who created it, who's affected by it, what its history is, and so on
3. Direct students to carefully select criteria for making their judgment.

Related Activities:

- Minilesson, Restaurant Review, TG 236
- Conventions: Sentence Fragments, TG 207
- Word Choice: Relative Clauses, TG 200

Write for College References

25 Shaping a Topic
82 Understanding Details
91 Mastering the Academic Essay
115 Writing with a Plan in Mind
219 Selecting a Topic
226 Using Graphic Organizers

Persuasive Writing

Write for College, 229–253

A main goal of your course work is to strengthen your students' reasoning ability so that they can construct persuasive arguments. You want them to be able to think and write logically, drawing sensible conclusions from solid evidence. This section of the handbook addresses four important forms of persuasive writing: editorials, personal commentaries, essays of argumentation, and position papers. Each time students develop one of these forms of writing, they will gain valuable insights into the process of thinking through an argument.

Of Special Interest

- Guidelines for writing editorials, personal commentaries, essays of argumentation, and position papers are provided. (pages 233–244)
- Samples of the above forms of persuasive writing are included. (pages 234–250)

Rationale

- Writing persuasive essays helps students learn how to form reasonable opinions or positions based on compelling evidence.
- Students must learn to anticipate and counter opposing points of view.

Major Concepts

- An editorial is a brief persuasive essay expressing an opinion about a timely issue. (pages 233–235)
- A personal commentary is a thoughtful reaction to some aspect of life. (pages 236–238)
- An essay of argumentation includes convincing evidence to support a proposition as well as reasonable counters to opposing points of view. (239–243)
- A position paper presents a thorough, extensive analysis of a noteworthy issue. (244–250)

Performance Standards

Students are expected to . . .

- form a clear position or opinion.
- include relevant and organized support.
- avoid fallacies of logic or thinking.
- anticipate and address opposing points of view.

Writing an Editorial (233–235)

DISCUSSION In editorials, writers add their viewpoint to a public discussion on a current issue—aiming to raise the awareness or change the minds of readers. For students, the process of writing an editorial refines their thinking skills and builds their awareness of current events and their right to respond. In a sense, the students join the press, becoming, in Douglas Cater's phrase, "the fourth branch of government." Here are keys to writing the editorial:

1. **Consider the publication and its readers (the rhetorical situation) in order to "target" your editorial.**
2. **Offer a thoughtful but boldly stated opinion supported with solid evidence and reasoning.**
3. **Get to the point in about 750 to 900 words.** Paragraphs and sentences should be short and the writing style concrete. Open by grabbing attention, follow with a sound argument, and close with energy.
4. **Enhance social dialogue by stating a clear position on a current issue.**
5. **Raise the levels of intelligence, civility, and commitment in public discourse.** Avoid writing editorials that simply offer an unresearched opinion or merely sound off.

Framing Questions

- What current issue am I interested in? How does it relate to me or to my community?
- What is the debate about? What are my initial thoughts/feelings on this issue?
- What recent events are related to this topic?
- What initial claim or point do I wish to make? How can I support it—with what evidence and reasoning? What are the opposing arguments?
- What do I already know about the issue, and what do I need to research?
- What audience am I writing for? How can I raise the readers' awareness or change their minds?
- How can I open with an effective lead, organize a logical argument, and close with energy?

Selecting Activities

Collaborative Activity Find and copy a newspaper or magazine article on an issue that interests your students. In groups, have them explore the issue and possible positions that could be supported in an editorial.

Warm-Up Have students read the local newspaper, national papers, weekly newsmagazines, and Internet sites. Ask them to copy two articles that sparked their interest and respond to this prompt: "What's the issue? Who should care, and why?"

Brainstorming Have students list communities they belong to: friends, school, generation, family, hometown, state, country, race or ethnic group, and so on. Then let students brainstorm each community's current events and central issues.

In-Process Activities

1. Ask students to bring in several editorials. In groups, let them debate each editorial's position and explore its purpose, claim, tone, support, lead, and ending.
2. Point students to "Thinking Through an Argument" (pages 251–253) for help with developing and supporting their theses and testing and sharing their first drafts.
3. Assign students to write three different leads and share them with classmates for feedback. (Leads inspire editors to publish and people to read editorials.)

Related Activities:

- Ideas: Supporting Your Points, TG 185

Write for College References

25 Shaping a Topic
112 Key Stylistic Reminders
115 Writing with a Plan in Mind
233 Selecting a Topic
251 Thinking Through an Argument
591 Using Clear, Fair Language

Writing a Personal Commentary (236–238)

DISCUSSION Like the editorial, the personal commentary allows students to join the public dialogue about current issues. However, while the editorial offers a boldly stated opinion in response to a current issue, the personal commentary reflects on an ongoing issue of daily life.

1. **Explore in a personal commentary.** Open a window on your world—exploring strong feelings, revising them, and taking a stand. The commentary gives you a chance to say, "This is the way I see the world."
2. **Employ rhetoric in a personal commentary.** Invite readers to say, "I hadn't seen this issue that way." Personal reflection often responds to and sometimes counters popular opinion.

"The life which is unexamined is not worth living."
—Plato

Framing Questions

- What issue in my own life do I want to explore?
- How does this topic relate to my experiences, values, and worldview? How can exploring this topic help me see things more clearly?
- What, exactly, is the issue? What do I know about it? What do I need to explore?
- What community of readers will I address? How will my perspective relate to their opinions? What tone should I adopt?
- How can I focus, develop, and support my commentary? How can I bring it to life?

Selecting Activities

Freewriting Have students read a news article and freewrite their personal responses. Then share and discuss their responses, getting at the issues behind the news event and its relationship to individual and community life. Encourage students to perform the same type of freewriting with other news stories as a way of discovering commentary topics.

Personal Responses Help students connect their lives and current issues in the following ways:

- Have students freewrite using the prompt "What's on my mind and in my heart?"
- Have students list major experiences they've had during the past year and explore how those experiences relate to personal, community, and life issues.
- Have students record a week's worth of daily activities in a journal and reflect on the connecting threads between those activities and broader issues.

Focused Assignment Offer students one of these topic options: (1) the reality versus the appearance of a place (for example, school, hometown); (2) the latest development on the Internet; (3) his or her relationship to a specific law, rule, or expectation.

In-Process Activities

1. Explore the handbook models and models from TV commentators and other news sources, keeping these issues in mind: (a) the commentary's topic and connection to news stories, (b) the importance of the piece for the writer, (c) ways the piece raises readers' awareness, and (d) ways the writer brings the commentary to life.
2. Have students think through the tension between the writer's perspective and the readers' by brainstorming two lists: My Perspective on the Issue, Popular Opinion on the Issue.

Related Activities:

- Minilesson, From My Perspective, TG 236
- Conventions: Sentence Errors, TG 208

Write for College References

25 Shaping a Topic
91 Mastering the Academic Essay
115 Writing with a Plan in Mind
236 Selecting a Topic
251 Thinking Through an Argument

Writing an Essay of Argumentation (239–243)

DISCUSSION Remind students that the argumentation essay isn't an intellectual fistfight. Rather, it explores and takes a reasonable stand on a debatable issue. Students should avoid writing papers that seek to promote either unexamined, set-in-concrete opinions or ambivalent positions of "It's all relative." Here are some keys to writing this type of essay:

1. **Start with a strong opinion, but be open to researching the topic until your position is fair and balanced.** Readers should not feel forced into accepting the argument.
2. **Include (a) a carefully worded claim; (b) reliable supporting evidence; and (c) logical thinking throughout.**

Framing Questions

- What debatable issues do I find intriguing or important for my life?
- What are the different sides of the issue? What claim do I want to make about it?
- How much do I know about the issue? What do I need to find out? Where can I find additional information?
- What are my reasons for making this claim? What evidence do I have to support my argument?
- What are the opposing arguments? How should I counter these arguments?
- How should I organize my ideas? Should I make my strongest points first? When should I deal with opposing views?

Selecting Activities

Warm-Up Have students discuss the following:

1. Topics they argue about with other students, coworkers, and family members
2. Hot topics such as divorce, immigration, sexual harassment, discrimination, private versus public schooling

Then discuss where arguments come from and how they get resolved.

Brainstorming Have students list communities they belong to and then explore issues, choices, and conflicts that divide each group.

In-Process Activities

1. Assist students so that they state their claims clearly.
   - Help students understand the different types of claims by giving them several controversial issues and asking them to draft claims of fact, value, and policy for each.
   - Have students test their claims with their peers.
2. Use "Thinking Through an Argument" (pages 251–253) to help students research and develop support for their claims and respond to each other's drafts.
3. Offer students the following traditional format for organizing their essays.
   - Introduce the topic and stress its importance.
   - Put the issue in context with background information.
   - Make your claim and develop a logical supporting argument.
   - Address counterarguments through concession and rebuttal.
   - Summarize main points and encourage the reader to accept your claim.

Related Activities:

- Minilesson, That's Debatable, TG 236
- Voice: Achieving Economy, TG 194
- Conventions: Pronoun-Antecedent Agreement, TG 210

Write for College References

Writing a Position Paper (244–250)

DISCUSSION A position paper stems from a student writer's stance on a meaningful issue. Rather than arguing for or against something, developing a position paper gives students an opportunity to deepen their understanding and refine their thinking about their writing idea. Students should attempt to be thoughtful but bold, encouraging the reader to respect their line of thinking. Here are some key instructions for your students.

1. **Develop a reasonable stand on an issue and then build a pathway to that position for your reader.** To convince the reader to follow your path, adopt a positive, thoughtful tone—not a "love it or leave it" attitude.
2. **Build on personal commitment, not abstract theory.** Choose topics that affect one of your communities.
3. **Be willing to develop and modify your position through research.**
4. **Soften your stance with qualifiers if necessary.** Let the evidence weigh in your favor.

"Though old the thought and oft expressed, 'tis his at last who says it best.' "

—James Russell Lowell

Framing Questions

- What issue is especially important for me? Why?
- What is my initial position on this issue? To what degree have I thought it through? What is the basis of my position—emotions, experiences, observations, ideas, readings?
- What research must I do to take a stand and convince my reader?
- What strategies should I use to present my position and build a path to it for the reader?

Selecting Activities

Brainstorming Have students brainstorm important issues in the current political, social, economic, cultural, environmental, and educational realms. Then have them rate each issue according to the strength of their feelings about it, their experience with it, and their knowledge about it.

Focused Assignment Focus the position paper on school issues, career issues, or issues affecting the writer's generation.

In-Process Activities

1. Help students think about their position papers by having them review the handbook models on pages 245–250.
   - What is your position on each essay's issue? In what ways is the issue debatable?
   - What stand does the essay take? Where is the stand stated?
   - Is the stand a "balanced" and reasonable one? How is it supported? How does the writer build a path between the reader and the position?
2. Encourage students to experiment with placement for their position statements. How does their paper change if they "state it" at the start or delay the position statement until the middle or the end?
3. Have students do peer reviews following these instructions:
   - **(a)** Write your paper's topic at the top of page one and then exchange papers.
   - **(b)** Read your classmate's topic label and draft a response to this prompt: "My first thoughts on this issue are . . . "
   - **(c)** Read your classmate's paper and complete a second prompt: "Your paper affected my initial position on this issue by . . . "

Related Activities:

- Minilesson, Standing Strong, TG 236
- Word Choice: Active vs. Passive Verbs, TG 197
- Conventions: Commas, TG 213

Write for College References

Writing About Literature

Write for College, 255–297

In a personal response, students freely explore their thoughts and feelings about a piece of literature. In a review, they discuss the merits of a particular book or series of stories. And in a literary analysis, they present their understanding or interpretation of a literary work. All three types of writing actively engage students in the literature that they read. When students are faced with an especially challenging text, writing serves as the perfect thinking aid. ("Challenging texts," of course, make up the suggested reading lists in all upper-level English curriculums.)

Of Special Interest

- Guidelines for personal responses to literature, book reviews, and literary analyses are provided. (pages 257, 263, 269, and 276)
- Samples of the above forms of writing about literature are also included. (pages 259–262, 264–268, 270–275, and 277–285)
- The section concludes with helpful glossaries of literary terms, poetry terms, and forms of criticism. (pages 287–297)

Rationale

- Writing about literature is a key component in upper-level English courses.
- Writing about literature helps students gain a better understanding of the texts they read.
- Students can improve their critical thinking skills by analyzing literature.

Major Concepts

- In a personal response to literature, students reply to something that a text says to them. (pages 257–262)
- In a book review, students pass judgment on a book or some other literary or artistic endeavor. (pages 263–268)
- In a limited literary analysis, students present a thoughtful interpretation of a text. (pages 269–275)
- In an extended literary analysis, students bolster their own understanding of a text with the viewpoint of important critics. (pages 276–285)

Performance Standards

Students are expected to . . .

- make a personal connection with literature.
- take a viewpoint and support it with references from a text.
- develop a thoughtful interpretation of a text.

Writing a Personal Response (257–262)

DISCUSSION Good literature relates to readers' lives. Writing personal responses helps students explore that relationship as the writing process engages them in clarifying and developing their thoughts and feelings. Such responses enrich class discussion and motivate future writing. Here are some tips:

1. **Understand the context of the response.** What are the guidelines? What types of responses are expected—journal entries, creative poems, dialogues, essays? Will the responses be evaluated and used in class? (See pages 95–100 and 132–141 in this manual for more on writing to learn.)
2. **Show meaningful interaction with a text.** Focusing on what grabs your attention, explore impressions, questions, and connections with your experiences and other stories. Personal responses can take you within and beyond yourself.
3. **Avoid responses that (a) simply say "I liked it" or "I hated it"; (b) focus only on your life or a summary of the plot; (c) try to say what the teacher wants to hear; (d) lack focus; or (e) preach.**
4. **Begin with a "conversational" attitude.** Approach any text with an open mind.

Framing Questions

- Why do I want to respond to this work?
- What thoughts and emotions are evoked by my first reading? Do I have a strong sense of what the author means and how the text works? What part of the work stands out for me? Why?
- Upon rereading, what impressions, connections, and questions am I most interested in exploring?
- What form should I use? How can this form expand, clarify, and deepen my thoughts and feelings about the text?

Selecting Activities

Warm-Up Model a practice response in class. Give students a short poem or story to read. After they freewrite a response, let them compare responses. Then have them reflect on how their ideas about the piece may have changed.

Creative Options Give students choices. Let them select one poem from a set of poems, or one story from a group of stories. Encourage students to challenge themselves by responding to works that impress, excite, or puzzle them.

Focused Assignment Match the response assignment to the text and to the class. For example, students could write journal entries during a poetry or novel unit. Afterward, they could write a response paper based on their journals. Be creative, flexible, and practical in your call for responses.

In-Process Activities

1. Discuss the handbook models, keeping these questions in mind: (a) In what ways are these pieces "personal"? (b) What strategies does each writer use to focus her response?
2. Help students focus their responses.
   - Direct them to "Starting Points for Journal Responses" (page 258), "Reacting to Fiction" (page 407), or "Reacting to Poetry" (page 406).
   - Give them time to discuss their initial responses with peers to move from individual concerns to the larger literary conversation.
   - Encourage note taking, annotating, journaling, and freewriting.

Related Activities:

- Minilesson, Touched by Words, TG 236
- Conventions: Usage, TG 216

Write for College References

286 Ideas for Literary Analyses
287 Literary Terms
295 Poetry Terms
297 Forms of Literary Criticism
406 Reacting to Poetry
407 Reacting to Fiction

Writing a Book Review (263–268)

DISCUSSION In a review, writers create a conversation about literature by discussing a text's merits with their readers. Here are some tips for the review:

1. **Evaluate a work using well-chosen criteria (standards of judgment).** The reviewer must know how literature works and what makes it work well. For example, a writer judging a novel must understand character, plot, setting, point of view, style, and theme to effectively gauge the work.
2. **Help readers decide whether they will or will not read the work.** A good review makes careful reference to the work and, without giving the story away, offers enough information to help the reader form a judgment. Well-crafted summarizing and carefully selected quotations are key.
3. **Avoid (a) judging without support, (b) providing an unbalanced evaluation, (c) using criteria that don't fit the work, or (d) simply presenting random thoughts on the work.**

Framing Questions

> "The literary work exists in the live circuit set up between reader and text: the reader infuses intellectual and emotional meaning into the pattern of verbal symbols, and those symbols channel his thoughts and feelings."
>
> —Louise M. Rosenblatt

- What work (novel, poem, play, or concert) do I want to review? Why?
- What is my attitude toward this author, this genre of writing? Have I read this type of writing or this author's works before?
- What criteria for evaluation make sense for this work?
- What's my initial measure of the quality of this text?
- How does my personal experience affect my understanding and appreciation of the work?
- Who will read my review?
- How should I organize my review?

Selecting Activities

Free Reading Make reviews part of students' independent reading. The shared reviews will assist their peers as they decide about future reading.

In-Process Activities

1. Have students review the handbook models and bring in reviews from periodicals.
   - Discuss the information reviewers provide about the work through a summary or a quotation. What information has been held back?
2. Help students develop appropriate criteria. Go over the basics of the literary genre they are reviewing. Then let them freewrite using this prompt: "A good novel (or short story, poem, play) should . . ."
3. Suggest students structure their reviews by trying the following:
   - Use the standard review format: (a) an introduction that puts the review in context and announces the writer's overall evaluation, (b) a summary of the work, (c) exploration of the work's strengths and weaknesses, and (d) a conclusion that restates the judgment and advises the reader.
   - Answer questions that readers want answered: What's this work about? Will it hold my attention—entertain, inform, enthrall, challenge? Is it worth reading? How does it compare with other works from the same author or genre?

Related Activities:

- Minilesson, A Book Review, TG 237
- Conventions: Colons, TG 214

Write for College References

219 Writing an Essay of Evaluation
286 Ideas for Literary Analyses
287 Literary Terms
295 Poetry Terms
297 Forms of Literary Criticism
406 Reacting to Poetry
407 Reacting to Fiction

Writing a Limited Literary Analysis (269–275)

DISCUSSION While a personal response explores impressions and a review evaluates a text, a limited literary analysis interprets a text—without relying upon secondary sources. Here are some tips for effective interpretation:

1. **Begin interpretation with personal response.** An analysis should be a committed exploration of a work's meaning.
2. **Seek to enrich understanding through analysis when the reader will already know the text.** Extensive plot summary is not necessary.
3. **Combine a firm grasp of literary concepts with a close reading of the text to demonstrate an understanding of its parts and the work as a whole in an insightful interpretation.**
4. **Choose an appropriate form for limited analysis.**
   - Explication—line-by-line, stanza-by-stanza, or section-by-section exploration of a work—of a part or the whole
   - Analysis—tracing one issue throughout a text
   - Comparison/contrast of two texts or of two elements within a text

"The world of the imagination is a world of unborn or embryonic beliefs."

—Northrop Frye

Framing Questions

- What is my first response to the text—impressions, questions, feelings?
- What is the text's meaning as a whole?
- What specific part, issue, or concept would I like to explore in depth? Is that focus manageable for this essay?
- What approach do I want to take—explication, analysis, comparison/contrast?
- What connections and patterns could I look for during rereading?
- What insightful thesis can I offer? How can I support it?

Selecting Activities

Clustering To help students match a text with an approach, have them (1) list texts they might write about, (2) select three, and (3) create a cluster of issues for each.

Review Have students review course readings, class notes, "Ideas for Literary Analyses" (page 286), and "Literary Terms" (pages 287–294).

Focused Assignment Choose one poem, story, or play; one specific theme; or one specific form, such as the sonnet.

In-Process Activities

In class, model the process of moving from an initial personal response to an analysis. Select a poem or story to work through.

- Respond through freewriting and note taking.
- Choose a focus by asking a pointed question or completing the sentence "This poem or story is one that . . . ."
- Reread, annotate, and take notes with the focus in mind.
- Review annotations and notes for patterns and connections.
- Write a working thesis statement.
- Outline support for the thesis.
- Draft an analysis with attention to opening, body, and closing strategies.

Related Activities:

- Minilesson, Never judge a book by its movie. , TG 237
- Organization: Limiting Your Topic, TG 190

Write for College References

Writing an Extended Literary Analysis (276–285)

DISCUSSION In the extended literary analysis, a writer interprets a text based on her or his own reading of it plus the observations of accomplished critics. Here are some tips:

1. **Develop a critical approach—reader response, formalist, historical, or so on.** (See pages 401–408.) Your approach should "match" the text, grow out of your critical questions, be attentive to literary elements, and be focused enough to be manageable.
2. **Use source materials effectively.** Ideas, not sources, should dominate the essay. Secondary sources should extend the interpretation—not substitute for it—by clarifying background, lending authoritative support, or offering alternative readings. All references and quotations must be carefully integrated.

> "The ability to interpret is not acquired . . . . What is acquired are the ways of interpreting and those same ways can also be forgotten or supplanted, or complicated or dropped from favor."
>
> —Stanley Fish

Framing Questions

- What text do I want to explore in depth?
- What questions should I ask?
- What do secondary sources say about the text? Do they offer background, support, or alternative readings?
- How can I organize my analysis integrating primary and secondary references?
- Is my tone respectful of both the text and the reader?
- Does my title identify the author or text and imply my focus?

Selecting Activities

Freewriting Encourage students to choose a text by freewriting about engaging works.

Critical Approaches Discuss page 297, "Critical Approaches to Literary Analysis." Have students list questions for their texts from a few of these approaches and then select an approach.

Focused Assignment Select one text and have students write analyses representing different critical approaches. Have students share their work; then discuss how the various approaches complement or clash with one another.

In-Process Activities

1. Have students refine thesis statements by allowing peers to test them for clarity and complexity. Students should also develop a forecasting statement about how the thesis will be proved.
2. Help students deal with sources:
   - Review types of secondary sources—author/work introductions; critical editions; periodical articles; CD-ROM's and online resources.
   - Model the pattern for using source materials in an essay: (a) make an interpretative point, (b) prepare for the quotation, (c) cite the quotation, and (d) comment on the quotation's significance.
3. Review drafts, asking students to answer the following questions about each other's work: What is the thesis, and is it thoroughly dealt with from the title through the conclusion? Does the introduction incite interest, introduce the thesis, and forecast the essay's direction? Are primary and secondary sources used to develop the analysis? Does the conclusion do more than repeat the thesis?

Related Activities:

- Minilesson, It all comes down to . . . and Under the Microscope, TG 237
- Organization: Devising a Writing Plan, TG 189

Write for College References

Business Writing

Write for College, 299–315

Good writing skills remain the bedrock for effective business communication. Whatever the task—writing a business letter or forming a memo or an e-mail message—it's important that students communicate clearly, accurately, and efficiently. Letter writing gives students an opportunity to connect with experts and organizations that offer information, provide internships, help solve problems, and more. Writing memos and e-mail messages allows students to create a flow of information within an organization, whether it's a classroom, an entire school, or a workplace.

Of Special Interest

- "Parts of a Business Letter" identifies the type of information that students should include in business letters. (page 302)
- "Guidelines—Résumé" explains the type of information that students should include in a résumé. (page 310)
- "Interviewing Tips" provides tips for preparing for and conducting an interview. (page 308)

Rationale

- Learning how to write business letters can help students in school and in the workplace.
- Résumés, memos, and e-mail messages help students take care of business in specific situations.

Major Concepts

- Business letters have a very businesslike appearance and follow a specific pattern of form, style, and spacing. (pages 300–309)
- A résumé is a vivid word picture of your skills, knowledge, and past responsibilities. (pages 310–311)
- E-mail messages and memos are quick forms of business communication that are usually less formal than a business letter. (pages 312–315)

Performance Standards

Students are expected to . . .

- use the writing process to produce and send a letter.
- follow conventional page formats to produce effective, readable workplace communications.
- choose appropriate workplace forms of writing for their purpose and audience.

Business Writing

Start-Up Activity

Create a list of possible summer jobs or internships available in your area. Have students choose one of these (or a position or opportunity of their own choosing) to apply for in a letter. Students should keep the following questions in mind as they plan their letter: *To whom will I address my letter? What are the employer's/official's needs? How can I fill those needs? What action do I want the recipient of my letter to take?*

ELL Considerations

Ask students how the accepted form for a business letter in the United States may differ from the form used in their country of origin. Also ask them about any differences that may exist for correctly addressing a business envelope.

Extension Activity

The following assignment is designed to give students practice with creating a résumé. You may also select activities from "Writing and Learning Across the Curriculum" in this guide on page 141.

Assignment: Write a résumé to accompany the letter of application that you completed in the Start-Up Activity.

Topic: You and your skills and achievements

Purpose: To convince an employer/program director to consider you for the position

Audience: Prospective employer or director

Form: Functional résumé

Voice: Formal

Minilessons

The World's Greatest Job, TG 237

Class Kudos, TG 237

The Research Center Teacher's Notes

Writing the Research Paper

Write for College, 317–326

"Research writing is one of the most complex intellectual activities we ask students to undertake. We are, in effect, asking them to perform the tasks of a scholar enroute to publication." This particular quotation comes from the Wisconsin Department of Public Instruction in its guide to curriculum planning for English. We, too, believe that writing a research paper is complex and challenging, even for the most committed and advanced high school students. With its easy-to-follow guidelines, this chapter is designed to help students meet the challenge of research writing.

Of Special Interest

- "Research Overview" gives the big picture in terms of writing a research paper. (page 318)
- "Guidelines for Writing a Thesis Statement" helps students form a focus for their research writing. (page 321)
- "Writing the First Draft" provides insights into forming the three main parts of a research paper: the introduction, the body, and the conclusion. (pages 324–325)

Rationale

- Effective research writing is the result of careful planning, searching, organizing, and evaluating.
- Writing a research paper involves students in higher-level thinking skills (analyzing, synthesizing, and evaluating).

Major Concepts

- A research paper is a carefully planned extended essay. (pages 317–326)
- The process of research writing involves selecting and limiting a topic, forming a thesis statement, taking notes, and more. (pages 319–326)

Performance Standards

Students are expected to . . .

- select relevant topics narrow enough to be effectively researched.
- support the thesis with facts, details, explanations, and examples from multiple sources.
- accurately convey information from primary and secondary sources.

Writing the Research Paper

Start-Up Activity

To make sure that students understand the difference between a research paper and a report, share the following creative writing conference:

Ms. Matthews: Your first draft is interesting, Allan, but it isn't really a *research paper*. I would call this a *report*.

Allan: Research paper—report—what's the difference? I went to an online encyclopedia and a book about the history of rock, and I wrote down everything there was about the origins of rock and roll. I wrote the same paper—I mean the same type of paper—last year.

Ms. Matthews: That was fine for a report. But a research paper requires a more active brand of thinking.

Allan: I was sure active. I wrote down a lot of facts.

Ms. Matthews: By "active" I mean intellectually active. In a research paper, you're no longer an observer, simply telling what others have said about something. You choose a topic that is open for debate. Then you gather information from multiple sources and develop your own position.

Allan: But half the time, they don't even agree!

Ms. Matthews: Exactly. That's why you must formulate your own position and develop it as no one has ever done before. You become an authority on your topic. That can be quite satisfying, Allan.

Allan: I get your point.

ELL Considerations

ELL students often know a great deal about the culture, history, and politics of their country of origin. As a result, consider allowing students to choose writing topics related to their native countries. This may help them deal more effectively with the research-writing process.

Enrichment Activity

At different points throughout the school year, share with students sample research papers or articles from scholarly journals for analysis. Have students identify the author's position, the effectiveness of his or her support, any concessions or counterarguments that are made, and so on.

Minilessons

Stellar Minds, TG 238
Card Games, TG 238

Writing Responsibly

Write for College, 327–332

A key skill students should learn through the research process is decision making. It is not enough that students find quality information. They must also make decisions about which information to use and how to use it. This is a difficult but ultimately rewarding part of the process because it lifts students' thinking to new levels of maturity. Of course, part of the decision making involves being an honest and responsible researcher, avoiding any forms of plagiarism. This chapter explains how students can avoid plagiarizing, write paraphrases, and use quoted material.

Of Special Interest

- "Examples of Plagiarism" illustrates different forms of plagiarism. (page 329)
- "Examples of Paraphrases" shows two samples of restating a text. (page 331)

Rationale

- Students need guidance for accurately paraphrasing and quoting the ideas and words of others.

Major Concepts

- Researchers avoid plagiarism by giving credit for the ideas of others that they include in their writing. (pages 328–329)
- When paraphrasing, writers use their own words to restate the ideas and words of others; the source of the paraphrase must be cited. (pages 330–331)

Performance Standards

Students are expected to . . .

- support a thesis with facts, details, explanations, and examples from multiple authoritative sources.
- provide clear and accurate documentation in their writing.

Writing Responsibly

Start-Up Activity

Be sure that students understand this important point about the research process: They must make their research their own. The chapter opener (page 327) addresses this point. To extend the discussion, share this information with your students:

> **When you (each student) make your research your own, two things will naturally follow: First, your writing will sound like it comes from you, a student researcher committed to presenting your findings as clearly and sincerely as possible. Second, your writing will be honest because you won't lean on the ideas of others for the main support of your research. Your writing, instead, will reflect the results of your planning, searching, and studying.**

If possible, share a few research papers that clearly sound like they come from the writer's own thinking.

ELL Considerations

It may happen that students use texts from their first language as resources. Remind students that if they translate information from one or more of these texts, they must set the information off with quotation marks and give credit to the author.

Extension Activity

As students develop their research papers, have them regularly reflect on the researching process in a writer's notebook or journal. These writings will help them think about, and connect with, their work in progress.

Minilessons

One Strike, You're Out, TG 238
In Your Own Words, TG 238
And I Quote, TG 239
Amusing Ourselves to Death, TG 239

MLA Documentation Style and Research Paper

Write for College, 333–360

Student researchers have always been burdened with the form of their finished product. For years, that meant dealing with endnotes or footnotes, a working or complete bibliography, title page, and so on. Current research styles, including the Modern Language Association (MLA) system, has alleviated some of the frustration and burden. A writer no longer has to struggle, for example, with footnotes or variations in line spacing. This chapter provides students with guidelines and examples for using the MLA documentation style.

Of Special Interest

- "Citing Sources" shows students how to make in-text citations. (pages 334–337)
- "Works-Cited Entries" shows students how to cite sources for the works-cited page. (pages 339–350)

Rationale

- Students need guidelines for accurately documenting their research essays.

Major Concepts

- In MLA style, students include parenthetical references in the body of their paper. (pages 334–337)
- Sample in-text citations and works-cited entries help students document their papers. (pages 339–350)

Performance Standards

Students are expected to . . .

- provide clear, accurate documentation both within the text of their papers and in works-cited pages.

MLA Documentation Style and Research Paper

Start-Up Activity

Remind students of the importance of citing sources in their work, but also point out that they shouldn't "overstock" their papers with the thoughts and feelings of others. The main part of their writing should reflect their own thoughts. If possible, show them two research papers (from previous years): (1) a paper in which the writer's own thinking is clearly the focus and (2) another paper that relies too heavily on the ideas of others.

ELL Considerations

Hold periodic conferences to monitor the students' documentation. Make sure that students record and keep track of all the publishing and documentation information they need to complete their papers.

Extension Activity

From time to time, while students are working on a research project, conduct documentation workshops, giving students practice in making parenthetical references and entries for a works-cited page.

Here is an example to get you started:

Directions: Paraphrase the passage below and refer to the source in a parenthetical citation. Also create a works-cited entry for the source.

> **"For two years Napoleon held (Europe) at bay, making up for his lack of soldiers by his marvelous skill and by the enthusiasm which he never failed to arouse in his troops. In 1814, however, surrounded by the troops of Austria, Prussia, Russia, and England, he had to confess himself beaten."**
>
> Source: *The World War and What Was Behind It* by L. P. Benezet, published in 1918 by Burnley Books in London. The passage is on page 146.

Minilesson

Laurel, According to Hardy, TG 239

- *Answer:* . . . (qtd. in Zinsser 55). *Note:* Students' sentences will vary, but the parenthetical reference will not.

APA Documentation Style and Research Paper

Write for College, 361–382

The research documentation style developed by the Modern Language Association (MLA) works well for papers in the humanities. However, for papers in the social sciences, the documentation style of the American Psychological Association (APA) is often used. If this chapter in *Write for College* doesn't answer all of your questions, refer to the Write Source Web site—thewritesource.com—for additional examples or to the *Publication Manual of the American Psychological Association,* the source text for APA documentation style.

Of Special Interest

- "Citing Sources" shows students how to make in-text citations. (pages 362–363)
- "Reference Entries" shows students how to cite sources for the reference page. (pages 365–370)
- "APA Research Paper" provides an example paper following APA documentation style. (pages 373–382)

Rationale

- Students need guidelines for accurately documenting their research papers.

Major Concepts

- In APA style, students include parenthetical references in the body of their paper. (pages 362–363)
- Sample in-text citations and reference entries help students document their research papers. (pages 365–370)

Performance Standards

Students are expected to . . .

- provide clear, accurate documentation in their essays and research papers.

APA Documentation Style and Research Paper

Start-Up Activity

Show the students two research papers—one paper documented according to MLA style and another paper documented according to APA style. (Use the two papers in *Write for College* or two papers of your choice.) Point out the difference between the two documentation styles. Also share with students the APA link for the Write Source Web site—thewritesource.com—for additional documentation examples.

ELL Considerations

Hold periodic conferences to monitor the students' research and documentation. Be sure that students keep track of all the publishing information they need to complete their research papers.

Extension Activity

From time to time, while students are working on a research project, conduct APA documentation workshops, giving students practice in making parenthetical references and entries for a reference page.

Here is an example to get you started:

Directions: Paraphrase the passage below and refer to the source in a parenthetical citation. Also create a reference entry for the source.

"He explained that they were all worried and resentful; they could not believe a young girl would come all the way from England just to look at apes, and so the rumor had spread that I was a government spy."

Source: page 16 of *In the Shadow of Man*
by Jane Goodall, published in 1971
by Houghton Mifflin Publishing in Boston

Using the Library

Write for College, 383–392

Because of the Internet, the library has lost some of its luster as a resource for information, but that shouldn't be the case. Libraries, managed by information specialists, contain reliable and reputable materials that are cataloged and easy to find—all of which makes libraries invaluable resources for student researchers. Libraries are especially helpful when students *begin* a research project. With the help of an information specialist, students will find it easier to gather initial information about a topic in the library than on the Net. This chapter covers the basic library skills, including using the electronic catalog, finding articles in periodicals, and selecting reference works.

Of Special Interest

- "Refining a Keyword Search" helps students use the electronic catalog. (page 386)
- "Finding Articles in Periodicals" provides guidelines for using the *Readers' Guide to Periodical Literature.* (page 388)

Rationale

- The library is an essential resource for research.

Major Concepts

- Electronic catalogs help student researchers use the library efficiently. (pages 385–386)
- Call numbers classify books, usually according to the Dewey decimal system. (page 387)
- The *Readers' Guide to Periodical Literature* allows researchers to search for articles in magazines, newspapers, and journals. (page 388)
- The reference section in the library contains dictionaries, encyclopedias, thesauruses, almanacs, and more. (pages 389–392)

Performance Standards

Students are expected to . . .

- use reference materials as an aid to writing.
- access information efficiently.

Using the Library

Start-Up Activity

Have an information specialist discuss sources of information in your school or community library. Ask the specialist to focus part of his or her discussion on helping students research a topic, starting with general information and progressing to more specific, specialized data. Also ask the specialist to discuss valuable research features and policies: library databases, reference books, interlibrary loan, and so on.

ELL Consideration

Some nonfiction books, periodicals, and reference materials may be challenging for a few ELL students, so ask an information specialist for help in locating appropriate materials. (There are specific catalogs for English language learners listing content-related materials that are simplified in terms of language, but not simplified in terms of content.)

Enrichment Activity

At different points during the school year, provide students with a topic (question) to research in the library. Ask students to develop a working bibliography of resources that they could use to learn about the topic. The bibliography should be organized from general to specific, specialized sources of information.

Minilessons

Grammar, Dahling, TG 240
Mochaloco, TG 240
Croak/Cash In/Kick the Bucket, TG 240

Using the Internet

Write for College, 393–399

The Internet is an effective research tool, one that student researchers eagerly access when it comes to searching and researching. Unfortunately, the Internet has its drawbacks: It is not that well organized, which can make searching the Net extremely time consuming. And it is open to all sorts of information, which makes evaluating the reliability of sources crucial, but often very difficult. This chapter serves as a basic guide for students conducting online research and communicating on the Net.

Of Special Interest

- "Evaluating Sources of Information" helps students check the reliability of online sources. (pages 394–395)
- "Researching on the Internet" identifies ways to find relevant information. (pages 396–397)

Rationale

- The Internet can be a valuable researching tool, but only if the user is aware of its drawbacks.
- The Internet has opened up new ways to communicate.

Major Concepts

- Before using online sources, students must consider the Internet's trustworthiness. (pages 394–395)
- To find quality information, students must know how to navigate the Net. (pages 396–397)
- Students can communicate via e-mail, chat rooms, blogs, message boards, and so on. (page 398)

Performance Standards

Students are expected to . . .

- efficiently access quality online information.
- communicate effectively on the Internet.

Using the Internet

Start-Up Activity

Identify a specific topic related to your course work or pose a thought-provoking question for your students to research on the Internet. Ask students to use more than one search engine to explore the topic or question and to list three or more sources that seem useful. (Refer to "Research Links" at thewritesource.com for a listing of popular search engines.) Afterward, discuss the various search engines that the students used and determine which were the most fruitful. Then ask volunteers to share a number of sources they found and to discuss the sources' value and reliability.

ELL Consideration

Because of their international experience, many ELL students may have added incentive to travel on the Internet. Students from highly industrialized countries will likely have strong computer and Internet skills, while those from poorer countries will not.

Enrichment Activity

On a regular basis, provide a number of online sources of information and ask students to review them for reliability, using the questions on pages 394–395 as a guide. This practice will help students select trustworthy sources when they develop their own essays and research papers.

Minilessons

From the Horse's Mouth, TG 239
Speaking Out, TG 239
Says Who?, TG 240

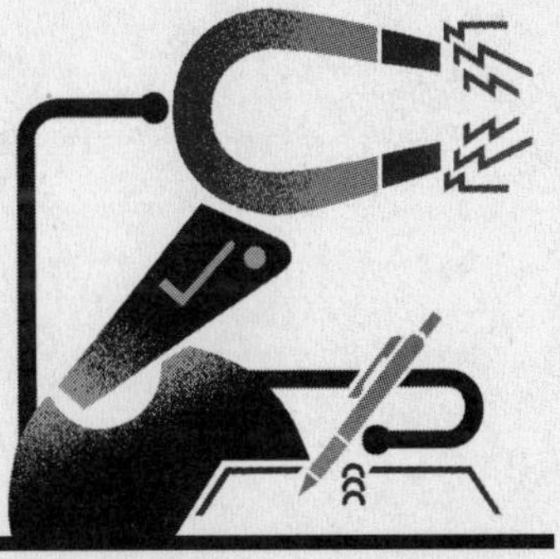

The Tools of Learning Teacher's Notes

Critical Reading

Critical Listening and Note Taking

Writing to Learn

Building a College-Sized Vocabulary

Speaking Effectively

Multimedia Reports

Critical Reading

Write for College, 401–408

Research supports the fact that when students read to learn, they engage their minds in a series of complex thought processes that help them to understand the written message. In each sentence, paragraph, chart, or graph students read, they must solve certain problems before arriving at the author's meaning. This chapter has been included in *Write for College* to help students meet any of their reading challenges, whether it's a difficult novel, a complex nonfiction text, or an ambiguous poem.

Of Special Interest

- "Reading to Learn" prepares students to read challenging texts. (page 402)
- "Using PQ4R" presents an active study-reading technique. (pages 403–405)
- "Reacting to Different Texts" shows how students can react to poetry, fiction, and nonfiction. (pages 406–408)

Rationale

- Students need guidelines and strategies to succeed as readers.
- Improving reading skills improves learning across the curriculum.

Major Concepts

- Critical reading skills help students improve their thinking and learning. (pages 401–402)
- PQ4R is a thorough reading strategy requiring a great deal of thinking. (pages 403–405)
- Memory techniques improve a student's ability to read and to learn. (page 405)

Performance Standards

Students are expected to . . .

- read, interpret, and evaluate information and data from a variety of print resources.

Critical Reading

Start-Up Activity

Begin by reading and discussing the opening two pages in the chapter (pages 401–402). Then ask students to explain this quotation by Richard Steel: "Reading is to the mind what exercise is to the body." *(Possible response: The quotation suggests that thoughtful reading is an interactive process that keeps the mind in shape.)* Afterward, have students identify reading selections that challenge them. Try to determine what makes these texts so difficult. Then have them identify texts that are easy to follow and what makes them so.

ELL Considerations

Remind students that textbooks use standardized conventions to help the reader understand the material. Use textbooks from different subject areas to demonstrate the way books and chapters are organized. Have students identify headings, graphics, boldfaced terms, and margin notes on the page. Also ask students to find the glossaries and indexes in each of their textbooks.

Extension Activity

Have students use the PQ4R strategy for the next challenging reading assignment in your class. Afterward discuss the results of the experience. Encourage students to make this strategy an important part of their reading and learning repertoire.

Minilesson

SQ3R, TG 241

Critical Listening and Note Taking

Write for College, 409–420

Learning according to Montaigne is "rubbing and polishing our brains against that of others." To aid in the "rubbing and polishing" process, students need to develop their classroom skills, including listening and note taking. These two skills work hand in hand: Note taking improves a student's listening, and, of course, effective listening leads to better note taking. This chapter includes guidelines for listening and note taking, as well as suggestions for taking electronic notes.

Of Special Interest

- "Improving Critical Listening Skills" provides a set of 10 helpful guidelines. (pages 410–412)
- "Using a Note-Taking Guide" demonstrates how to keep text and class notes together. (pages 415–417)

Rationale

- Listening is an important communication skill.
- Taking quality notes helps students improve their learning.

Major Concepts

- To listen well, students must concentrate on the speaker's words. (pages 410–412)
- Note taking requires careful listening and high-level thinking skills (responding, questioning, summarizing, organizing, and evaluating). (pages 413–420)

Performance Standards

Students are expected to . . .

- take notes from sources such as teachers, content-related reading, special presentations, and online sites.
- summarize and organize new ideas gained from multiple sources.

Critical Listening and Note Taking

Start-Up Activity

Before introducing the note-taking part of this chapter, ask students to share or demonstrate their note-taking technique. Discuss these techniques using these questions as a guide: *Why do you take notes? How do you use them? Do you follow the same technique each time you take notes? What problems do you encounter when taking notes? Do you use shorthand symbols? Have you ever tried electronic note taking?* Then review the note-taking guidelines presented in the handbook. Ask students to consider how their own technique compares to this information.

ELL Consideration

Help students create a shorthand system for note taking, starting with the information provided on page 418. This will help them become faster note takers.

Extension Activity

Provide students with lectures that coordinate with reading assignments so they can practice keeping text and lecture notes together (pages 415–417).

Minilessons

In the News, TG 241
Fact Check, TG 241
yr spcl dctnry, TG 241

Writing to Learn

Write for College, 421–428

Students are all too familiar with writing to show what they have learned. They may not be as familiar with writing to learn, which is based on the following premise: Learning, in one form or another, occurs anytime a student chooses words to put on paper in response to her or his course work. As writing theorist James Britton stated, "The productive use of language, and especially writing, is a valuable tool for learning for all students in all subjects at all ages." Writing to learn is often freely written and seldom graded. This chapter includes guidelines and examples for four types of writing to learn: learning-log entries, summaries, paraphrases, and abstracts.

Of Special Interest

- Learning logs involve students in their own learning. (pages 422–423)
- "Writing a Summary" (pages 424–426), "Writing a Paraphrase" (page 427), and "Writing an Abstract" (page 428) help students write condensed versions of texts.

Rationale

- In a learning log, students explore their thoughts and feelings about what they are studying.
- Paraphrasing and summarizing the ideas of others are skills that connect the reading and writing processes.
- Learning to write a summary helps students make important connections in all content-area reading.

Major Concepts

- Learning logs personalize the learning process. (pages 422–423)
- Writing a summary helps students read critically to understand and remember a topic. (pages 424–426)
- A paraphrase is a type of summary that may include a student's interpretation of a passage. (page 427)

Performance Standards

Students are expected to . . .

- use writing as a learning tool.
- write summaries that contain the material's main ideas and most significant details.

Writing to Learn

Start-Up Activity

Ask students to write a learning-log entry in response to something that was discussed or covered in class. You may want to participate in this writing as well. Afterward, have each student underline one discovery they made in their writing. Ask for volunteers to share their work with the rest of the class. Encourage students to keep learning logs in all of their classes. You could also have students compare their writing to the sample entries on page 423 in the handbook.

ELL Considerations

Learning logs can be especially helpful for ELL students, allowing them to make connections between the subject matter and their lives. Such writing helps them both to understand what they are learning and to verbalize any areas in which they are struggling—a first step in resolving problems. Explain the uses for this type of writing: summarizing main ideas, exploring questions, making predictions, reflecting on new concepts, and so on. Make sure to model the process before you ask students to work on their own.

Extension Activity

Throughout the semester, have students complete the following types of writing-to-learn activities:

- **Admit slips** are brief pieces of writing called for at the beginning of class. An admit slip can be a summary of last night's reading, a review of yesterday's lecture, a preview of a lesson to come, and so on.
- In a **dialogue,** students create imaginary conversations between themselves and someone else. Dialogues can bring information to life, helping students better understand it.
- With **first thoughts,** students write down their immediate impressions about a topic you are preparing to study. These writings will help students focus on new subject matter.
- **Nutshelling** is the process of writing down, in one sentence, the importance of something covered in class.
- When **predicting,** students stop at a key point in a book or lesson and write what they think will be presented next.

Minilessons

Captain's Log, TG 241
Dramatic Scenarios, TG 242
Why? Why? Why?, TG 242

Building a College-Sized Vocabulary

Write for College, 429–444

Novelist Stephen King appreciates the value of vocabulary for aspiring writers. As he says, "Put vocabulary, along with grammar, on the top shelf of your [writer's] toolbox." A healthy vocabulary makes it easier for a student writer to express him- or herself. This chapter offers strategies for building vocabulary, including using context and working with prefixes, suffixes, and roots.

Of Special Interest

- The "Quick Guide" lists eight ways for students to improve their vocabulary. (page 430)
- "Using Context" provides strategies for learning unfamiliar words in a text. (pages 431–432)
- The glossary of prefixes, suffixes, and roots helps students learn new words. (pages 435–444)

Rationale

- As students progress in school, building an effective vocabulary becomes more and more important.
- Knowing how to improve their vocabularies makes students more confident and capable writers, readers, and learners.

Major Concepts

- Keeping a vocabulary notebook, using flash cards, and learning the origin of words will help students improve their vocabulary skills. (page 430)
- Using context clues helps students figure out some unfamiliar words. (pages 431–432)
- When students know the meaning of prefixes, suffixes, and roots, they can figure out the meaning of many words. (pages 434–444)

Performance Standards

Students are expected to . . .

- learn vocabulary-building strategies.
- understand the different parts of words.

Building a College-Sized Vocabulary

Start-Up Activity

During your discussion of the opening two pages (429–430), point out that an individual actually has four vocabularies, one each for reading, listening, speaking, and writing (listed here from largest to smallest). Although there is a great deal of overlap, students will always be able to recognize more words than they can produce. Ask students how having four overlapping vocabularies impacts their ability to learn.

Then, after reviewing pages 434–444, have students read a preselected text containing five or six challenging words. Ask students to study each word in context and write down what they think each one means. As a class, discuss possible meanings for each word and arrive at the correct definition.

ELL Consideration

Many English prefixes, suffixes, and roots come from other languages and may be familiar to some of your students. When studying vocabulary, ask students to identify word parts they already know.

Extension Activity

Have students set aside a portion of their notebooks to record new words. For each word, they should also write down the sentence in which the word is used. Students should then analyze the word using its context, word parts, a dictionary, and a thesaurus.

Minilessons

Medical Terminology 101, TG 242
Getting to the Root, TG 242
Vocabulary Pro, TG 243

Speaking Effectively

Write for College, 445–458

Most experts in the field of communication agree that there are five basic communication functions: expressing feelings, ritualizing (greetings, taking leave, and so on), imagining, informing, and persuading. The last two functions should receive serious attention in any secondary language arts curriculum. "Speaking Effectively" will best serve students when they are preparing speeches to inform and to persuade, the two communication functions requiring the most planning.

Of Special Interest

- "Preparing a Speech" is the first step in the speaking process. (page 446)
- "Writing the Speech" requires careful attention to each main part: the introduction, the body, and the conclusion. (pages 447–448)
- "Rehearsing and Delivering the Speech" is the publishing step in the speaking process. (page 449)

Rationale

- Speaking is a way to inform and to persuade.
- Effective speeches need careful preparation and practice.

Major Concepts

- Preparing a speech requires close attention to purpose, topic, audience, and details. (page 446)
- Speeches can be delivered in three different forms: impromptu presentations, outlined speeches, and written speeches. (page 449)
- Rehearsing is an important part of the speaking process. (page 450)
- Using special appeals can control the tone of a speech. (pages 455–456)
- Conducting an interview is a valuable information-gathering technique. (pages 457–458)

Performance Standards

Students are expected to . . .

- choose appropriate patterns of organization.
- use various techniques to develop an effective introduction.
- present a clear thesis and include valid supporting details to keep the attention of the audience.
- conclude a speech in a way that helps the audience understand what they have learned.

Speaking Effectively

Start-Up Activity

Have everyone (instructor included) freewrite for 10 minutes about his or her speech-making experiences: Consider the preparation for each speech, what worked well, what did not go as planned, and so on. Discuss these writings as a class. Then review the speech-making process as outlined in the handbook. Pay special attention to the style section (pages 455–456) to make sure that students understand the classic stylistic techniques used in formal speeches.

ELL Consideration

If the model speech on pages 452–454 seems too challenging to students, provide them with a simpler model to analyze. Focus their attention on the three main parts of the speech: the introduction, body, and conclusion.

Extension Activity

Invite a guest speaker to give a speech to the class. Ask this speaker to share her or his preparation notes, the written format of the speech, information about making and using visual aids, and so on. If possible, also show taped speeches for response and evaluation.

Minilessons

Being Narrow Minded, TG 243
Oh, Captain, My Captain, TG 243
Speaking Up, TG 243

Multimedia Reports

Write for College, 459–463

Albert Einstein once said, "Computers are incredibly fast, accurate, and stupid; humans are incredibly slow, inaccurate, and brilliant; together they are powerful beyond imagination." This combined "power" will help students turn their essays and speeches into compelling multimedia reports. The chapter contains writing guidelines for creating a multimedia presentation plus an interactive report. Samples of each are available on the Write Source Web site: http://www.thewritesource.com/.

Of Special Interest

- "Writing Guidelines" and "Creating a Presentation Storyboard" take students through the process of developing a multimedia presentation. (pages 460–461)
- "Writing Guidelines" and "Creating an Interactive Storyboard" take students through the process of developing an interactive report. (pages 462–463)

Rationale

- Today's students—and tomorrow's businesspeople—need to be able to use technology to deliver reports and presentations.

Major Concepts

- Students can turn an essay or a speech into a multimedia presentation by adding visuals and/or sound to the basic text. (pages 460–461)
- Students can turn an essay or a speech into a computerized interactive report through the use of hypertext. (pages 462–463)

Performance Standards

Students are expected to . . .

- incorporate technology into the presentation of their essays and speeches.

Multimedia Reports

Start-Up Activity

If at all possible, invite an expert in business communications to share a multimedia presentation with the class. Afterward, have the expert explain the process he or she used to develop the presentation. Also ask your school's technology teacher to share her or his expertise related to incorporating technology into presentations or speeches.

ELL Consideration

For students who have had little experience in preparing presentations, provide the following checklist as a basic guide for their work.

Multimedia Report Checklist

Ideas

____ **1.** Have I included the main ideas of my essay or speech in my multimedia report?

____ **2.** Does each slide or sound bite suit the audience and the purpose of the presentation?

Organization

____ **3.** Do I state the topic in the introduction?

____ **4.** Do I include the main points in the body?

____ **5.** Do I restate my focus in the closing?

Voice

____ **6.** Do I sound interested and enthusiastic?

Media and Word Choice

____ **7.** Are the words and pictures on each slide easy to see?

____ **8.** Have I chosen the best audio and visual clips?

Presentation Fluency

____ **9.** Does my oral report flow smoothly from point to point?

Conventions

____ **10.** Is each slide free of errors in grammar, spelling, capitalization, and punctuation?

Extension Activity

If any of your students are especially knowledgeable about multimedia software programs, assign them to an advisory board to help other students learn how to use the programs.

Minilesson

More Power!, TG 243

The Testing Center Teacher's Notes

Writing on Demand

Answering Document-Based Questions

Taking Exit and Entrance Exams

Taking Advanced Placement* Exams

Writing on Demand

Write for College, 465–472

Writing on demand has become an essential element in today's English classrooms. As co-authors Anne Ruggles Gere, Leila Christenbury, and Kelly Sassi state in *Writing on Demand,* "Today, writing on demand is not an occasional, in-some-cases situation but an omnipresent one that faces all students at all levels of skill and ability." The ability to write on demand is especially critical for juniors and seniors faced with advanced placement and college-entrance exams. This chapter helps students prepare for writing-on-demand experiences and provides a strategy for responding to a prompt in a timed writing.

Of Special Interest

- "Analyzing a Prompt" provides tips for preparing for writing-on-demand experiences. (page 466)
- "Understanding the Purpose of a Prompt" offers a strategy for identifying the key information in a prompt. (page 467)

Rationale

- Writing on demand has become important because of high-stake testing.
- Reviewing the basics of writing on demand helps students prepare for timed writings.
- Analyzing a writing prompt is the critical first step in any writing-on-demand situation.
- Crafting an effective response to a prompt requires a working knowledge of the writing process.

Major Concepts

- In timed writings, "short-term" time management is essential. (page 465)
- The STRAP questions help students analyze a prompt. (page 466)
- Writing a thesis (focus) statement is an important first step when planning a response. (page 468)
- Writing an effective response requires clear, quick thinking. (pages 469–470)

Performance Standards

Students are expected to . . .

- craft effective responses in timed writings.
- apply proven strategies in writing-on-demand situations.

Writing on Demand

Start-Up Activity

After reviewing the first part of the chapter (pages 465–468), have students analyze the following two prompts using the STRAP questions. (Remind students that some prompts may not include answers for every STRAP question. They should use their best judgment to answer those questions.)

Prompt 1

Former Green Bay Packers coach Vince Lombardi knew a lot about teamwork. According to Lombardi, "People who work together will win, whether it be against complex football defenses, or the problems of modern society." Drawing on your own experience, write an essay for your classmates explaining how a project you worked on benefited from teamwork.

Prompt 2

In response to problems with traffic in your community, a city council member has proposed assessing a $50 fee on each car. The money collected will be used to reduce the cost of local bus service. As a concerned member of the community, write a letter to the city council to persuade them to vote for or against this new fee.

ELL Considerations

Review effective responses to prompts to show students what is expected of them. Make sure that they understand how to organize their limited time for responding and how writing on demand is evaluated (with an emphasis on ideas, organization, and voice).

Extension Activity

Have students plan, write, and revise a response to one of the prompts that they analyzed in the start-up activity. Ask them to complete their work within a prescribed amount of time (the SAT essay allows students 25 minutes). Afterward, discuss the responding process or have students reflect on the experience in a notebook or journal entry. (Repeat this activity throughout the semester.)

Minilesson

Ready, Set, Go! TG 244

Answering Document-Based Questions

Write for College, 473–480

Answering document-based questions (DBQ's) is now an important feature on advanced placement (AP) exams. DBQ's ask students to approach problems in a way similar to that of professional researchers. Students must identify the sources of documents they cite, check for consistencies between documents, and establish a thesis that thoughtfully addresses the problem based on the available research (the documents). Because DBQ's are so intellectually stimulating, instructors should try to use them in a number of situations—to prompt discussion at the beginning of a unit, as a summary at the end of a unit, and so on.

Of Special Interest

- "Responding Tips" helps students answer DBQ's. (page 474)
- "Sample Documents" provides example documents linked to a timely problem. (pages 475–478)
- "Sample DBQ and Response" shows how one writer draws key details from the example documents in an essay response. (pages 479–480)

Rationale

- Students need an understanding of all types of test questions, including DBQ's.
- Learning how to use primary and secondary sources of information helps students with their academic writing.

Major Concepts

- Answering DBQ's helps students think and write like a historian, social scientist, or physical scientist. (page 473)
- Documents can be print excerpts from books and other text sources as well as visual items such as graphs and editorial cartoons. (pages 475–478)
- Answering a DBQ requires interpreting and synthesizing information. (pages 479–480)

Performance Standards

Students are expected to . . .

- read and interpret information and data from a variety of resources.
- establish a central idea (thesis) and gather information to support it.

Answering Document-Based Questions

Start-Up Activity

Share with students three sources of information (a news article, a photograph, an editorial cartoon, an opinion letter, and so on) about a timely topic. Determine how the sources are similar and different in treatment. Then, as a class, establish a thesis that thoughtfully expresses the central idea reflected in the documents. Also have students identify information from the sources that supports the thesis. Upon completion of this activity, students should be in the right frame of mind to review the chapter.

ELL Considerations

Remember that the students' ability to synthesize and evaluate information from documents depends on (1) whether they have practiced these skills in their first language, (2) their level of English competency, and (3) their overall experience with thinking and writing in their new language. To help them along, regularly demonstrate the process of *synthesizing* (combining, predicting, proposing, and so on) and *evaluating* (recommending, assessing, criticizing, and so on).

Enrichment Activity

For additional DBQ practice, have students submit three or more documents discussing an interesting topic. (Preferably, documents should be taken from periodicals so that copies can easily be made.) At different points during the year, supply a particular set of documents to students and have them answer a document-based question you have created. Specify a time limit for students to complete their work.

Minilesson

Exploring the Unknown, TG 244

Taking Exit and Entrance Exams

Write for College, 481–494

For better or for worse, education in today's classrooms is all about assessment and accountability. The importance placed on testing puts a great deal of stress on teachers and students. For those students who believe that they are bad test takers, their problem may be preparation. If students keep up with their daily work, study effectively, and employ test-taking strategies, they have a good chance to perform well on any exam. Guide students through the material in this chapter to help them improve their test-taking strategies. This information will help students take high school exit exams, college entrance exams, and other district- or state-level tests.

Of Special Interest

- Writing-related multiple-choice questions test students' ability to decide if a sentence or passage contains some type of error. (pages 482–488)
- Responding to a writing prompt requires students to write an essay, a narrative, or a letter. (pages 489–494)

Rationale

- Understanding the presentation of writing-related questions and prompts on exit and entrance exams helps students prepare for these tests.

Major Concepts

- Successful test taking requires careful reading and understanding of each question. (pages 481, 483, and 489)

Performance Standards

Students are expected to . . .

- perform to their best ability on exit and entrance exams.

Taking Exit and Entrance Exams

Start-Up Activity

Ask students to take out a piece of paper and number it from 1 to 10. (Assure them that they are not taking a pop quiz.) Have them list their top 10 reasons for not liking tests. (Examples: *"I don't ever feel prepared." "Tests make me feel dumb." "So much hinges on tests."*) Afterward, discuss their responses as a class. Then guide students through the chapter to help them prepare more effectively for all testing situations.

ELL Consideration

Until students reach an advanced level of language mastery, they are very literal readers. As a result, they may have difficulty with certain test questions and may not be able to interpret key words *(all, except, not)*. To address this problem, review with students the construction of all types of test questions.

Extension Activity

Throughout the school year, regularly give students opportunities to respond to prompts in timed writings. Remind students to review "Responding Tips" on page 474 before they do their writing. Afterward, have them evaluate their writing using the "Checklist for Effective Writing" on page 20.

Minilesson

Key Questions, TG 244

Taking Advanced Placement* Exams

Write for College, 495–507

George Orwell once said, "Great literature is simply language charged with meaning to the utmost possible degree." It is "great literature" of all types that serves as the focus for the exams in the two AP English courses—Language and Composition and Literature and Composition. This chapter in the handbook can serve as a review guide prior to either exam. Additional information related to test taking can be found in the other chapters of the "The Testing Center" section of the handbook. (See pages 465–494.)

Of Special Interest

- "AP English Language and Composition" provides guidelines and samples to help students complete both parts of the exam. (pages 497–501)
- "AP English Literature and Composition" provides guidelines and samples to help students complete both parts of the exam. (pages 502–507)

Rationale

- Students need strategies to help them prepare for AP exams.
- Studying examples helps students understand what to expect on the exams.

Major Concepts

- Multiple-choice questions test students' ability to analyze literary passages. (pages 497–498 and 502–503)
- Responding to prompts requires students to defend a position and/or articulate a clear understanding of a literary text. (pages 500–501 and 505–507)

Performance Standards

Students are expected to . . .

- perform to their best ability on AP exams.

Taking Advanced Placement* Exams

Start-Up Activity

Ask students to take out a piece of paper and write a paragraph about someone they know or have read about who has achieved some level of success. Ask for volunteers to read their paragraphs aloud for discussion. Focus the discussion on important lessons that can be learned from each story, inspiring students as they prepare for the AP examinations.

ELL Consideration

Until students reach an advanced level of language mastery, they are very literal readers. As a result, they may have difficulty with certain exam questions and may not be able to interpret key words *(all, except, not)*. To address this problem, review with students the construction of a multiple-choice question and a writing prompt.

Extension Activity

During one of your in-class timed writings (just prior to the AP test event), stop students after one-third of the time has passed. Ask them to explain exactly what they have done so far so you can see who is and who isn't actually planning before they write. This discussion will allow students to share their prewriting and writing strategies. (During another timed writing, consider stopping students close to the end of the allotted time. Ask them to explain exactly what they have done up to that point.)

Minilesson

Testing Yourself, TG 244

Proofreader's Guide Teacher's Notes

Marking Punctuation

Checking Mechanics

Understanding Idioms

Using the Right Word

Parts of Speech

Using the Language

Proofreader's Guide

Write for College, 509–593

The conventions of language take on real meaning when students are ready to share (publish) what they have learned. Standard use and presentation of the language is essential to communicating effectively. To provide students with a handy reference, the "Proofreader's Guide" is separated into five main parts: "Marking Punctuation," "Checking Mechanics," "Using the Right Word," "Parts of Speech," and "Using the Language." Each section contains explanations with examples to illustrate the basic rules.

Of Special Interest

- The "Proofreader's Guide" provides explanations with examples to illustrate the basic rules, or conventions. (pages 509–560)
- This teacher's guide provides minilessons for the proofreader's section of the handbook. (pages 245–246)

Rationale

- Learning the conventions of the English language builds fluency and effective communication skills.

Major Concepts

- "Marking Punctuation" helps students use punctuation correctly in their writing. (pages 509–528)
- "Checking Mechanics" provides a reference for students to check their mechanics and spelling for correctness. (pages 529–544)
- "Using the Right Word" lists words that are frequently confused and misused. (pages 551–560)
- "Parts of Speech" presents the eight parts of speech with examples (pages 561–579)
- "Using the Language" helps students learn standard syntax for the English language and use fair language in communications. (pages 580–593)

Performance Standards

Students are expected to . . .

- use punctuation and the mechanics of writing.
- write complete sentences varying in length and structure.
- identify and use the parts of speech correctly.
- use standard English to communicate effectively.

Almanac Teacher's Notes

Language

Common Parliamentary Procedures

Six-Year Calendar

Weights and Measures

Periodic Table of the Elements

Historical Time Line

Almanac

Write for College, 595–616

The "Almanac" helps make *Write for College* a general, all-purpose reference book that students can use in all of their classes. This section includes language, common parliamentary procedures, a six-year calendar, weights and measures, the periodic table of the elements, and a historical time line.

Of Special Interest

- The "Almanac" provides helpful, generic information that is useful in all content areas. (pages 595–616)

Rationale

- Students should be able to access and interpret visual information.
- Learning to use reference tools is a necessary life skill.

Major Concepts

- The "Language" page features the manual alphabet and a map of languages that influenced English. (page 595)
- "Common Parliamentary Procedures" used to keep meetings orderly and efficient are listed. (page 596)
- A "Six-Year Calendar" makes long-range planning easier. (page 597)
- "Weights and Measures" includes metric and standard systems used in the United States. (pages 598–601)
- "Periodic Table of the Elements" lists the basic elements of matter (page 602)
- A historical time line lists some cultural, political, and social changes or events of the last 500 years. (pages 603–616)

Performance Standards

Students are expected to . . .

- use reference materials to increase their understanding of a particular subject area and expand their knowledge of relationships between content areas

Approaches to Writing

The approaches to writing described on the following pages offer you a variety of ways to meet the individual needs of your students.

Effective Writing Instruction

Contemporary writing research shows us that writing isn't really taught. That is, writing isn't a set of facts, forms, or formulas that a teacher imparts, and it certainly isn't worksheet busywork. We know that it is (or should be) a student-centered activity that is learned through a variety of writing experiences.

The teacher's role in effective writing programs changes from lecturer to mentor as teachers and students write and learn together. By providing the proper mixture of freedom, encouragement, and guidance, writing teachers create environments that promote writing as a student-centered learning activity. Writing approaches that demonstrate this philosophy share two basic goals:

1. **Students learn to write.** Students learn to write in the same way all writers learn—by practicing the craft. The best writing programs give students frequent, significant, and varied writing opportunities that explore a variety of purposes and audiences. They receive constructive, supportive, and challenging responses to their writing.

2. **Students write to learn.** Writing is thinking on paper. Through writing, students explore ideas and questions—about themselves, about the world, and about subjects they're studying in order to understand concepts, discover facts, clarify thinking, and pass along information.

In addition to sharing these two goals, effective writing programs exhibit the following characteristics:

No Textbook Needed Most textbooks by their very nature are prescriptive. They are designed to teach writing skills, but they are also intended to tie the teacher and student to the textbook. Good writing programs encourage independent thinking and use the students' own writing as the text. Supported by the necessary reference materials (including a handbook), students and teachers help one another develop and grow as writers.

Individualized Because all writers are unique, one formula for writing instruction doesn't work for all students. Strong writing programs allow students to write and work individually, supported as needed by a 10- to 15-minute minilesson about a basic skill or rhetorical concept.

Interactive Classroom Structure Strong writing programs promote active learning. Writing classrooms are structured to reflect real writing experiences. Students interact with one another and with the teacher to discuss their writing. On a given day, a student might spend time in a group critiquing session, work on a project of his or her own, or help a classmate sort out a writing problem.

Well Planned Even the most motivated students will take advantage of too much freedom. Deadlines, support materials, methods of instruction, methods of measuring writing progress, and classroom management procedures all have to be established for a program to be successful.

Adaptable and Integrated Curriculum A good writing program is flexible. It must accommodate new methods of writing instruction or assessment. Likewise, a good writing program combines various approaches to provide the best writing opportunities for the students. What follows is a brief description of five significant approaches to writing.

An Overview of the Approaches

As you begin your search for an appropriate writing approach, remember that these five approaches are not exclusive. One approach can be used in conjunction with other writing approaches. When designing a writing program, choose an approach (or a combination) that fits your needs and those of your students. Remember, you must provide students with guidelines and strategies for approaching writing as well as numerous opportunities to practice what they learn.

1 The Personal-Experience Approach

The focus of this approach is simple: Students enjoy writing and find it meaningful if it stems from their personal experiences and observations. Students usually keep a journal in a personal-experience (experiential) program so that they always have a number of potential writing ideas to draw from. Often the writing process and some form of writing workshop are incorporated into the program.

Freewriting (spontaneous writing) also plays a key role in this approach to writing. Both freewriting and journal writing help students write honestly about their personal experiences when they do assigned writing. And these techniques help students eventually produce writing that readers will find interesting.

Review the forms of writing in *Write for College* (page 141), and you will note that we generally address personal forms of writing before we address content-oriented forms of writing. The more students write from personal experience, the better able they are to address increasingly complex experiences in more sophisticated forms of writing. (See page 125 in this guide for more information.) For more about the personal-experience approach, read Ken Macrorie's *Writing to Be Read* and *The I-Search Paper* as well as James Moffett's *Active Voice: A Writing Program Across the Curriculum*.

2 The Process Approach

While using the process approach, students learn that writing—real writing—is a process of exploration and discovery rather than an end product or a series of basic skills. As students develop their writing, they make use of all steps in the writing process—prewriting, drafting, revising, editing and proofreading, and publishing. And the writing they develop, for the most part, stems from their own experience and thinking.

"Like stones, words are laborious and unforgiving, and the fitting of them together, like the fitting of stones, demands great patience and strength of purpose and particular skill."

—Edmund Morrison

Students use prewriting activities to discover writing ideas they know and care about. They are encouraged to talk about their ideas and create a classroom community of writers. They write first drafts freely and quickly, and they revise carefully. After editing and proofreading, students share or publish their work.

Write for College discusses the writing process (starting on page 1). Also note that the guidelines for the specific forms of writing are organized according to the steps in the writing process. (See pages 126–127 in this guide for more on the writing process.) For more about the writing process, read *What a Writer Needs* by Ralph Fletcher and *Teaching Grammar in Context* by Constance Weaver.

3 The Trait-Based Approach

Students who use a trait-based approach to writing become confident, competent managers of their own writing process. In particular, they learn how to approach revision because they know what makes writing work.

Trait-based instruction focuses on key features—or traits—that most writers, editors, and thoughtful readers agree are essential to effective writing:

- ideas
- organization
- voice
- word choice
- sentence fluency
- conventions

Students are taught each trait individually, but eventually they address all of them as they revise and edit their own work. The strength of trait-based instruction lies in its power to make writing and revision manageable for students. Like an athletic coach, a trait-based writing instructor helps students develop overall proficiency one critical skill at a time. (See page 128 in this guide.) For more about the trait-based approach, read *Creating Writers* by Vicki Spandel.

4 The Thematic Approach

When using this approach, the teacher (with student input) chooses a theme (such as *change, power, courage,* and so on) that serves as the focal point for an intense, integrated language experience—an experience that immerses students in integrated reading, writing, and speaking activities that may cross into other curricular areas.

The writing teacher provides pieces of literature and other prewriting activities as starting points for the thematic study. Students then explore the theme from different perspectives and eventually focus on one aspect of the theme. Writing projects evolve from these activities.

Thematic teaching isn't just for English class. Teachers of any other content area can also be thematic teachers. In addition, teams of teachers from various disciplines can work together by choosing a theme and integrating writing, reading, speaking, and listening activities in different content areas. These interdisciplinary thematic units can provide students with complete language experiences that will actively involve them in learning. (See page 129 in this guide.) For more about interdisciplinary teaching and the thematic approach, read *Aims and Options: A Thematic Approach to Writing* by Rodney D. Keller.

"The maker of a sentence launches out into the infinite and builds a road into chaos and old night, and is followed by those who hear him with something of wild, creative delight."

—Ralph Waldo Emerson

5 The Writing Workshop Approach

In a writing workshop, students write or work on writing-related issues every day (reading, researching, critiquing, participating in collaborative writing, and so on). They keep all of their writing in folders, and they produce a specified number of finished pieces by the end of the term. They are encouraged to take risks and to experiment with new forms and techniques. Support during each writing project comes from both peer and teacher conferences. Students use the steps in the writing process to develop their writing and share it with the group.

The teacher acts as a guide and facilitator, creating a classroom environment that is conducive to a workshop. Desks are arranged for student interaction, and the classroom is stocked with relevant reading and writing materials. Instruction and advice are given as they are needed—on an individual basis, in small groups, or to the entire class. (See pages 146 and 158 in this guide.) For more about the writing workshop approach, read *Using the Workshop Approach in the High School English Classroom* by Cynthia D. Urbanski.

The Personal-Experience Approach

The focus of this approach is simple: Students enjoy writing that stems from their own experience and observation. Developing personal-writing skills prepares students to address more complex content-oriented writing.

Getting Started

Before you begin to implement this approach, remember these key points:

- The personal approach incorporates the writing process and the writing workshop.
- Journals, a key component of the personal approach, can be used in many ways to accomplish different goals.
- The audience and purpose for this type of writing change as the writer moves from a personal to a more formal style of writing.

Implementation Guidelines

- Establish a classroom environment that invites students to write by providing stimulating topic ideas—through books, magazines, posters, displays, and so on.
- Establish a weekly routine for journal writing.
- Explore a variety of purposes and audiences for student writing. Will the writing be shared with the teacher? With other students?

Teaching Strategies

In addition to the strategies provided in *Write for College*, try these ideas:

Journals

Diary In this journal, students record their thoughts and feelings. Due to the private nature of this type of writing, it may or may not be shared.

Freewrite Journal This teacher-directed journal offers writing prompts that direct students to explore ideas in daily 10-minute quick writes.

Dialogue Journal The teacher and student (or two students) write back and forth to one another in this type of journal. Dialogue may be personal or related to a subject area being studied. This lends itself to classroom pairing in other cities, states, or countries.

Personal Notebook In this journal, students record ideas, observations, and insights that they may use in future writing pieces.

Class or Project Journal In this journal, students respond to what they are reading or studying in class. Questions, predictions, and commentary are common in this type of journal. For a group project, students document their participation and responsibilities as well as evaluations of the group's performance.

Learning Log In this journal, students record what they are learning. In science, this could be an observation log for a lab experiment. In social studies, this could be a freewrite exploring the relationship between what is being studied and students' past experience or knowledge.

Research (I-Search)

Journals After students choose a topic that interests them, allow them to explore the topic through mapping or brainstorming. Then have them write to explore different perspectives on their topic—by taking notes as they conduct an interview or talk with an "expert." They should keep a log, recording questions that arise during the process as well as answers and other discoveries. Students should also record their responses to and summaries of background reading on the topic.

Research Report This formal report includes personal connections students make with the topic. As they improve their research skills, their research reports become more sophisticated.

Informal to Formal

Transitions from personal to more complex forms could include the following:

Informal	Formal
Sensory freewriting	Observation reports Descriptions
Discussions of topics Brainstorming Mapping	Essays Speeches Editorials
Dialogue journals Freewrite monologues	One-act plays Argumentation essays
Story starters Dreams Writing prompts	Short stories Poetry Narratives

The Process Approach

This approach emphasizes the process of exploring and discovering rather than the end product. In the process approach, writing is viewed as a developmental process rather than an accumulation of skills. *Write for College* divides the process into these steps: prewriting, writing, revising, editing and proofreading, and publishing.

Getting Started

Before you begin to implement the process approach, remember these key points:

- The writing process is not linear; it is cyclical. Steps are repeated in different order depending on the writers and the writing assignments.
- The writing process is unique for each writer.
- Writing is not a neat, formulaic, or orderly process.
- Not all writing needs to progress through all the stages of the writing process. Considering audience and purpose helps writers develop a piece of writing.
- Because the writing process helps turn thinking into writing, it's valuable in all content areas.

Implementation Guidelines

- Give students many opportunities to practice the steps of the writing process—especially prewriting and revising.
- Write with your students to show them that you are not just an evaluator, but also a writer.
- Encourage students to think about their writing process and write reflectively about it as they develop a piece.
- Emphasize creativity and exploration (rather than perfection) during prewriting and drafting; stress organization during revising; focus on refinement during editing and proofreading.
- Use writing folders to store "works-in-progress."

Teaching Strategies

In addition to the prewriting, drafting, revising, editing and proofreading, and publishing strategies offered in *Write for College,* try these ideas:

Prewriting

While prewriting strategies are designed to stimulate the flow of ideas before any structured writing begins, they can also help writers explore ideas throughout the writing process. In prewriting, the writer discovers expected and unexpected relationships between ideas and experiments with ways of developing and supporting these ideas.

Color-Coded Cluster Color coding can help identify related ideas during the exploration process. For example, students may explore and cluster a topic by using the five senses, coding each sense by color. Such coding can also be used to highlight ideas according to patterns of organization—cause and effect, problem and solution, pro and con, comparison and contrast.

Branching Organizers and graphs provide a tighter structure for the exploration process. (See pages 27–28 in *Write for College* for more on graphic organizers.)

Musical Freewriting Accompany student writing with music to create a specific mood. This prewriting activity encourages students to explore a topic from different perspectives.

Question Clusters Have students cluster by focusing on the journalist's questions (who? what? when? where? why? and how?) to develop their ideas.

Drafting

The drafting stage should be spontaneous and creative—the process of shaping and connecting ideas. In this stage, writers learn what they have to say about a topic. This experimental, chaotic, and often messy process takes time, energy, patience, and persistence.

Great Authors, Great Ideas Read aloud some great leads and endings. Choose different styles so that students don't become convinced that there is only one way to write an introduction or ending. Put examples from various forms of writing on the overhead, read them, and discuss what makes these introductions and conclusions work. Then give students opportunities to experiment with different introductions and conclusions of their own.

Teacher Drafters Share one of your own drafts with your students. Allow them to see how messy and disorganized this stage can be for you.

For Whom Am I Writing? Practice writing to different audiences and for different purposes. Have students write letters or directions on the same topic to elderly relatives and friends, to students in other classes, and to younger students. Discuss how the audience affects the writing.

Sound Check Good writing is communication between the writer and the reader. Ask students to explain their topic to someone else by pretending to be talking to the reader. Have them focus on making their ideas understandable and interesting.

Revising

Revision is the act of "looking again" at a piece of writing with an eye for improving it. Remind students that any writing they take to finished form must be thoroughly revised before it will be effective.

Teacher Revisers Make a transparency of one of your first drafts and discuss its strengths and weaknesses with students. Then show them your revision work and your second draft.

Expanding and Contracting Ask students to expand a professional writing model by adding concrete details and specific support. Compare it to the original and discuss reasons for expanding a piece of writing. Then ask students to narrow the focus of a writing model to be more specific.

Building Strong Connections Take a short story with strong transitions, cut it into sections, and mix them up. Then have students reassemble the story by using the transitions to connect ideas. The story "Charles" by Shirley Jackson works well for this activity. Another idea is to cut a paragraph into sentences and have students reassemble it in outline form.

Freewriting Frenzy Have students choose from their own journal freewrites and experiment with writing for a different audience, changing the form or purpose, experimenting with different patterns of organization, or changing the point of view.

Editing and Proofreading

Editing and proofreading involve line-by-line changes that make a piece of writing readable and accurate. Editing is most effective when students learn to approach it as a process of fine-tuning and correcting a piece of writing after it has been revised.

Read It Out Loud Assign student partners to read each other's draft out loud, or have students tape-record their own drafts. Hearing a piece of writing is an effective way to check for sentence fluency, word choice, and accuracy.

Model Correctness Provide editing and proofreading practice by putting sample paragraphs on a transparency and correcting them together.

Bloopers Have students target errors in newspapers, magazines, newsletters, and advertisements. Offer rewards to "typo terminators."

Focus Have students edit for one kind of error at a time. As they become adept at seeing errors, they may concentrate on more than one type of error at a time.

Publishing

Publishing is the driving force behind writing. It makes all of a student's prewriting, drafting, revising, and editing worth the effort. Publishing can take many forms.

Publishing in Process When students read their writing to a partner, they get immediate feedback and reaction; this directs further writing. Read out loud from your own work and solicit responses from the class, using appropriate response guidelines on pages 49–51 in *Write for College.*

Quotable Quotations Each week, put a passage of student writing on the board as a model of good writing. (Get permission first and allow the writer to remain anonymous.)

Literary Magazine Have the class publish stories, poems, and essays in a literary magazine made available to the entire student body.

Real-World Writers Have students write letters of inquiry or application to an individual outside of the school setting.

The Trait-Based Approach

Trait-based writing can be integrated into the writing process and a writing workshop. This approach focuses on helping students identify, in their own writing and in the writing of others, those qualities that make writing strong.

Getting Started

Before you begin implementing the trait-based approach, remember these key points:

- The trait-based approach helps students to become good assessors of all writing and to improve their own writing.
- Check *Write for College* (pages 15–20) and page 123 in this guide for more information on the traits.

Implementation Guidelines

- Use writing models from books, newspapers, menus, travel brochures, and the workplace. Discuss how the traits of effective writing are (or are not) demonstrated in each model.
- Display posters featuring each trait.
- Give students rubrics (scoring guides) before they begin writing so that they understand what is expected for each writing task.
- Once a week, as a class, score a piece of anonymous writing to help refine students' assessment skills.
- Use trait language to respond to student writing; ask students to use trait language to respond to one another's writing.
- Hold peer-response sessions during which students can discuss their writing according to the traits.

Teaching Strategies

Ideas

Textbook Ideas In small groups, have students find a textbook section that shows good idea development. As a class, discuss this trait.

Pick a Paragraph Using paragraphs from newspapers, recipes, advertisements, and so on, discuss the idea development of each sample.

Organization

From the Pros Choose a professional piece of writing with excellent transitions, cut it into pieces, and have small groups reassemble it. Discuss how transitions aid organization.

From Start to Finish Look at introductions (and conclusions) by professional writers. Discuss what makes the introductions and conclusions "work."

Voice

Imaginary Conversations Have students freewrite about a news event using two different voices. Share the freewrites and discuss how the voices affect the writing.

Audience Adjustment Have students write three sets of instructions for the same task: one set for a child, one for an elderly friend, and one for a classmate. How do the three voices vary?

Word Choice

Workouts with Words Using pieces of their own writing, have students identify strong and weak word choices. Then have them revise their work by replacing general words with vivid ones.

Theme Dictionaries Have students create dictionaries according to their areas of interest: music, sports, technology, and so on.

Sentence Fluency

Paragraph Makeovers Give students two paragraphs: one with short, choppy sentences and the other with only one long sentence. Ask them to rewrite each paragraph by changing the sentence lengths.

Test Textbooks Using textbooks, have students chart sentence lengths, beginnings, and transitions. Discuss the differences and similarities among the texts.

Conventions

Reward Offered Reward students for finding mechanical errors in your work.

Editor's Desk Have students use copy editors' symbols in their editing work.

The Thematic Approach

The thematic approach to writing helps students use language meaningfully to identify relationships within and between content areas. With this approach, a teacher or team of teachers chooses a theme to serve as the focus of an integrated learning experience that combines writing, reading, speaking, and listening skills.

Getting Started

Before you begin to implement the thematic approach, remember these key points:

- The thematic approach can be used to study one discipline or it can span the disciplines.
- Thematic writing provides an avenue for students to write to learn—to connect their learning (synthesize and integrate), to apply it to new situations, and to think creatively.
- While students contribute to decisions about the type of writing project, its length, its audience, and the time schedule, teachers guide them through the writing process.

Implementation Guidelines

- Thematic projects may be written individually, in small groups, or as a class.
- This approach incorporates the process approach. Familiarize students with the steps of the writing process before you begin.
- Writing activities should reflect clear objectives and target areas in which students are grounded in the content or theme.
- A topic should be selected that is neither too general nor too specific, one that is relevant and interesting to students.
- As a framework for exploration, specific questions can provide a "table of contents," a scope and a sequence for the thematic study.
- Writing assignments in different content areas should involve inquiry, discovery, and synthesis.

Teaching Strategies

Choosing a Theme or Topic

Teacher-Chosen Theme Discuss interesting material about the theme. Then collaborate with students about how to explore the theme.

Student-Chosen Theme Brainstorm for interesting topics. In small groups, have students cluster a theme. List the topic in the center with spokes representing other subjects or areas of literacy (writing, speaking, listening, thinking, reading).

Continue Exploring Talk about and list various audiences and how they would affect the handling of this theme.

Resources Provide reading material relevant to the theme. Encourage the use of both primary and secondary sources.

Organizing the Thematic Study

Create a Framework Discuss and develop questions that the thematic study will answer to keep the scope and focus of the exploration in view.

During the Thematic Study

Other Voices Have students interview community members who are familiar with the theme. Invite speakers. Schedule video presentations.

Synthesize and Integrate Information Have students write to enlarge their perspectives. Employ whole-class and small-group activities:

- speeches
- magazines
- one-act plays
- newspapers
- poetry anthologies
- debates
- multimedia presentations

Assign individual writing activities:

- journals
- editorials
- cartoons
- book reviews
- research papers
- interviews
- proposals
- personal essays
- problem-solution essays
- argumentation essays
- letters of complaint
- observation reports
- song compositions

After the Thematic Study

Publish Create a class newspaper, anthology, magazine, research report, or multimedia presentation.

Perform Present plays, speeches, or debates.

Display Design a bulletin board or Web site.

The Writing Workshop Approach

The writing workshop approach offers students a writing experience that is similar to a real-world writing experience. In this approach, students write independently; they choose their own topics and spend the class period working through stages of the writing process that apply to their topics and writing needs. Like professional writers who get feedback on their writing from editors and publishers, student writers get support for their writing from their peers and teacher during conferences.

Getting Started

Before you begin to implement this approach, remember these key points:

- This approach establishes a writing community as students and teacher work collaboratively through the writing process.
- In an informal workshop classroom, the teacher serves as a writing mentor.
- Each class period focuses on providing students with a large block of time to work on writing projects of their choice.
- Depending on the group's needs, the teacher may use class time to discuss writing issues, address questions, and share professional models to guide the writing process.
- Students work through the steps of the writing process at their own pace, conferring with other students and the teacher as necessary.
- Students write daily for a set period of time.
- Students use writing folders for both finished and unfinished pieces. For each marking period, students choose two or three pieces to develop for a grade assessment.

Implementation Guidelines

- Despite the relaxed classroom structure of this approach, routines must be maintained. (See the class schedule in the next column.)
- Establish areas for certain tasks: writing area, conferencing area, editing and proofreading area, publishing area.
- Share examples of your own writing, including problems you've encountered as well as ways you've tried to solve them.
- Establish your role as a facilitator—responding to, encouraging, and even challenging students as they develop their ideas through the writing process.

Teaching Strategies

The sample schedule below shows how one teacher organized a writing workshop. Since the schedule was designed for one of the first weeks of the workshop, all students were asked to participate in the minilessons. This plan would change, of course, according to the group's needs. One teacher might conduct writing workshops for three days a week and reading workshops for the other two days. Another might vary the routine to conduct an extended lesson on an important writing skill. Another might conduct minilessons two or three days a week and have students write in a journal on the other days.

My Weekly Planner

<table>
<tr><th>Mon.</th><th>Tues.</th><th>Wed.</th><th>Thurs.</th><th>Fri.</th></tr>
<tr><td colspan="5">Writing Minilessons
(10 minutes as needed)</td></tr>
<tr><td colspan="5">Status Checks
(5 minutes)
Find out what students will work on for the day.</td></tr>
<tr><td colspan="5">Individual Work
(30 minutes)
Prewriting, Writing, Revising, Editing, Conferencing, or Publishing</td></tr>
<tr><td colspan="5">Whole-Class Sharing Session
(5 minutes)</td></tr>
</table>

Writing and Learning **Across the Curriculum**

The strategies and guidelines discussed in this section will help you make writing an important part of your curriculum, whether you teach mathematics, science, social studies, or English.

Introducing Writing Across the Curriculum

"I hear and I forget;
I see and I remember;
I write and I understand."
—Chinese proverb

Q. What is writing across the curriculum?

A. Writing across the curriculum (WAC) is the use of writing as a teaching and learning tool in all courses. Based on his or her course content and learning goals, each teacher chooses which writing activities to use and how to use them.

Q. How is writing a tool for learning in all subject areas, including technology?

A. Cross-curricular writing helps students in three ways. It helps them . . .

1. to think through and find meaning in their learning,
2. to retain what they learn, and
3. to develop their learning skills.

When students find meaning in their learning, they have the incentive to work hard and to retain what they learn. (See the cluster diagram on page 133.)

Q. How does *Write for College* support WAC?

A. *Write for College* is an all-school handbook—a guide to writing, thinking, and learning across the curriculum. The diagram on the following page shows how *Write for College* supports writing and learning.

The framework on page 134 suggests which forms of writing featured in *Write for College* can be used in writing across the curriculum. *Write for College* provides guidelines, strategies, and writing models for many forms of writing, and most of them—from journals to research writing—could be an effective learning activity in any course. In addition, this "Writing Across the Curriculum" section presents activities designed for specific courses (see pages 139–141).

Q. How does this teacher's guide support teachers who assign writing projects in their classrooms?

A. "Writing Across the Curriculum" (pages 132–144 in this guide) is designed to help every teacher who assigns writing. In this section, you will find many easy-to-implement writing-to-learn activities that promote learning in all subject areas. (See "Writing to Learn Activities" on pages 138–139.) "Designing Writing Assignments" (pages 142–144 in this guide) offers ideas and strategies on designing and presenting writing assignments using a variety of forms of writing.

To give students experience in writing persuasively in all subject areas, "Research" on page 143 suggests assigning the position paper.

Q. How does writing enhance learning in my subject area?

A. Whether you assign a 10-minute freewrite to explore ideas on a topic or a full-blown research paper, writing helps all students learn . . .

1. to develop and record their thoughts,
2. to connect and analyze their ideas, and
3. to carefully craft their writing and take ownership for what is said and how it is said.

Q. To grade or not to grade?

A. Teachers choose whether and how to grade their writing assignments by considering issues such as the goals of the course, the assignment objectives, and the type of writing project. For ideas on how to assess all types of writing, see the "Assessing Writing" section in this guide (pages 146–160).

Write for College in a Schoolwide Program

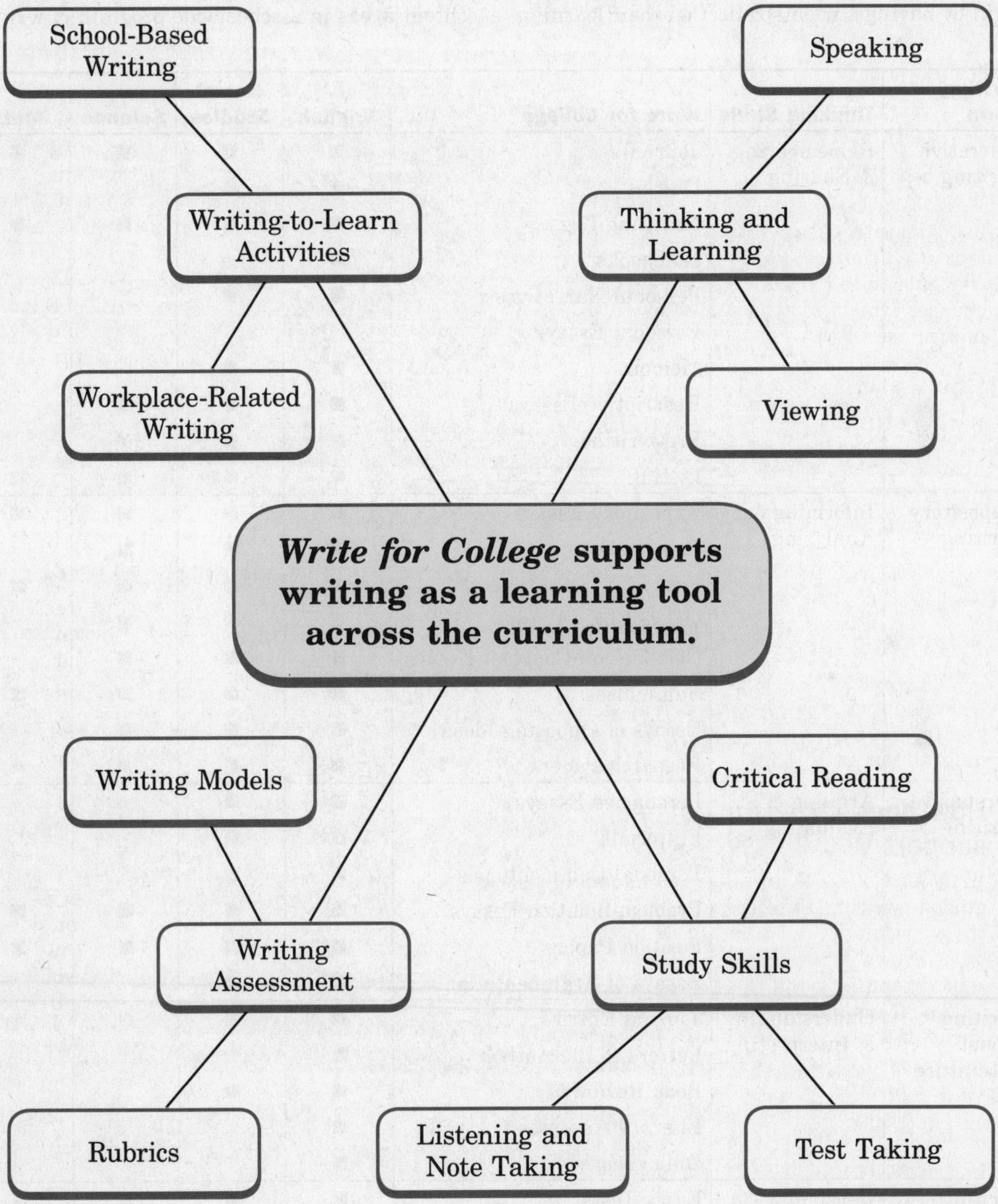

Writing Forms Across the Curriculum

Write for College supports almost every type of writing—formal and informal—that students are asked to do (see page 135 in this guide). To make writing an essential part of the curriculum, begin by having students reflect on their learning informally in response journals and learning logs. Students can use additional forms of writing in all subject areas. This framework suggests how the forms of writing might be utilized by the core content areas in a schoolwide program of writing.

Writing Form	Thinking Skills	*Write for College*	English	Social Studies	Science	Math
Narrative Writing	Remembering & Sharing	Journals	■	■	■	■
		Diaries	■	■		
		Learning Logs	■	■	■	■
		Notebooks	■			
		Personal Narratives	■	■		
		Personal Essays				
		Memoirs	■	■		
		Descriptive Essays	■	■	■	
		Freewriting	■	■	■	
		Listing	■	■	■	■
Expository Writing	Informing & Analyzing	Expository Essays	■	■	■	■
		Process Essays	■	■	■	
		Essays of Definition	■	■	■	■
		Cause-Effect Essays	■	■	■	
		Comparison-Contrast Essays	■	■	■	
		Summaries	■	■	■	■
		Essays of Opposing Ideas	■	■	■	
		Research Papers	■	■	■	■
Persuasive Writing	Arguing & Evaluating	Persuasive Essays	■	■		
		Editorials	■	■		
		Personal Commentaries	■	■		
		Problem-Solution Essays	■	■	■	■
		Position Papers	■	■	■	■
		Essays of Argumentation	■	■		
Writing About Literature	Understanding & Interpreting	Journal Entries	■	■	■	■
		Letters to the Author	■			
		Book Reviews	■	■		
		Literary Analyses	■			
		Dialogues	■			
Writing Tests	Reasoning	Essay Tests	■	■	■	■
		AP Exams	■	■	■	■
		Entrance/Exit Exams	■	■	■	■
		Document-Based Question		■	■	

Setting Up a WAC Program

Writing across the curriculum (WAC) is the whole faculty's assignment—teachers and administrators alike. Therefore, the material on the following pages is addressed to the entire faculty. Use it in department or faculty meetings to discuss how to build and implement a successful WAC program.

A Formal WAC Program

Your school may have an informal, undeveloped writing-across-the-curriculum program, or a formal, more refined program. In an informal program, individual teachers decide whether to use writing and how to use it. While individuals may use writing effectively, often their efforts are not coordinated with the work of other teachers and may lack the supportive elements of a formal program. In a formal WAC program, teachers and administrators establish a coordinated, schoolwide writing program.

Elements of a formal WAC program:

- **Tools** to build a unified, schoolwide writing program: (1) a writing handbook used by all teachers and students and available to parents; (2) a writing-skills grid showing skills that students will develop; (3) a writing-forms framework showing forms of writing in core subject areas; and (4) student portfolios used to store, revise, and show writing
- **Periodic Faculty-Development Workshops** on topics like designing assignments, teaching the writing process, conferencing with student writers, and evaluating writing
- **An Assessment Strategy** like "traits of effective writing" taught to all students and faculty and used in all classes
- **A Writing Center** staffed with trained teachers to help students plan and complete their writing assignments

- **Collaboration** between English teachers and other teachers regarding how to use writing as a teaching and learning tool
- **Team-Taught Courses** sponsored by two or more departments and taught by teachers from these departments
- **Parent-Teacher Communication** that includes (1) posting assignments and projects on a classroom Web site or voice-mail service; (2) holding portfolio conferences with both parents and student; and (3) publishing a student-written newsletter for parents

Write for College Supports Your Schoolwide Writing Program

Put *Write for College* in every classroom (not just the English department). Use the handbook and the *Teacher's Guide* to make writing a learning tool in all courses. To make your schoolwide writing program work, be sure that every student has a personal copy of *Write for College* to use in all classes and that every faculty member has *Write for College* and the *Teacher's Guide* to the handbook.

Writing Helps Students Achieve Learning Goals

Following are five reasons teachers want students to write. To choose the best writing activity for a course or unit, think about which concepts most closely reflect your learning goals.

1 Writing to Learn New Concepts and Ideas

Popular writing-to-learn activities are usually ungraded (see examples on pages 138–139 of this guide). The purpose is not to produce finished writing, but rather to help record one's thoughts on paper in order to organize and refine them.

2 Writing to Share Learning

Having students share their writing lets them interact with an audience and builds a healthy learning community. The school-based activities on pages 139–141 of this guide are often used for this purpose.

3 Writing to Show Learning

The most common reason content-area teachers have for asking students to write is to show learning. For these forms of writing, see the following headings in the index of *Write for College:* Argumentation, Cause and effect (Essay), Classification, Compare-contrast (Essay), Definition, Essay test, Journal writing, Learning logs, Note taking, Paraphrase, Process (Explaining), and Summary.

4 Writing to Explore Personal Thoughts

Exploring personal thoughts and feelings helps students connect course content and their personal questions, ideas, and plans. For these forms of writing, see the following headings in the index of *Write for College:* Journal writing, Learning logs, Personal (Essay), Personal (Narrative), and Persuasion (Essay).

5 Writing to Plan and Complete Tasks

When assigning writing to help students plan and complete their work, you can use memos and e-mail messages to help students (1) organize writing projects, develop plans, and budget their time; and (2) correspond with others regarding progress on their course work. (See pages 312–315 in *Write for College*.)

Schoolwide Writing Helps Students Learn Course Content

For example, writing an expository essay (see pages 161–185 in *Write for College)* helps students develop and present a contemporary topic. Many of the writing samples in *Write for College* demonstrate writing done in courses other than English.

Workplace-Related Writing Helps Students Plan Ahead

The classroom is your students' workplace, and *Write for College* provides guidelines and models for workplace writing. Workplace-writing practice prepares students for the workplace they will soon enter.

Guidelines, Models, and Rubrics Help Students with Assignments

Students sometimes struggle to understand how to develop an assigned piece of writing or how to distinguish an unfinished piece from a finished piece. Guidelines, models, and rubrics for writing help clarify what students need to do and how to do it for the forms of school-based writing. There are guidelines and models in *Write for College.*

For example, the cause-and-effect organizers on pages 27 and 227 of the handbook will help students organize information for a cause-and-effect essay. The assessment rubric for expository writing on page 162 will help them revise their essays. Look through the lists below to find other helpful tools.

Additional Writing Tools

	Write for College pages
Organizing Strategies	
• analogy	84
• classification	84
• chronological	85
• illustration, climax	86
• comparison	87
Graphic Organizers	
• for writing	27–28
Rubrics	*Teacher's Guide*
• personal narrative and essay	151
• expository writing	152
• persuasive essay	153
• responding to literature	154
• research writing	155
• business writing	156
Working with Information	*Write for College*
• evaluating	394–395
• searching for	322–323, 385–392
• services	384
• transitions	88–89
Writing About . . .	
• terms (definitions)	203–206
• memorable events	145–150
• literature	255–297
• places	149–150
Special Forms of Writing	
• essay test	465–479
• learning log	422–423
• note taking	413–419
• paraphrase	427
• summary	424–426
• video review	268

Quick Guides, Strategies, and Writing Guidelines

Write for College has advice to save you time and improve students' writing. For example, if students are writing a persuasive essay, teach them how to build a clear argument by first developing a thesis statement (see *Write for College* pages 30 and 94). It will pay dividends: (1) the papers will be stronger and (2) you'll save hours evaluating them. Here are some other helpful tools.

Quick Guides

- (see the handbook index) 618

Strategies

- forming a thesis statement 30
- group advising 49–51
- critical reading 401–408
- supporting a thesis 100
- word-search tips (Web) 396

Writing Guidelines

- book reviews 263–267
- business letters 301–309
- definition 203–206
- expository 161–185
- literary analysis 269–297
- personal essay 151–155
- personal narrative 143–159
- persuasive 229–253
- position paper 253
- research paper 317–325
- response to literature 255–297
- workplace 299–315

Checklists

- (see the handbook index)

Link Writing Assignments to Course Goals and Assessment

Design a writing assignment so it is clearly linked to course goals and an assessment rubric. When presenting the assignment, point out this link and explain how students can use the assignment, the writing guidelines, and the rubric to revise and edit their work. (See "Designing Writing Assignments" on page 142 in this guide.)

"In literate society, business involves skillful writing, reading, speaking, listening, and thinking. Writing across the curriculum helps students practice the ground rules for citizenship in such a society."

—Verne Meyer

WAC Resources

Add books to the faculty's professional library. For example, you could discuss the following tips offered by Donald Graves in his book *Investigate Nonfiction:*

- Students need sustained periods of time to immerse themselves in their writing in class.
- When students have opportunities for sharing sessions about their writing-in-progress, they generally put more effort into their work.
- Encourage students who are writing reports about a subject to complete at least two rounds of data gathering, discussion, and exploratory writing before they establish a definite form and focus for the writing.
- Give students many information-gathering experiences. Make firsthand data-gathering experiences (like interviewing and direct observation) a priority.
- Help students learn to analyze and interpret the data they gather.

Implementing Writing-to-Learn Activities

Any writing activity (from listing information on a topic to writing a long research paper) is a form of writing to learn. (See "Writing to Learn" on pages 421–428 in *Write for College*.) Try these short writing-to-learn activities to encourage thinking and learning in your classroom:

Admit Slips These brief pieces of writing (usually on half sheets of paper) are collected as "admission" into class. An admit slip can be a summary of last night's reading, a question about class material, a request to review a particular point, or anything else that promotes meaningful dialogue and learning. To help students focus on the day's lesson, the teacher may read several admit slips aloud.

Brainstorming Brainstorming is done to collect as many ideas as possible on a particular topic. Students will come away with ideas that might be used to develop a writing or discussion topic. In brainstorming, everything is written down, even if it seems to be weak or irrelevant.

Class Minutes One student is selected each day to keep minutes of the day's lesson (including questions and comments) and to write them up for the next class. Reading and correcting these minutes serves as a review and a listening exercise.

Clustering Clustering begins by placing a key word (nucleus word) in the center of the page and circling it. Students then record other words related to this word. Each word is circled, and a line connects it to the closest related word. (See examples on pages 2 and 22 of *Write for College* and page 133 in this guide.)

Completions Students complete an open-ended sentence starter or interpret a symbol in as many ways as possible. Writing completions and interpreting symbols help students to look at a subject in different ways or focus their thinking on a particular concept.

Correspondence One of the most valuable benefits of writing to learn is that it provides many opportunities for students to communicate with their teachers, often in a sincere, anonymous way. Teachers should set up a channel (suggestion box, special reply notes, e-mail address) that encourages students to communicate freely and honestly.

Creative Definitions Students are first asked to write out definitions of new words. Then they read their definitions to the class, and the group discusses which definition is most accurate. The writing and discussion help students remember the correct definitions.

Dialogues Students create an imaginary dialogue between themselves and a character (a public, historical, or literary figure). The dialogue brings to life information on the subject.

Dramatic Scenarios Students imagine themselves to be historical characters (during key moments in these people's lives) or people involved in world current events, and then they write dialogues that capture the moment. For example, students might put themselves in President Truman's shoes in 1945 when he decided to bomb Hiroshima or in Rosa Parks's shoes in 1955 when she refused to take a backseat on a bus in Montgomery, Alabama.

Exit Slips At the end of class, students write a short piece in which they summarize, evaluate, or question something about the day's lesson and then turn in their exit slips before leaving the classroom. Use the slips to assess the success of a lesson and to plan a follow-up lesson.

First Thoughts Students write their immediate impressions (or what they already know) about a topic they are preparing to study. The writing helps students focus on the topic, and it serves as a reference point for measuring their learning.

Focused Writing Writers concentrate on a single topic (or one particular aspect of a topic) and write nonstop for a time. Like brainstorming, focused writing allows students to see how much they have to say on a particular topic.

How-To Writing To help students clarify how to accomplish a task, have them write instructions. Ideally, they then test their writing on someone who is unfamiliar with the task.

Learning Logs A learning log is a journal (notebook) in which students keep their notes, thoughts, and personal reactions to a subject. (For examples, see pages 422–423 in the handbook.)

Listing Students can begin with any idea related to the subject and list thoughts and details that come to mind as a quick review or progress check.

Nutshells The teacher stops class activity and asks students a question like this: "In a nutshell, what is the meaning or importance of the concept or idea that we're talking about?" Students write on the topic for 3 minutes, and then individuals share their writing. The teacher uses the writing to help the class refine its thinking on the topic.

Predicting Students are stopped at a key point in a lesson and asked to write what they think will happen next. This technique works well for lessons that have a strong cause-and-effect relationship.

Question of the Day Writers respond to a "What if?" or "Why?" question that is important to a clear understanding of the lesson. To promote class discussion, the writing is usually read in class.

Stop 'n' Write At strategic points during a class discussion, students are asked to stop and write to evaluate their understanding of the topic, to reflect on what has been said, to make connections with previous learning or experience, and to question anything that may be unclear.

Student Teachers Students construct their own math word problems, science experiments, and discussion questions (which can be used for reviewing or testing). Replace routine end-of-the-chapter or workbook reviews with these questions that students feel are worth asking.

Summing Up Students are asked to sum up what was covered in a particular lesson by writing about its importance, a possible result, a next step, or a general impression of the topic.

Warm-Ups Students write for the first 5 to 10 minutes of class—question-of-the-day, a freewrite, or a focused writing to begin class discussion of the day's lesson. Have volunteers read their writing.

Writing Activities for Specific Courses

The following activities focus on the arts, family and consumer science, language arts, psychology and social work, mathematics, science, social studies, and the workplace. (Page numbers indicate guidelines and models in *Write for College.*)

Arts (Music, Theater, Visual Art)

Art for Life Write a personal commentary on how the arts do or do not enrich life in your community. (See "Personal Commentary," pages 236–238.)

Arts in Review Write a review of an art exhibit, a concert, a play, a movie, or a film. For models, refer to reviews in newspapers and magazines. (See "Film Review," page 268.)

Guess Who's Coming to School? Choose an artist whom you'd like to see perform at a school assembly. Write a memo to the principal or to the school's program committee describing the person's work and explaining why she or he should be invited to perform. (See "Memo," pages 312–313.)

Photography and Painting Study landscape paintings of the 1850s, photographs made with early cameras, and expressionist and impressionist paintings of the late 1800s. Then write an essay in which you explain how the invention of photography may have influenced expressionist and impressionist styles. (See "Essay of Comparison," pages 193–197.)

Technology and the Arts Investigate some aspect of technology and its role in visual art, theater, or music. Write your findings in an essay. (See "Report Writing," pages 161–185.)

Family and Consumer Science

Counting Your Bucks Choose an occupation that you may pursue and research your expected income. Then, based on the location of the job, assess the cost of housing, utilities, food, clothing, retirement account, auto expenses, health insurance, life insurance, and taxes. Compose your findings in a report. (See "Compiled Report," pages 165–169.)

Diet Log Maintain a diet log for two weeks, noting everything you have eaten. As part of each entry, reflect briefly on how you feel. (See "Journal," page 135.)

Making Policy Write an essay of argumentation to promote a policy or practice that would help alleviate a serious health problem. Include specific, health-related details. (See "Essay of Argumentation," pages 239–243.)

Paraphrasing Lifestyles Read a magazine or an Internet article that describes some aspect of a healthful lifestyle. Write a paraphrase of the material. (See "Writing Paraphrases," pages 330–331.)

Language Arts

My Process The next time you develop a story, play, poem, or essay, keep a record of your process by writing each day in your learning log. (See "Learning Logs," pages 422–423.)

Slice of Life Interview an elderly family member, neighbor, or acquaintance about growing up or working in an earlier time; report your findings in an essay. (See "Conducting Interviews," page 457.)

You-Were-There Stories Write a short personal commentary on a human-interest story in the newspaper. Publish it in your school newspaper or classroom. (See "Personal Commentary," pages 236–238.)

Psychology and Social Work

Acting Strangely Harmlessly break one or two social rules. (Examples: Wear your shirt backwards. Stand very close to the person talking to you.) Then write a report explaining (1) what you did, (2) how people reacted, and (3) how their reactions made you feel.

Cents vs. Sense Analyze five or six TV, Internet, or print ads related to patterns of eating or taking medications. Then write an essay on your findings and share it with the class. (See "Report Writing," pages 161–185.)

Who's Laughing? Select 10 daily comic strips and read them for a two-week period, noting how males and females are portrayed (smart, clumsy, dominant, important, assertive, and so on). Then write a summary of your observations.

Why People Help Do an informal survey asking people, "Why do you do volunteer work?" Then choose a community program that needs and uses volunteers. Analyze the form, content, and style of the group's requests for help. Write an essay exploring effective appeals for volunteer help.

Mathematics

Backed into a Corner Keep a daily learning log in which you ask yourself a question about a significant concept discussed in class that day and then answer the question. (See "Learning Logs," pages 422–423.)

Problem Solved Research the development of an invention (ink pens, cell phones, and so on) designed to solve a specific communication problem. Write an essay on the topic. (See "Problem-Solution Essay," pages 213–218.)

Testing 1, 2, 3 With a writing partner, take turns writing an essay test question based on a concept discussed in class. Then exchange questions and list the main points you would cover in the answer. (See "The Testing Center," pages 465–507.)

This Year in Sports Compile an accurate and comprehensive manual of one year's records and statistics for one sport at your school. Compare these statistics to those of another school in your conference or to a previous year in your school.

Science

Both Sides Now Choose a controversial science-related issue to present in an essay. Use a Venn diagram to identify the opposing ideas. (See "Venn Diagram," page 226, and "Essay of Comparison," pages 193–197.)

Careers Research a career related to a specific field of science, technology, or electronics. (See "Writing the Research Paper," pages 317–326.)

Dear Mr. Galileo In an e-mail message to a scientist who died at least 50 years ago, explain how his or her work is impacting science today. (See "E-Mail Messages," pages 314–315.)

Newsworthy Science Read and summarize an important science-related article in either a newspaper or magazine. Read your summary to the class and answer classmates' questions. (See "Writing a Summary Report," pages 163–164.)

Science Write an essay about whether there is a crisis in science education today and, if so, what should be done about it. (See "Persuasive Writing," pages 229–253.)

Teach It! Choose a process learned during this course (like a weather-related phenomenon) and write a process essay to help next year's students learn the process. (See "Process Essay," pages 190–193.)

Working Together Write an essay that focuses on how your community is trying to solve an environmental problem, such as loss of wildlife habitat, industrial pollution, or pesticide use. (See "Problem-Solution Essay," pages 213–218.)

Social Studies

Carried Downstream Write a report explaining how a river in the United States influenced the outcome of a major historical event. (See “Writing the Research Paper,” pages 317–326.)

Civil Rights Compare and contrast the contributions of two key individuals in the African American civil rights movement. (See “Comparison Essay,” pages 194–197.)

Fiction and Fact Read a novel about a significant historical event or issue. Then write a book review focusing on how the book did or did not help you understand the event or issue. (See “Book Review,” pages 266–267.)

Good Causes Interview key people at a nonprofit agency in your community to learn how the agency contributes to community life; write a report on your findings. (See “Conducting Interviews,” page 457.)

Movers and Shakers Write an editorial in which you advocate making the birthday of an important social thinker, spiritual leader, or humanitarian a national holiday. (See “Editorial,” pages 233–235.)

To the Boats Imagine that you are George Washington about to lead your troops across the Delaware. Write an e-mail message to Thomas Jefferson explaining why this action is necessary. (See “E-Mail Messages,” pages 314–315.)

Take Two Watch “The Seeds of War,” volume I of the documentary *World War II,* and then write a review in which you analyze how well the video identifies the economic causes of the war. (See “Film Review,” page 268.)

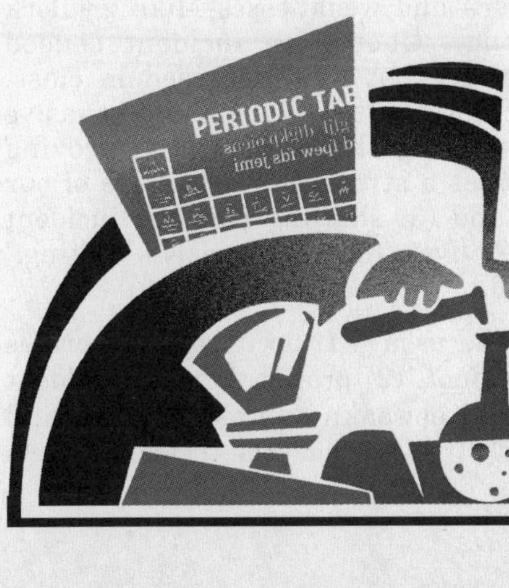

Workplace

Acquisition Interview a key person at a local business or institution about its newest piece of equipment. Learn why the item was purchased, how it works, and how it has affected the business. Report your findings in a brief report. (See “Conducting Interviews,” page 458.)

High Tech Interview five businesspeople about how they use technology in their work. (See “Conducting Interviews,” page 458.)

Make an Appointment Interview five businesspeople about how writing helps them do their work, and write a short report on your findings. Share your findings in class. (See “Conducting Interviews,” page 458.)

No Malfunction Research a politician you think is qualified for his or her office, and write a functional résumé that shows this person’s qualifications. Be prepared to present your résumé as a report to the class. (See “Résumé,” pages 310–311.)

Think I’ll Apply Write an application letter for a college-sponsored summer camp in physics. Include with your letter the proposal for your physics project, along with your project report. (See “Application Letter,” page 305.)

Designing Writing Assignments

Add value to your next assignment by designing meaningful course goals, connecting the assignments to the goals, and evaluating the assignments with goal-related criteria. When students see that doing an assignment helps them achieve something valuable to you and them, they are more likely to succeed.

For example, you will find an assignment below for four courses. For each course, trace the connection between one of the course's goals; a writing assignment that helps students achieve the goal; and evaluation criteria that will help writers, peer editors, and the teacher.

English

Course Goal: To respond to literature by writing a variety of forms, including book reviews, literary analyses, character sketches, and freewrites

Assignment: For the next three class periods, read and trace the development of a leading character (in a play of your choice). After you finish reading each act, write in your journal for 15 minutes to record and explore new information and insights that you have gained about the character that are related to behavior, motivations, or changes. (See "Personal Response" to literature, pages 259–262.)

Evaluation: The writing shows that the student has (1) read the assignment, (2) identified information in the text revealing character development, and (3) reflected on what this information suggests about the character.

Math

Course Goal: To learn basic concepts or techniques of math and to understand how to use them to solve daily problems

Assignment: Each Friday, choose one concept discussed during the week and explain in your journal (1) what the concept is and (2) how someone in the workplace uses that concept to do his or her work.

Evaluation: The journal entry accurately describes (1) a math concept discussed in class and (2) how the concept is used in the workplace.

Science

Course Goal: To learn how plants grow and how scientific methods of assessment can measure that growth

Assignment: Over several weeks, study the effects of sunlight on plant life. Working with a lab partner, do the following:

1. Plant the Wisconsin fast plant (http://www.fastplants.org) in the soil tray provided. (Soil in all trays is the same.)
2. Set the timer on your grow light for the number of hours and minutes stated on the tab attached to the tray. (Each team's plant will be lit for a different span of time.)
3. Each day, analyze plant health by counting leaves, grading leaf color, and measuring leaf sizes and plant height.
4. After the experiment, write an essay explaining what you learned. (See "Cause-Effect Essay," pages 208–211.)

Evaluation: The notes and essay (1) are well organized and clear, (2) include accurate information requested in the assignment, (3) show that the writer understands factors involved in plant growth, and (4) show how scientific methods can measure plant growth.

Social Studies

Course Goal: To learn how strengths and weaknesses of the checks-and-balances structure in our three branches of government affect our lives.

Assignment: The checks-and-balances structure of government has strengths—like limiting the abuse of power—and weaknesses—like gridlock and inefficiency. Choose an incident caused by this structure that was discussed in class. After researching the topic, write a persuasive essay (1) describing the incident, (2) proving that it illustrates a strength or weakness of our government, and (3) showing how the incident affects people's lives. (See "Persuasive Writing," pages 229–253.)

Evaluation: The essay (1) accurately describes a relevant incident, (2) proves that the incident reflects a strength or weakness in our governmental structure, and (3) shows how the incident affects people's lives.

Research

One of the best forms of writing for practicing research skills is the position paper. The form requires the writer to take a positive and assertive stand on a significant issue of local, national, or global importance. Avoid giving broad or vague topic areas that may invite students to purchase or plagiarize online research papers. After selecting a topic (usually a specific contemporary issue), the writer gathers data from a variety of sources: books, periodicals, newspapers, Web sites, news reports, documentaries, interviews, and meetings.

Getting Started To get started, brainstorm for a list of important issues related to your subject area. List ideas as fast as they are suggested. Then have students chart their attitudes or feelings about each topic.

To do this, students should first list the topics on their own paper. Next to each topic, they put the letter *A, B, C,* or *D,* depending on their reaction to each one. An *A* means students have strongly held beliefs about the topic, *B* means students are quite knowledgeable about the topic, *C* means students have little or no interest in the topic, and *D* means they have little or no knowledge about it. (Each topic can be marked with two letters.) A topic marked with an *A* or a *B* is certainly worth considering as a possible topic for writing.

Presenting the Assignment Provide students with your evaluation guidelines at the time the assignment is given. This way students will know what you expect of them before they begin writing. (See "Assignment Format" on page 144 in this guide.) Assessment rubrics also provide guidelines for specific forms of writing.

Focusing the Research Once students have decided on a topic, provide questions based on the 5W's and H strategy to focus their research. Propose the following questions:

- *Who* or *what* is or will be affected by this issue?
- *What* are the opposing arguments for resolving this issue?
- *When* did the issue first emerge?
- *Where* does (or will) this issue have the greatest impact or consequence?
- *Why* is this issue controversial?
- *How* can it be resolved?

Writing a Position Statement After gathering details from reliable sources, the writer is ready to develop a position statement that expresses the idea or argument she or he intends to support. Students can use a checklist like the one on page 94 or 321 in *Write for College* to make sure their position statement is accurate and effective.

Supporting a Position The writer supports the position statement by providing essential background information on the topic, interpreting data from various sources, evaluating the facts and addressing counterarguments, and expanding on the idea put forth in the position statement. (If you require a working outline, refer students to the model on page 97 in *Write for College.*)

Students may explore different viewpoints through role-playing. One student reads his or her position statement, and a partner states one of the opposing viewpoints addressed in the paper. Allow a 3- to 5-minute discussion to enhance the writer's understanding of the counterargument.

Writing the First Draft When students understand the steps in the process of writing, they become more confident about getting started on their first draft. Schedule writing conferences as needed. (See "Conducting Conferences" on page 147 in this guide.)

Using Writing Samples A position paper succeeds when it presents and supports a claim that readers find interesting and worthy of thoughtful consideration. Present a sample paper. (See page 253 in the handbook.)

Assignment Format

Students complete writing assignments more successfully if they have the following information: topic, audience, purpose, form of writing, ideas for prewriting, and criteria for evaluation. Based on your course goals, choose which of these items you should provide and which the students should come up with themselves. Then present the information in an assignment form like the one below.

If your goals call for writing that is prescriptive in focus and form, you may supply all the information called for. However, if you want students to respond freely to an idea, you may supply only a writing prompt and evaluation guidelines.

In either case, this information will give students a clear view of the assignment and help them complete it successfully.

Topic: ....

Audience: ....

Purpose: ....

Form of Writing: ....

Prewriting Activities: (Prewriting is important if the assignment does not grow out of information or concepts already covered in class. See pages 21–30 in *Write for College*.)

1. ....

2. ....

3. ....

Evaluation Guidelines: (Refer to guidelines and assessment rubrics in *Write for College*.)

1. ....

2. ....

3. ....

4. ....

Assessing Writing

The information in this section covers a number of areas related to assessment, including linking assessment to instruction and using rubrics to assess different modes of writing. (Reproducible copies of six rubrics are provided.)

An Overview—Assessment and Instruction

In past decades, writing assessment was generally held to be the province of the teacher. Students turned in work—then they waited to see what grades they would receive. Now it is widely recognized that learning to be a good assessor is one of the best ways to become a strong writer. In order to assess well, students must learn to recognize good writing. They must know and be able to describe the difference between writing that works and writing that does not work. Students learn to assess, generally, by following three key steps:

1. Learning about the traits of writing by which their work—and that of others—will be assessed
2. Applying the traits to a wide variety of written texts
3. Applying the traits to their own work—first assessing it for strengths and weaknesses and then revising it as needed (See page 149 in this guide for additional information.)

Why should students be assessors?

Students who learn to be assessors also . . .

- learn to think like professional writers,
- take responsibility for their own revising, and
- make meaningful changes in their writing—instead of simply recopying a draft to make it look neater.

"We must constantly remind ourselves that the ultimate purpose of evaluation is to enable students to evaluate themselves."

—Arthur Costa

Role of Teachers and Students

Here is a quick summary of the kinds of activities teachers and students usually engage in while acting as assessors in the classroom.

Teachers

As assessors, teachers often engage in . . .

- roving conferences, in which they roam the classroom, observing students' work and offering comments or questions that will lead students to subsequent steps.
- one-on-one conferences, in which students are asked to come prepared with a question they need answered.
- informal comments—written or oral—in which they offer a personal response or pose a question a reader may have.
- reading student work, using a general *rating sheet*, such as the one on page 149 in this guide, or an *assessment rubric*, such as one of those on pages 151–156.
- tracking scores over time to calculate a final grade for a grading period.

Students

As assessors, students often engage in . . .

- reviewing scoring guides such as the rubrics in this guide.
- using a *rating sheet* (page 149 in this guide) or a *peer response sheet* like the one on page 51 in *Write for College.*
- assessing and discussing written work that the teacher shares with the class.
- assessing their own work, using a scoring guide or rubric.
- compiling a portfolio and reflecting on the written work included.

Effective Assessment in the Classroom

Good assessment gives students a sense of how they are growing as writers. It indicates to teachers which students are finding success and which need help. To ensure that assessment is working in your classroom, you should do the following things:

- Make sure all students know the criteria you will use to assess their writing. If you are going to use a rating sheet or rubric, provide them with copies.
- Make sure your instruction and assessment match. You cannot teach one thing and assess students on another—if you expect them to be successful.
- Involve students regularly in assessing . . .
  - published work from a variety of sources,
  - your work (share your writing—even in unfinished draft form), and
  - their own work.
- Don't grade *everything* students write, or you'll be overwhelmed with stacks of papers to assess. Instead, encourage students to write *often*; then choose a few pieces to grade.
- Respond to the content *first*. Then look at the conventions. Correctness is important, but if you comment on spelling and mechanics before content, the message to the student is, "I don't care as much about what you say as I do about whether you spell everything correctly."
- Encourage students to save rough drafts and to collect pieces of work regularly in a portfolio. This type of collection gives students a broad picture of how they are progressing as writers.
- Ask students if they mind having comments written directly on their work. For some students, comments on sticky notes may seem less obtrusive.

Conducting Conferences

"Good assessment starts with a vision of success."
—Arthur Costa

Conduct conferences to maintain an open line of communication with student writers at all points during the development of a piece of writing. Here are three common practices that you can employ to communicate with student writers during a writing project:

- **Desk-side conferences** occur when you stop at a student's desk to ask questions and make responses. Questions should be open ended. This gives the writer "space" to talk and clarify his or her own thinking about the writing.
- **Scheduled conferences** give you and a student a chance to meet in a more structured setting. In such a conference, a student may have a specific problem to discuss or simply want you to assess her or his progress on a particular piece of writing.

NOTE: In a typical 3- to 5-minute conference, try to praise one thing, ask an appropriate question, and offer one or two suggestions.

- **Small-group conferences** give three to five students who are at the same stage of the writing process or are experiencing the same problem a chance to meet with you. The goal of such conferences is twofold: first, to help students improve their writing and, second, to help them develop as evaluators of writing.

Formative vs. Summative Assessment

Formative assessment is ongoing and is often not linked to a letter grade or score. It may be as simple as a brief one-on-one conference or an informal review of the beginning of a student's draft to suggest possible next steps. **Summative assessment**, on the other hand, is a summing up of a student's performance. Formative assessments usually occur in the form of a comment—oral or written. Summative assessments take the form of . . .

- a letter grade,
- total points earned,
- a percentage score, or
- some combination of these.

Responding to Student Writing

Responding to Nongraded Writing

(Formative)

- React noncritically with positive, supportive language.
- Use marginal dialogue. Resist writing on or over the student's writing.
- Respond whenever possible in the form of questions. Nurture curiosity through your inquiries.
- Encourage risk taking.

Evaluating Graded Writing

(Summative)

- Ask students to submit prewriting and rough drafts with their final drafts.
- Scan final drafts once, focusing on the writing as a whole.
- Reread them, this time assessing them for their adherence to previously established criteria.
- Make marginal notations, if necessary, as you read the drafts a second time.
- Scan the writing again and note the feedback you have given.
- Complete your rating sheet or rubric, and, if necessary, write a summary comment.

Approaches for Assessing Writing

The most common forms of direct writing assessment (summative) are listed below.

Analytical assessment identifies the features, or traits, that characterize effective writing and defines them along a continuum of performance. Many analytical scales run from a low of 1 point to a high of 5 or 6 points. This form of assessment tells students exactly where their strengths and weaknesses lie: "Your writing has strong ideas but needs work on voice," or "Your writing has a powerful voice but lacks accuracy." See the rating sheet on page 149. It can be adapted as a teacher or peer response sheet.

Mode-specific assessment is similar to analytical assessment except that the rating scales or scoring guides (rubrics) are designed specifically for particular modes of writing, such as narrative, expository, persuasive, and so on. This kind of assessment works best in a structured curriculum where students will be assigned particular forms and subjects for writing. (See pages 151–156 in this guide for sample rubrics.)

Holistic assessment focuses on a piece of writing as a whole. Holistic assessors often use a checklist of traits to remind themselves of the kinds of characteristics they're looking for; this is called focused holistic assessment. The assessors do not, however, score traits separately, and this means that student writers do not know where they were most or least successful in their work.

Portfolio assessment gives students a chance to showcase their best writing or to document their growth as writers over time. In assembling a portfolio, students generally choose which pieces of writing they will complete and which ones they will include in their portfolios. (See page 157 in this guide for more information.)

Rating Sheet

Ideas

- Fuzzy and disjointed
- General, sketchy

- Clear and focused
- Rich in detail

1 2 3 4 5

Organization

- No real lead, just dives in
- Confusing order
- Ideas not connected
- Just stops, no conclusion

- Great opening
- Logical organization
- Clear transitions
- Powerful ending

1 2 3 4 5

Voice

- Inappropriate voice for audience and purpose
- Sounds bored by topic
- Feels distant, disconnected

- Right voice for audience and purpose
- Enthusiastic about topic
- Holds reader's attention

1 2 3 4 5

Word Choice

- Overused, tired words
- Modifier overload!
- Meaning lost in unclear phrasing

- Ear-catching phrases
- Strong verbs, clear nouns
- Well-chosen modifiers
- Meaning very clear

1 2 3 4 5

Sentence Fluency

- Hard to read
- Bumpy—or strung out
- Overlong sentences add to confusion

- Easy to read aloud
- Smooth, fluent
- Varied sentence beginnings and lengths

1 2 3 4 5

Conventions

- Numerous, distracting errors
- Careless mistakes
- Ineffective layout

- Editorial correctness
- Attention to detail
- Effective layout

1 2 3 4 5

Assessment Rubrics

There are six rubrics to assess the different forms of writing covered in the handbook. Use these rubrics as indicated below:

Narrative Writing

Use this rubric to assess personal narratives and personal essays. (See page 151.)

Expository Writing

Use this rubric to assess informational writing, including expository essays, summaries, and basic reports. (See page 152.)

Persuasive Writing

Use this rubric to assess persuasive essays, pet peeves, editorials, personal commentaries, and position papers. (See page 153.)

Responding to Literature

Use this rubric to assess literary analyses. (See page 154.)

Research Writing

Use this rubric to assess research papers and personal research reports. (See page 155.)

Workplace Writing

Use this rubric to assess business letters, memos, brochures, and so on. (See page 156.)

Using Rubrics to Assess Writing

Before using these rubrics, read the following list of important points. (Also read pages 146–160 in this manual.)

- Each rubric lists the six traits of effective writing explained in *Write for College*, pages 16–20, and used to assess writing on many state writing-assessment tests.
- Specific descriptors listed under each trait help you assess the writing for that trait.
- Writing doesn't have to exhibit all of the descriptors for each trait to be effective.
- Each rubric is based on a 5-point scale. A 5 means that the writing addresses a particular trait in a masterful way (**excellent**); a 4 means the trait has been handled well (**good**); a 3 means that the writing is average or competent (**fair**); a 2 indicates a weak handling of a trait (**poor**); and a 1 means the trait was not addressed (**incomplete**).
- The rubrics can be used to assess works-in-progress and final drafts.
- Students should know beforehand how their writing will be assessed. (They should understand the traits of effective writing.)
- Change each rubric as needed to meet the needs of the students or the requirements of the writing being assessed.

Using Rubrics as a Teaching Tool

Have students evaluate the effectiveness of published or student writing using a rubric as a basic guide. (Use excerpts or complete pieces for these evaluating sessions.) At first, have students focus on one specific trait (such as *organization*) during these sessions. Later on, ask them to evaluate a piece of writing for all of the traits. Have students discuss their evaluations after each session.

Assessment Rubric Narrative Writing

____ Ideas

The writing . . .

- focuses on a specific experience or time in the writer's life.
- presents an appealing picture of the action and the people.
- uses dialogue and sensory details.
- makes the reader want to know what happens next.

____ Organization

- begins by pulling the reader into the narrative.
- gives events in an order that is easy to follow.
- uses transition words and phrases to connect ideas.

____ Voice

- creates a tone and mood that fit the topic.
- shows the writer's personality.

____ Word Choice

- contains specific nouns, vivid verbs, and colorful modifiers.

____ Sentence Fluency

- flows smoothly from one idea to the next.
- uses a variety of sentence lengths and structures.

____ Conventions

- applies the basic rules of writing.
- uses the format provided by the teacher or another effective design.

Scoring Guide

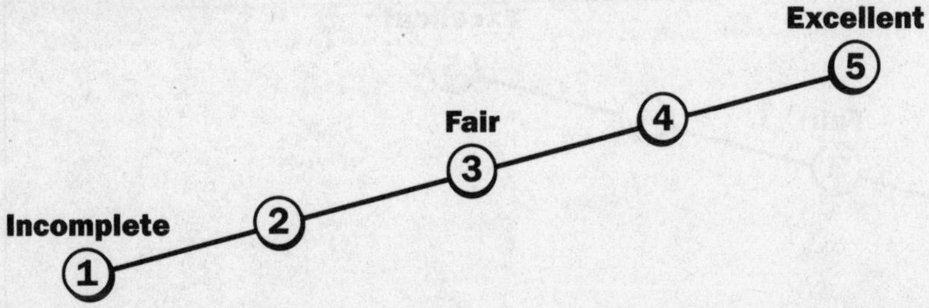

(Add any summary comments on the back of this sheet or at the bottom of the student paper.)

Assessment Rubric Expository Writing

____ Ideas

The writing . . .

- develops a clearly expressed thesis statement.
- contains specific facts, examples, anecdotes, paraphrases, or quotations to support the thesis.
- thoroughly informs the reader.

____ Organization

- includes clear beginning, middle, and ending parts.
- presents ideas in logically ordered paragraphs.
- uses transitions as needed to link sentences and paragraphs.

____ Voice

- speaks clearly and knowledgeably.
- shows that the writer is truly interested in the topic.

____ Word Choice

- explains or defines unfamiliar terms.
- contains specific nouns and active verbs.

____ Sentence Fluency

- flows smoothly from one idea to the next.
- shows a variety of sentence lengths and structures.

____ Conventions

- adheres to the basic rules of writing.
- follows the appropriate guidelines for presentation.

Scoring Guide

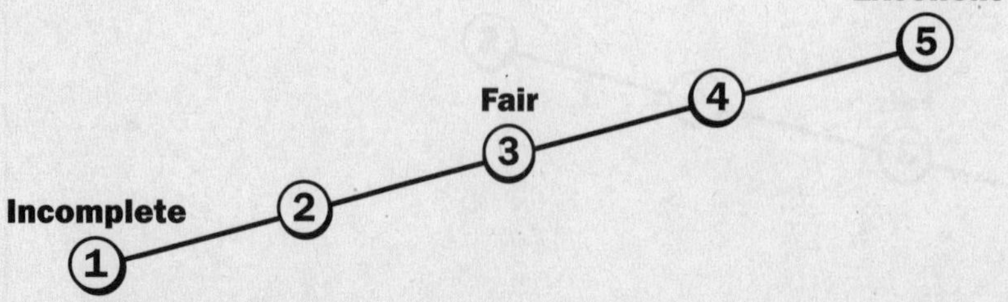

(Add any summary comments on the back of this sheet or at the bottom of the student paper.)

Assessment Rubric Persuasive Writing

____ Ideas

The writing . . .

- addresses a timely, debatable topic.
- presents a clear opinion and logical argument.
- counters opposing points of view.

____ Organization

- follows a logical plan from paragraph to paragraph.
- uses transitions to connect ideas.

____ Voice

- sounds confident and convincing.
- demonstrates the writer's knowledge about the topic.

____ Word Choice

- defines and explains unfamiliar terms.
- uses specific nouns and verbs with appropriate connotation.

____ Sentence Fluency

- creates a smooth flow of thought from sentence to sentence.
- includes different types and lengths of sentences.

____ Conventions

- follows the basic rules of writing.
- accurately cites sources in the essay.
- adheres to the appropriate guidelines for presentation.

Scoring Guide

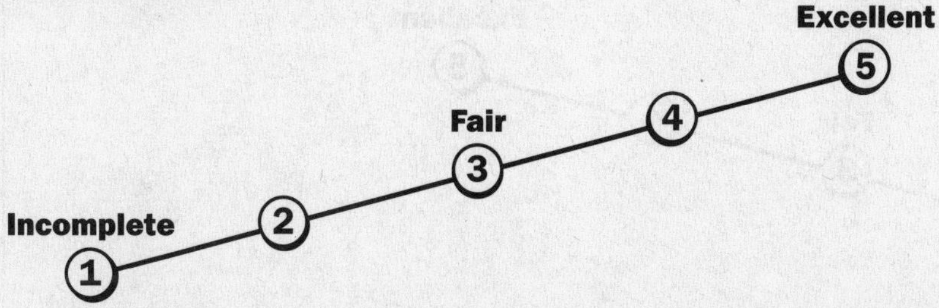

(Add any summary comments on the back of this sheet or at the bottom of the student paper.)

Assessment Rubric Responding to Literature

____ Ideas

The writing . . .

- addresses a single piece of literature.
- focuses on one or more important elements (plot, character, setting, or theme).
- contains supporting details and examples from the work.
- maintains a clear and consistent view from start to finish.

____ Organization

- includes an effective beginning, strong supporting details, and a convincing conclusion.
- presents ideas in an organized manner (perhaps offering the strongest point first or last).

____ Voice

- speaks in a convincing and knowledgeable way.
- shows that the writer clearly understands the piece.

____ Word Choice

- explains or defines any unfamiliar terms.
- pays special attention to word choice.

____ Sentence Fluency

- flows smoothly from one idea to the next.

____ Conventions

- observes the basic rules of grammar, spelling, and punctuation.
- follows the appropriate formatting guidelines.

Scoring Guide

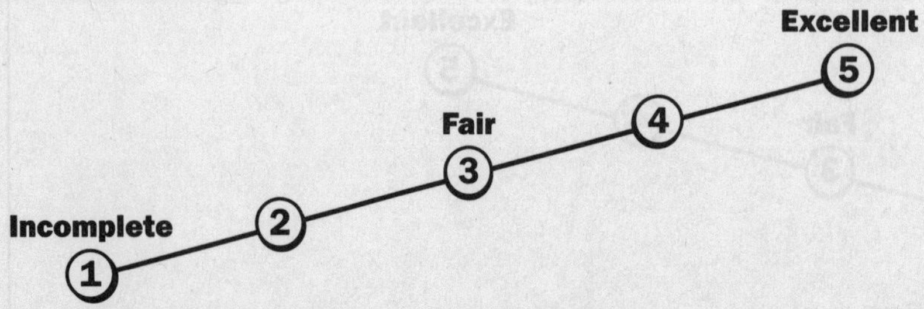

(Add any summary comments on the back of this sheet or at the bottom of the student paper.)

Assessment Rubric Research Writing

____ Ideas

The writing . . .

- focuses on an important part of a topic, expressed in a thesis statement.
- effectively supports or develops the thesis with facts and details from a variety of sources.
- gives credit, when necessary, for ideas from other sources.

____ Organization

- includes a clearly developed beginning, middle, and ending.
- presents supporting information in an organized manner (one main point per paragraph).

____ Voice

- speaks in a sincere and knowledgeable voice.
- shows that the writer is truly interested in the subject.

____ Word Choice

- explains or defines any unfamiliar terms.
- employs a formal level of language.

____ Sentence Fluency

- flows smoothly from one idea to the next.
- shows variation in sentence structure.

____ Conventions

- adheres to the rules of grammar, spelling, and punctuation.
- follows MLA or APA guidelines for documentation.

Scoring Guide

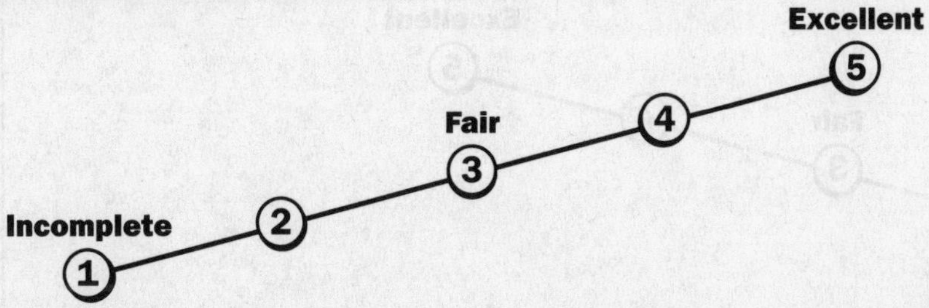

(Add any summary comments on the back of this sheet or at the bottom of the student paper.)

Assessment Rubric Workplace Writing

____ Ideas

The writing . . .

- focuses on an appropriate topic.
- develops a clearly expressed goal or purpose.
- includes details the reader needs to know.

____ Organization

- includes a clear beginning, middle, and ending.
- arranges details logically, using appropriate transitions.

____ Voice

- speaks knowledgeably and sincerely about the topic.
- uses a voice that fits the purpose (persuasive, informative, and so on).
- uses a level of language appropriate to the reader.

____ Word Choice

- uses plain language, specific nouns, and vivid verbs.
- defines terms the reader might be unfamiliar with.

____ Sentence Fluency

- flows smoothly from one thought to another.
- includes sentences with varied beginnings and lengths.

____ Conventions

- adheres to the basic rules of writing.
- follows the appropriate format.

Scoring Guide

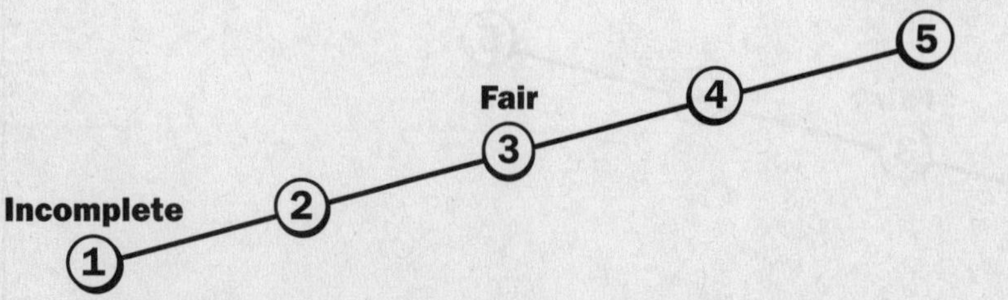

(Add any summary comments on the back of this sheet or at the bottom of the student paper.)

Using Writing Portfolios

More and more, English teachers are making portfolios an important part of their writing programs. Will portfolios work for you? Will they help you and your students assess their writing? Read on and find out.

Q. What is a writing portfolio?

A. A writing portfolio is a limited collection of a student's writing for evaluation. A portfolio is different from the traditional writing folder. A writing folder (or working folder) contains all of a student's work; a portfolio contains only selected pieces.

There are two basic types of portfolios to create. A showcase portfolio is usually presented for evaluation at the end of a grading period. As the name implies, it should contain a selection of a student's best work. A growth portfolio notes the way in which a writer is changing and growing. This type of portfolio is usually collected regularly—say, once a month—over a long period of time.

Q. Why should students compile writing portfolios?

A. Having students compile a portfolio makes the whole process of writing more meaningful to them. They will put forth their best efforts more willingly as they work on various writing projects, knowing that they are accountable for producing a certain number of finished pieces for publication. They will approach writing more thoughtfully, recognizing it as an involved and recursive process of drafting, sharing, and rewriting, and knowing that this process leads to more effective writing. And they will craft finished pieces (for showcase portfolios) more responsibly, since their final evaluation will depend on the finished products they include in their portfolios.

Q. How many pieces of writing should be included in a portfolio?

A. Although you and your students will best be able to decide this, we advise that students compile at least three to five pieces of writing in a showcase portfolio each quarter. (The number of pieces in a growth portfolio may vary from month to month.) All of the drafts should be included for each piece. Students should also be required to include a reflective writing or self-critique sheet that assesses their writing progress.

"Portfolios have become each student's story of where they are as readers and writers."
—Linda Rief

Q. When do portfolios work best?

A. Students need plenty of class time to work on writing if they are going to produce effective portfolios. If they are used right, portfolios turn beginning writers into practicing writers. And practicing writers need regularly scheduled blocks of time to "practice" their craft—to think, talk, and explore options in their writing over and over again. Portfolios are tailor-made for language arts classrooms that operate as writing workshops.

Q. How can I help students with their portfolio writing?

A. Allow students to explore topics of genuine interest to them. Also have them write for many different purposes and audiences and in many different forms.

In addition, expect students to evaluate their own writing and the writing of their peers as it develops—and help them to do so. Also provide them with sound guidance when they need help with a writing problem.

Q. How do I grade a portfolio?

A. Base each grade or assessment on goals you and your students establish beforehand and on what is achieved as evidenced in the portfolio. Many teachers develop a critique sheet for assessment based on the goals established by the class.

Peer Assessment

All writers learn to write by writing. No one questions that. But their ability to improve increases significantly if they read a lot. Any writer would tell students that it is essential to become an avid reader in order to learn the craft of writing.

It is also advisable to become part of a writing community. Writers need to talk about writing with other writers. They also need to know that someone just like them—a writer writing—is available when they need help. That's why it's important that student writers share their work throughout the process of writing. They need to feel that they are among writing colleagues—all committed to helping one another improve as writers.

A Community of Writers

The reason some teachers find the workshop approach to writing so effective is that it naturally creates a feeling of comradeship among the writers in the classroom. (See page 174 in this guide for more information.)

The exchange of ideas among fellow writers is especially important once they have produced early drafts of their work. Writers generally get so close to their writing that they can't always evaluate it objectively themselves. They need their fellow writers, their peers, to ask questions, make suggestions, and offer encouragement. (Use the following minilesson as a possible starting point for group assessing.)

Peer Editing Minilesson

Provide a writing sample from a previous year for students to evaluate using the peer response sheet on page 159 in this guide.

As a class, discuss the strengths and weaknesses of the paper after the students have finished their individual evaluations. During this discussion, tell students how you would assess the paper and your reasons for doing so.

Types of Evaluating

There are three types of assessment that are generally employed during a peer conference: (1) peer revising, in which two or more student writers share ideas about a piece of writing-in-progress (see the peer response sheet on page 159); (2) peer editing, in which two student writers help each other with editing a revised draft; and (3) peer assessment, in which fellow writers actually rate the finished pieces of writing (see the rating sheet on page 149). (See the guidelines below for editing conferences. Also refer students to the editing and proofreading checklist on page 54 in *Write for College*.)

NOTE: Peer assessment does not replace teacher assessment. Teachers will want to help their student writers as much as they can during the writing process. They will also want to assess the students' final products.

Editing Conference

When conducting an editing conference, a peer editor should . . .

1. sit next to the author so that both students can see the piece of writing.
2. read the piece of writing back to the author exactly as it is written (mistakes and all).
3. allow the author to stop the reading at any time in order to edit her or his piece.
4. use a highlighting marker to point out other problems after the author has completed her or his corrections.
5. sign her or his name in the upper left-hand corner of the author's first page so that the teacher will know who helped edit the piece.

Peer Editing Technology

To build and improve writing and editing skills, have students regularly respond to the writing of others, using the reviewing tool on newer word-processing programs.

Peer Response Sheet

Use a response sheet like the one below to make comments about another person's writing-in-progress. (You may not always have comments for both categories.)

Responder's Name ....

Writer's Name ....

Title ....

What I liked about your writing: ....

....

....

....

....

....

....

....

....

Changes I would suggest: ....

....

....

....

....

....

....

....

....

....

....

What About Grammar?

In the late 1980s, researchers George Hillocks, Jr., and Michael W. Smith completed a thorough study of the teaching of grammar. The purpose of their study was to determine the effectiveness of grammar instruction in school curriculums. Their research indicates that the study of grammar has no real impact on writing quality (except for the implementation of the types of activities listed on this page).

However, Hillocks and Smith do point out that students need a basic understanding of grammar and mechanics to produce accurate final drafts: "We assume that to proofread with any care, some knowledge of grammar must be necessary." But they go on to say that no one knows for sure what that body of knowledge is and how it is acquired.

Until such knowledge is determined, the researchers suggest that what will help student writers the most is a handy reference or guide to the rules of grammar and usage (such as the "Proofreader's Guide" in *Write for College*).

Teaching Grammar in Context

The following procedures or types of activities will help students gain a better understanding of grammar and mechanics:

- Link grammar work as much as possible to the students' own writing.
- Make editing of the students' writing an important part of classroom work. They should also have practice editing and proofreading cooperatively.
- Use minilessons for grammar instruction rather than hour-long grammar activities. (See pages 245–246 in this guide.)
- Make grammar instruction fun as well as instructive. For example, develop grammar games and contests.
- Immerse students in all aspects of language learning: reading, writing, speaking, listening, and thinking. Educator James Moffett says the standard dialect is "most effectively mastered through imitating speech."
- Make sure students understand why proper attention to standard English is important. Have experts (professionals, medical workers, businesspeople, attorneys, and so on) share their thoughts on the importance of accuracy, consistency, and appropriateness in communication.
- Also make sure students understand what is meant by the study of grammar—the eight parts of speech, usage, agreement, and so on.
- Don't overwhelm students with too much grammar. Find out which skills give students the most problems and focus your instruction accordingly.
- Emphasize grammar instruction during proofreading, because that's when students should think about it.

Approaches to Use

Sentence Combining—Use the students' own writing as much as possible. The rationale behind combining ideas and the use of proper punctuation for combining should be stressed.

Sentence Expansion and Revising—Have students practice adding and changing information in sentences that they have already created. Also have them expand and revise each other's writing.

Sentence Transforming—Have students change sentences from one form to another (from passive to active, beginning a sentence in a different way, using a different form of a particular word, and so on).

Sentence Imitation—Provide opportunities for students to imitate writing models. According to James Moffett, this activity teaches grammar naturally as it exposes young writers to the many possibilities of English grammar beyond the basic forms. (See page 73 in *Write for College* for guidelines and models.)

Critical Reading Skills

The strategies in this section will help you promote personalized, active reading in your classroom.

Improving Critical Reading Skills

Teachers in every subject area can help students improve their reading skills by teaching effective reading strategies. Educators Fran Claggett, Louann Reid, and Ruth Vinz, authors of the *Daybook of Critical Reading and Writing* series, and Jim Burke, author of the *Reader's Handbook* and *Reading Reminders,* describe many techniques for teaching critical reading strategies. Here are seven effective approaches that are easy to implement:

1 Interact with the text.

A successful reader interacts with a text by highlighting important or startling lines, writing notes or questions in the margins, circling words that are puzzling, or noting his or her reactions while reading. Through this interaction, the reader becomes much more attentive and engaged in the reading and gains more from the experience. (See page 163 in this guide for an example.)

2 Make connections with the text.

A text takes on more significance if the reader makes personal connections with it. The most obvious way for the reader to connect with a text is to ask (and try to answer) the following types of questions:

- *Have I faced a situation similar to the one faced by the main character?*
- *Have I known similar characters?*
- *Have I encountered similar problems?*
- *Would I have reacted in the same way?*
- *Do I have the same beliefs as ________?*
- *Have I read or heard about similar events?*

3 Explore multiple perspectives.

An inexperienced reader typically thinks about a text in one way, taking everything at face value. But if the reader steps back and asks "what if" questions, a text often opens up in new ways. Here are some sample questions that can help a reader see a text in new ways:

- *What if a different character told the story?*
- *What if this story took place in a different time or place?*
- *What if the main character held different beliefs?*

4 Study the style and craft of a text.

Writers deliberate very carefully about word choice, character development, plot development, and so on. Good critical readers constantly ask themselves questions about the writer's style and craft:

- *Why did the writer use that word?*
- *Why is this character introduced?*
- *Why did the story end here?*
- *Why weren't more details included about ________?*

By thinking about a writer's choices, a reader can better understand what the writer is trying to express.

5 Focus on a writer's life and work.

A writer's life often affects how she or he views the world, so exploring background information about a writer may help the reader understand a text more fully. In addition, a writer's beliefs and interests become clearer by reading more than one of his or her titles. (See "Critical Reading," pages 401–408 in *Write for College.*)

6 Use a before/during/after strategy for reading nonfiction.

Before starting, the reader should consider the text and activate prior knowledge. *During* reading, the reader should jot down questions and pause often to reflect on what the writer is saying. *After* reading, the reader should reread challenging parts of the text in order to connect with the material. A reader needs to be able to summarize the reading and state the writer's purpose and point of view. (See pages 403–405 in *Write for College.*)

7 Learn content-related vocabulary.

A careful reader records new words and definitions in a vocabulary notebook, utilizes a book's glossary, index, annotations, and illustrations to understand specialized vocabulary and important concepts in textbooks and course materials. A serious reader refers to a dictionary and thesaurus while reading in order to learn new words.

Responding to a Text

For the following poem, the reader used a copy on which to jot down initial responses, line by line. In books one owns, responses can be made right on the page.

For textbooks or online sources, always make a photocopy or printout for taking notes. Unfamiliar words can be circled and interesting phrases can be highlighted.

My November Guest

MY Sorrow, when she's here with me, a
Thinks these dark days of autumn rain b
Are beautiful as days can be; a
She loves the bare, the withered tree; a
She walks the sodden pasture lane. b

Her pleasure will not let me stay.
She talks and I am fain to list:
She's glad the birds are gone away,
She's glad her simple worsted gray
Is silver now with clinging mist.

The desolate, deserted trees,
The faded earth, the heavy sky,
The beauties she so truly sees,
She thinks I have no eye for these,
And vexes me for reason why.

Not yesterday I learned to know
The love of bare November days
Before the coming of the snow,
But it were vain to tell her so,
And they are better for her praise.

—Robert Frost

Margin notes:

- Sorrow is personified.
- iambic tetrameter and regular rhyme scheme throughout
- sodden: heavy, soaked
- not let me stay: will not leave me alone
- fain to list: gladly listen (can't help but listen)
- worsted: heavy, dense wool fabric
- Poem moves from "she loves . . ." to "I learned to know the love . . ."
- Something of love in sorrow—love of what is gone, lost . . .
- Sorrow as inevitable as the natural cycle of seasons
- vexes me: will not leave me alone
- Not yesterday: not suddenly, but gradually
- –The "s" sounds repeated throughout the poem are like the incessant hiss of wind and rain. They abate in the final stanza as the poet moves from resisting to embracing his November guest.

Insights into Critical Reading

Listed below are six categories and the types of insights that a critical reader gains over time through many reading experiences. Sharing these insights with students may help them become more insightful and skillful readers themselves.

Short Fiction

- Studying the characters helps the reader connect with a story.
- Establishing point of view—the vantage point from which a story is told—helps to determine how much the reader will learn about each character.
- Understanding the basic structure of a plot leads to a more thoughtful analysis of a story.
- Showing how the setting contributes to the tone or mood in a story adds depth to a literary response.
- Connecting a story's theme to one's own life reveals the deeper meaning of a story.

Poetry

- Analyzing the layout adds to an overall appreciation of a poem.
- Studying the sensory details in a poem leads to a better understanding of the poet's message or purpose.
- Exploring figures of speech deepens the reader's insights into a poem.
- Studying the rhyme and rhythm in a poem helps the reader appreciate its "music."
- Responding personally to a poem leads to better understanding.
- Noting the sound patterns—*alliteration, repetition,* and so on—in a poem gives the reader insights into its tone or mood.

Nonfiction

- Employing effective reading strategies can "unlock" the text and connect it more thoughtfully to the reader. (See approaches listed on page 162 in this guide.)
- Sorting out the main ideas and supporting details is the basis for understanding nonfiction texts.
- Making generalizations based on the reading leads to better understanding.
- Considering causes and effects helps the reader make connections between ideas.

Persuasive Writing

- Knowing the basic structure of an argument (see pages 239–243 and 251–253 in *Write for College*) leads to a more thoughtful analysis of persuasive texts.
- Identifying the writer's viewpoint is the starting point for analyzing and understanding a persuasive piece.
- Knowing that persuasive writers may use loaded words and stories that appeal to the emotions helps the reader judge the quality of an author's argument.

Authors

- The writer often draws on personal experiences and relationships to create believable characters and situations in a story.
- The writer of historical fiction blends events that happened in history with fictional details to make history come alive.
- The writer tackles tough issues to show that there are lessons to be learned from difficult situations.
- The writer uses exaggeration to entertain, add humor, and give insight into characters and their actions.

Themes

- The reader should always ask, "What is the writer trying to say to me?" The theme lies in the answer to that question.
- The reader should look for additional themes beyond the primary one. These secondary themes can add to the understanding and appreciation of a text.

Reading-Writing Connection

The next six pages list high-interest titles that you may want to use when planning units for different sections in *Write for College*. We gratefully acknowledge Vicki Spandel for this list of books that exemplify the traits of effective writing.

The Process of Writing

Bird by Bird: Some Instructions on Writing and Life
Anne Lamott

A Book of Your Own: Keeping a Diary or Journal
Carla Stevens

Creating Unforgettable Characters
Linda Seger

Daily Sentence Composing
Don and Jenny Killgallon

Everyday Use: Rhetoric at Work in Reading and Writing
Hephzibah Roskelly, David A. Jolliffe

Fiction Writer's Workshop
Josip Novakovich

How to Write a Movie in 21 Days
Viki King

On Writing: A Memoir of the Craft
Stephen King

The Reviser's Toolbox
Barry Lane

10,000 Ideas for Term Papers, Projects, Reports, and Speeches
Katheryn Lamm

What's There to Write About?
Kalli Dakos

Words Fail Me
Patricia T. O'Conner

The Writing Life
Annie Dillard

Writing with Purpose and Passion: A Writer's Guide to Language and Style
Jeff Stalcup and Michael Rovasio

Books That Exemplify the Traits of Effective Writing

Ideas

Alien Invaders: The Continuing Threat of Exotic Species
Sneed B. Collard, III

All Over but the Shoutin'
Rick Bragg

The Book of Qualities
Ruth Gendler

Growing Up in Coal Country
Susan Campbell Bartoletti

Guns, Germs, and Steel: The Fates of Human Societies
Jared Diamond

How the Irish Saved Civilization
Thomas Cahill

Ironman
Chris Crutcher

Kindred
Octavia Butler

Monster
Walter Dean Myers

Books That Exemplify the Traits of Effective Writing (continued)

The New Way Things Work
David Macaulay

Sweet Words So Brave: The Story of African American Literature
Barbara K. Curry and James Michael Brodie

The Things They Carried
Tim O'Brien

When Human Heads Were Footballs: Surprising Stories of How Sports Began
Don L. Wulffson

Wild Thoughts from Wild Places
David Quammen

Organization

The Great Automatic Grammatizator and Other Stories
Roald Dahl

My Life in Dog Years
Gary Paulsen

Seedfolks
Paul Fleischman

Steven Caney's Invention Book
Steven Caney

Voice

The Boys War: Confederate and Union Soldiers Talk About the Civil War
Jim Murphy

The Burnt Stick
Anthony Hill

The Emperor's Embrace: Reflections on Animal Families and Fatherhood
Jeffrey Moussaieff Masson

Essays That Worked: 50 Essays from Successful Applications to the Nation's Top Colleges
Boykin Curry and Brian Kasbar

Home
Sharon Sloan Fiffer and Steve Fiffer, editors

Instant Physics: From Aristotle to Einstein, and Beyond
Tony Rothman

Out of the Dust
Karen Hesse

Soldier's Heart
Gary Paulsen

Tuesdays with Morrie
Mitch Albom

Word Choice

The Beauty of the Beastly: New Views on the Nature of Life
Natalie Angler

Crazy English: The Ultimate Joy Ride Through Our Language
Richard Lederer

Forgotten English
Jeffrey Kacirk

It Was a Dark and Stormy Night: The Final Conflict
Scott Rice

Nature's Numbers
Ian Stewart

Where the Bluebird Sings to the Lemonade Springs
Wallace Stegner

Sentence Fluency

The Block
Langston Hughes

E. E. Cummings
S. L. Berry

Hear, Hear, Mr. Shakespeare
Bruce Koscielniak

The House on Mango Street
Sandra Cisneros

I Know What the Red Clay Looks Like: The Voice and Vision of Black Women Writers
Rebecca Carroll

River Teeth: Stories and Writings
David James Duncan

Versed in Country Things
Robert Frost

What It Took for Me to Get Here
San Francisco WritersCorps, editors

Conventions & Layout

Anguished English
Richard Lederer

Jazz: My Music, My People
Morgan Monceaux

The Journey Is the Destination: The Journals of Dan Eldon
Kathy Eldon, editor

Metamorphosis: The Ultimate Spot-the-Difference Book
Mike Wilks

The Forms of Writing: Personal and Fiction Writing

All Quiet on the Western Front
Erich Maria Remarque

Angela's Ashes
Frank McCourt

Anna Karenina
Leo Tolstoy

The Canterbury Tales
Geoffrey Chaucer

Catch 22
Joseph Heller

Cold Mountain
Charles Frazier

The Complete Works of William Shakespeare
William Shakespeare, David Bevington, editor

The Count of Monte Cristo
Alexander Dumas

Cyrano de Bergerac
Edmond Rostrand

Death in Venice
Thomas Mann

Dr. Faustus
Christopher Marlowe

Emma
Jane Austen

Farewell to Arms
Ernest Hemingway

Favorite Folktales from Around the World
Jane Yolen

The Fountainhead
Ayn Rand

Giants in the Earth
O. E. Rölvaag

The Grapes of Wrath
John Steinbeck

Great Expectations
Charles Dickens

The Great Gatsby
F. Scott Fitzgerald

The Hobbit
J. R. R. Tolkien

In a Sunburned Country
Bill Bryson

The Forms of Writing: Personal and Fiction Writing (continued)

Jane Eyre
Charlotte Bronte

Les Miserables
Victor Hugo

Lord of the Flies
William Golding

A Man for All Seasons: A Play in Two Acts
Robert Bolt

Native Son
Richard Wright

The Old Man and the Sea
Ernest Hemingway

On the Beach
Nevil Shute

The Once and Future King
T. H. White

The Phantom of the Opera
Gaston Leroux

Reach for the Moon
Samantha Abeel

Rocket Boys
Homer Hickam

Schindler's List
Thomas Keneally

Seabiscuit: An American Legend
Laura Hillenbrand

The Secret Diary of Anne Boleyn: A Novel
Robin Maxwell

She Stoops to Conquer
Oliver Goldsmith

Shizuko's Daughter
Kyoko Mori

Siddhartha
Hermann Hesse

Stones from the River
Ursula Hegi

The Stranger
Albert Camus

A Thousand Acres
Jane Hamilton

To Kill a Mockingbird
Harper Lee

Winterdance
Gary Paulsen

Wuthering Heights
Emily Bronte

The Forms of Writing: Poetry

Native American Songs and Poems
Brian Swann, editor

Nine Horses
Billy Collins

100 Best Loved Poems
Philip Smith, editor

The Oxford Treasury of Classic Poems
compiled by Michael Harrison and Christopher Stuart-Clarke

The Poet's Companion: A Guide to the Pleasure of Writing Poetry
Kim Addonisio and Dorianne Laux

Things I Have to Tell You: Poems and Writing by Teenage Girls
Betsy Franco, editor

You Hear Me? Poems and Writing by Teenage Boys
Betsy Franco, editor

The Forms of Writing: Academic Writing

Absolute Zero: And the Conquest of Cold
Tom Shachtman

Amazon Journal: Dispatches from a Vanishing Frontier
Geoffrey O'Connor

Band of Brothers
Stephen E. Ambrose

The Diary of Victor Frankenstein
Roscoe Cooper

Founding Brothers
Joseph J. Ellis

Hiroshima
John Hersey

Innumeracy: Mathematical Illiteracy and Its Consequences
John Allen Paulos

Man's Search for Meaning
Viktor Frankl

Postcards from France
Megan McNeill Libby

They All Laughed . . . From Light Bulbs to Lasers
Ira Flatow

The True Story of Two Friends Separated (for a Year) by an Ocean
Hilary Liftin and Kate Montgomery

21st Century Earth: Opposing Viewpoints
O. W. Markley and Walter R. McCuan, editors

Undaunted Courage: The Pioneering First Mission to Explore America's Western Wilderness
Stephen E. Ambrose

Wealth of Nations
Adam Smith, Alan B. Krueger (introduction)

When I Was Your Age
Amy Ehrlich, editor

Working Women: Opposing Viewpoints
Mary E. Williams, editor

A World at Arms: A Global History of World War II
Gerhard L. Weinberg

The Forms of Writing: Workplace Writing

Business Writing: What Works, What Won't
Wilma Davidson

Résumé Writing Made Easy, 7th Edition
Lola Brown

Write for Business
Verne Meyer, Pat Sebranek, John Van Rys

The Tools of Learning

The Craft of Research
Wayne C. Booth et al.

The Curious Researcher: A Guide to Writing Research Papers
Bruce Ballenger

Great American Speeches
Gregory Suriano, editor

Oxford Dictionary of Phrases, Proverbs, and Quotations
Elizabeth M. Knowles, editor

Readings on the Comedies of Shakespeare
Clarice Swisher, editor

Vocabulary for Achievement
Margaret Ann Richek

Proofreader's Guide

Eats, Shoots & Leaves
Lynne Truss

The Elements of Style Illustrated
William Strunk, Jr., E. B. White, and Maira Kalman (illustrator)

The Elephants of Style: A Truckload of Tips on the Big Issues and Gray Areas of Contemporary American English
Bill Walsh

The Wordwatcher's Guide to Good Writing & Grammar
Morton S. Freeman

Student Almanac

National Geographic Concise Atlas of the World (2003)
Carl Mehler, editor

Women's Almanac
Linda Schmittroth and Mary Reilly McCall, editors

World Almanac Book of Facts 2007
Ken Park, editor

Thinking and **Learning** Strategies

The thinking and learning strategies in this section cover important areas in a comprehensive writing program.

Teaching Thinking

"Let your students know that thinking is a goal. Create the right climate and model it."
—Arthur L. Costa

Outstanding proponents of broader and better integrated approaches to thinking—leaders such as David Perkins, Art Costa, Richard Paul, Robin Fogarty, Barry Beyer, Robert Marzano, and others—have been writing, speaking, and inspiring teachers all over the country to "rethink" their classrooms.

Many teachers successfully challenge their students to think more analytically and creatively. These teachers teach critical thinking skills—skills that will serve their students for a lifetime—as a matter of course in their content areas. Educators who incorporate thinking skills into their curriculum believe that critical thinking skills are communicated and refined during collaborative learning opportunities. We learn from and with others all our lives. We learn to converse and get along; tie our shoes and make our letters; ride a bicycle and drive a car; plan a party and build a complex structure; swim a relay race and dance a jig; read a play and write a letter; paint a picture and play a musical instrument—all with the help of family, friends, and teachers.

Creating a Thinking Climate in Your Classroom

For educators who believe that thinking can be taught, it is helpful to consider the classroom strategies suggested by those who have done extensive research in this field. In *Developing Minds: A Resource Book for Teaching Thinking* (ASCD publications, 2001), Arthur L. Costa collected ideas and advice about teaching thinking from outstanding thinkers. The book presents three components in teaching thinking: teaching *for* thinking (by creating the right classroom climate), teaching *of* thinking (by teaching thinking skills), and teaching *about* thinking (by helping students to become more aware of their own thinking).

Teaching *for* Thinking

Q. How can I create a thinking climate in my classroom?

A. To create a thinking climate, teachers connect their classrooms to the real world. Here are several strategies to consider:

- Personalize the learning in your classroom. Students will approach learning more thoughtfully when the subject matter means something to them personally. Common sense (plus plenty of studies) tells us students won't become thoughtfully engaged in work that is not relevant to them. What does this mean to you? Don't rely solely on the textbook. Convey your enthusiasm for topics in your subject area by inviting your students' questions and observations and including their interests as starting points for thinking and learning.
- Engage students in collaborative learning projects. Have them produce a class or school newspaper or magazine. Have them write and produce a play or a news show. Have them develop instructional manuals on a variety of activities, such as skateboarding or troubleshooting on a computer. Establish writing groups in which students regularly read and respond to the ideas and words of others. There are any number of challenging thinking activities built into long-range projects. (For more information on collaborative learning, see "Peer Reviewing" on pages 49–51 in *Write for College* and "Collaborative Learning" on page 174 in this guide.)
- Promote thinking and writing activities that have heretofore been considered fillers: writing and publishing stories and poems, producing pamphlets and brochures, writing letters on issues that affect the community in which you live, encouraging discussion and debate. These activities get students actively thinking and learning. (Remember, basic-skills sheets generally do not promote critical thinking.)
- Promote active learning in your classroom. Give your students every opportunity to explore, take risks, and make mistakes. Ask them more open-ended questions. Initiate class discussions and use more writing-to-learn activities. (See pages 421–428 in *Write for College* and pages 138–141 in this guide.)

- Help your students learn to think about and respond thoughtfully to the ideas and opinions of others. (See "Peer Reviewing," pages 49–51 in *Write for College.*)

In other words, get students thinking *for* thinking.

Teaching *of* Thinking

Q. How do I work thinking skills into my curriculum?

A. Introduce thinking skills into the classroom by focusing on one skill at a time.

- Review a taxonomy of thinking skills and select a limited number to emphasize throughout the year—perhaps one comprehension skill, such as summarizing; one analyzing skill, such as classifying; and one evaluating skill, such as persuading.
- Produce your own activities for teaching thinking skills, or use reputable materials that are commercially produced. Instruction that is infused with the "call to think" requires students to immerse themselves in the learning process.
- Arthur Costa suggests that these skills be worked into the general content area *and* be taught independently. He suggests spending two or three hours per week in the direct teaching of thinking skills.

In other words, get students thinking *of* thinking.

Teaching *About* Thinking

Q. How can I help students think about their own thinking?

A. Teachers share their own learning experiences and present other ways of thinking in order to get students thinking about their own process.

- Help students think about their own learning process. Have them estimate how long an assignment will take, determine what materials they will need, and break down assignments into manageable tasks. Help students find partners who can help them if they get stuck. Have them keep track of their progress during an extended project and relay their progress to you in memos or e-mail messages. (See pages 312–315 in *Write for College.*)
- Discuss with students how the brain works. Provide an overview of important studies on brain research and summarize what we have learned about how humans think. Introduce the topic of artificial intelligence and discuss the scientific advances in this area and the technological implications for future generations.
- Read to your students about important developments in your field and recommend biographies of famous thinkers. Pique your students' curiosity about the life and work of a famous thinker by asking them to find how early discoveries by this person affect the way we think about the topic today.
- Encourage students to take pride in their own work. Remind them that their work is a reflection of their own thinking. Use assignment guidelines and peer response groups to help them refine their ideas. Set aside time to have them evaluate their completed work. Students in every course should consider what they would do differently in the future on a similar writing or research assignment and record their reflections in a learning log. (See pages 422–423 in *Write for College.*)
- Remind students that it's all right to start over or reach dead ends. We all do. Give students opportunities to talk or write about their thoughts and feelings when things aren't going as planned. Help them learn from these experiences.
- Encourage students to connect what they have already learned to new information. Also take every opportunity across the curriculum to connect what they are learning to their personal lives. Have students evaluate popular products or events; ask them to analyze the progress and results of local, national, or global initiatives; and frequently ask them to reflect on and summarize their contributions to and participation in class, school, and the community.

In other words, get them thinking *about* thinking.

Collaborative Learning

Collaborative (cooperative) learning is a powerful classroom strategy for both teachers and students. It involves working together as we have always tried to do, but with new knowledge about group dynamics, borrowed largely from the areas of communication and psychology.

Obviously, you already know a lot about cooperative learning. You have been or are a member of many groups—families, sport teams, community groups, faculty committees, and so forth. Sometimes when we look at these groups, we tend to remember how ineffective they can be. We may have knowledge about what not to do. If nothing else, this is an incentive toward discovering what to do.

What should a teacher do?

First, we suggest that you experiment with collaborative learning before deciding if this classroom strategy is for you and your students. We provide three strategies you can use for this experimentation. The group skills you will want to work with are described in *Write for College.*

As you experiment, keep these advantages of collaborative learning in mind:

- Allows teachers to move away from the front of the room and rely less on lecturing.
- Provides students with one of the most powerful ways to learn—verbalization.
- Gives students more ownership of their learning and therefore motivates them to become better students.

Three Strategies That Work

The three strategies you can use for experimentation follow:

Tell/Retell Groups

Application: Any reading-to-learn activity

Recommended group size: 2 (3 in one group if you have an uneven number of students)

Group skills to emphasize: Listen actively, listen accurately, and offer words of encouragement.

STEP 1: One member reads a portion of the assigned material; the second member becomes an "active listener."

STEP 2: The second member tells what he or she heard; the first member becomes the "active listener." They decide together what the essential information is. (It's okay for them to look back at the reading material.)

STEP 3: Reverse roles and read the next portion.

Smart Groups

Application: Any reading-to-learn activity

Recommended group size: 2

Group skills to emphasize: Request help or clarification when needed, offer to explain or clarify, and never use put-downs.

STEP 1: Both students read assigned material. While reading, they put a faint check mark beside each paragraph they understand and a question mark beside any sentence, word, or paragraph they do not completely understand.

STEP 2: At each question mark, team members ask for help and clarification. If they both have questions, they try together to make sense of the material. If they both agree to seek outside help, they may consult another team or the teacher. If time allows, they may share what they remember about the passages they both understand. (See "Critical Reading," pages 401–407 in *Write for College.*)

Up-with-Your-Head Groups

Application: Checking comprehension

Recommended group size: 4-5

Group skills to emphasize: Reach a decision.

STEP 1: Ask each student to number off within each group.

STEP 2: The teacher or a panel of students asks a question about the material that has been read.

STEP 3: Each group makes sure every member in their group knows the answer. When the question is open-ended, the group reaches a consensus of opinion.

STEP 4: The questioner calls a number (1, 2, 3, 4, 5), and students with the corresponding number raise their hands to respond. When the question requires "the" answer, only one student need reply; but when the question is open-ended, a member from each group may reply.

Building Vocabulary

What do we know about vocabulary development?

For one thing, we know there is a strong connection between a student's vocabulary and her or his reading ability. The same is true for a student's ability to listen, speak, and write. In fact, we now recognize that each person actually has four vocabularies, one each for reading, listening, speaking, and writing (listed here from largest to smallest). Although there is much overlap, students will always be able to recognize more words than they can produce. This is important to keep in mind as you develop a program of vocabulary development for your students.

Vocabulary development must also occur across the curriculum. Students must read, hear, speak, and write with the words they are attempting to learn in their classes. If they do not do this, the words will not become part of their permanent "producing" vocabulary.

Existing studies tell us two things: (1) giving students lists of vocabulary words with little or no context is not an efficient way to teach vocabulary; (2) students must be actively involved with the words they are attempting to learn.

Vocabulary-Building Strategies

The following vocabulary-building strategies have taken all of these points into consideration:

Previewing in Context

1. Select five to six words from a chapter or selection students are about to read.
2. Have students open their books to the page and paragraph in which each word is located. Ask them to find the word, read it in context, and try to figure out the meaning.
3. Have each student write down what they think each word means.
4. Discuss possible meanings and arrive at the correct definition in this context.
5. Confirm your consensus by checking a dictionary.

Self-Collection

1. Students should set aside a portion of their journals or notebooks to collect personal vocabulary.
2. Students can collect new and interesting words from any source, preferably outside of school.
3. Each journal entry should contain the word and the sentence in which it was used.
4. The student can then analyze the word using its context, word parts, and dictionary definitions.

Prefix, Suffix, Root Study

1. Students should learn the most common prefixes, suffixes, and roots. (See "Using Word Parts," pages 434–444 in *Write for College.*)
2. For a complete study of the prefixes, suffixes, and roots, assign three to four word parts each week during the year and teach the following strategies for learning them (see word parts lists on page 176 of this guide):
   - Assign students one word part daily. As you are taking roll, students can write out the word part, the definition, a sample word, and a sentence using this word, which can then be exchanged and corrected.
   - Brainstorm afterward for familiar words that include the word part to reinforce the meaning of each word part.
   - Challenge students to combine the word parts they have studied into as many words as possible (in 5 minutes or as a challenge assignment for the next day). Special cards can also be used for this purpose.

Word Card

de		ion
	flex	
re		or
	flect	
in		ible

- Students can also be challenged to create "new" words using the word parts they have learned. To qualify, a new word should be one that makes sense and might actually be used.
- Students can be asked to share the "new" word and challenge other students to guess what it means and to write a sentence using this word.
- Students can start a special section in their notebooks for word parts they come across in newspapers, magazines, and their other classes.

> "Words are one of our chief means of adjusting to all situations of life. The better control we have over words, the more successful our adjustment is likely to be."
>
> —Bergan Evans

Word Parts Study List

These lists of word parts can form the basis of a vocabulary-building program.

On Your Mark

Prefixes: anti (ant), bi (bis, bin), circum (circ), deca, di, ex (e, ec, ef), hemi (demi, semi), hex, il (ir, in, im), in (il, im), intro, mono, multi, non, penta, post, pre, quad, quint, re, self, sub, super (supr), tri, un, uni

Suffixes: able (ible), ade, age, al, an (ian), ary (ery, ory), cule (ling), en, er (or), ese, ess, ful, hood, ic, id (ide), ion (sion, tion), ist, ity (ty), ize, less, ology, ship, ward

Roots: anni (annu, enni), anti, aster (astr), aud (aus), auto (aut), bibl, bio, brev, centri, chrom, chron, cide (cise), cit, clud (clus, claus), corp, crat (cracy), cred, cycl (cyclo), dem, dent (dont), derm, dict, domin, dorm, duc (duct), erg, fin, fix, flex (flect), form, fort (forc), fract (frag), geo, graph (gram), here (hes), hydr, hydra, hydro, ject, join (junct), juven, lau (lac, lot, lut), magn, mand, mania, meter, micro, migra, multi, numer, omni, ortho, ped (pod), phon, pop, port, prehend, punct, reg (recti), rupt, sci, scrib (script), serv, spec (spect, spic), sphere, tele, tempo, terra, therm, tract (tra), typ, uni, ver (veri), vid (vis), zo

Get Set

Prefixes: ambi (amb), amphi, bene (bon), by, co (con, col, com), contra (counter), dia, dis (dif), eu, extra (extro), for, fore, homo, inter, mis, ob (of, op, oc), para, per, peri, poly, pro, se, sup, sus, syn (sym, sys, syl), trans (tra), ultra, under, vice

Suffixes: algia, ance (ancy), ant, ate, cian, escent, fic, fy, ish, ism, ive, ly, ment, ness, ous, some, tude

Roots: ag (agi, ig, act), anthrop, arch, aug (auc), cad (cas), cap (cip, cept), capit (capt), carn, cause (cuse, cus), ced (ceed, cede, cess), civ, clam (claim), cord (cor, cardi), cosm, crea, cresc (cret, crease, cru), deca, drome, dura, dynam, equi, fac (fact, fic, fect), fer, fid (fide, feder), gam, gen, gest, grad (gress), grat, grav, hum (human), hypn, leg, liter, log (logo, ogue, ology), luc (lum, lus, lun), man, mar (mari, mer), medi, mega, mem, mit (miss), mob (mot, mov), mon, mor (mort), nov, onym, oper, pac, pan, pater (patr), path (pathy), pend (pens, pond), phil, photo, plu (plur, plus), poli, portion, prim (prime), psych, salv (salu), sat (satis), scope, sen, sent (sens), sign (signi), sist (sta, stit), solus, solv (solu), spir, string (strict), stru (struct), tact (tang, tag, tig, ting), test, thesis (thet), tort (tors), vac, vert (vers), vict (vinc), voc, volvo

Go!

Prefixes: a (an), ab (abs, a), acro, ante, be, cata, cerebro, com, de, dys, em, en, epi, hyper, hypo, infra, intra, macro, mal, meta, miso, neo, oct, paleo, pseudo, retro, sesqui, sex (sest), suf, sug

Suffixes: cy, dom, ee, ence (ency), esis (osis), et (ette), ice, ile, ine, ite, oid, ure, y

Roots: acer (acid, acri), acu, ali (allo, alter), alt, am (amor), belli, calor, caus (caut), cognosc (gnosi), crit, cur (curs), cura, doc, don, dox, endo, fall (fals), fila (fili), flu (fluc, fluv), gastr(o), germ, gloss (glot), glu (glo), greg, helio, hema (hemo), hetero, homo, ignis, levi, liber (liver), loc (loco), loqu (locut), matri, morph, nat (nasc), neur, nom, nomen (nomin), nox (noc), pedo, pel (puls), phobia, plac, pneuma (pneumon), pon (pos, pound), proto, ri (ridi, risi), rog (roga), sacr (sanc, secr), sangui, sed (sess, sid), sequ (secu, sue), simil (simul), somnus, soph, sume (sump), ten (tin, tain), tend (tent, tens), the (theo), tom, tox, trib, tui (tuit, tut), turbo, ultima, vale (vali, valu), ven (vent), vic (vicis), viv (vita, vivi), vol, volcan (vulcan), vor

Expanding Technology

Access to the World Wide Web and the Internet offers the user an endless source of facts and opinions. Because virtually anyone can publish virtually anything on the Web, it can be a challenge to locate reliable sources. Even so, students need to learn how to use technology effectively in order to become fully literate. Solutions to multifaceted problems facing future generations may lie in how well students learn to explore complex issues today.

Using Technology in the Classroom

Advances in technology have made it possible to bring the world into the classroom. Today's students use technology to find, read, and respond to the ideas of prominent thinkers in all fields of study. More teachers routinely plan cross-curricular projects that require the use of computer technology for conducting research. Many high school teachers utilize computer technology to establish and maintain regular communication with their students on reading, research, and writing topics. Computer labs in many high schools offer sophisticated writing programs to assist students in producing polished pieces on topics they have selected for research.

Advancements in technology also help students publish their work. Students regularly use computer programs to plan and prepare multimedia reports. Students can easily enhance their presentations with data and visuals that help explain complex concepts. They can revisit, revise, and edit their work using software programs that troubleshoot areas in need of improvement.

Teachers who help their students prepare for the future integrate technology instruction into their daily lesson plans. They utilize technology as an essential and continuously evolving tool for teaching thinking across the curriculum. They understand that teaching technology literacy is really about teaching people to solve problems. By teaching their students to use technology effectively, today's teachers help prepare their students for tomorrow's challenges.

As the realm of communication expands to include the global community, Netiquette (Network etiquette) guidelines that are sensitive to cultural differences become increasingly important.

Problem Solving with Technology

Teachers who use technology to teach literacy establish a list of criteria or skills for students to master. Here is a task-oriented list that educators, employers, and parents commonly identify:

1 Identify the Problem

For students to become self-directed, lifelong learners, they must become problem solvers. They must be able to identify the problem and acquire the knowledge to intelligently find a solution.

2 Predict and Find Sources of Information

In order to efficiently find needed information, students must be proficient in traditional skills, such as interviewing and library use, and in electronic skills, such as accessing a database and searching the Internet.

3 Evaluate Information

With the proliferation of online information sources—many of them unreliable—critical-thinking skills are needed to recognize misinformation.

4 Credit Sources

With the rapid expansion of information sources on the Internet, students must recognize their responsibility to the larger community to give proper credit for information used.

5 Formulate a Plan

Having identified and researched a problem or need, students must be able to plan a response, whether to find a solution to a problem or to report new knowledge they have acquired. Often, they will need to use information-processing technology, such as spreadsheets and topic web (cluster) programs.

6 Collaborate with Others

In many cases, in order to accomplish their plans, students will need to work with peers in teams and groups of teams (often across the curriculum). They need to know how to divide the work appropriately, how to carry out their own roles, and how to communicate effectively when they have information for others in the group or need information from them. It may be helpful to use resource management programs.

7 Communicate Results

When communicating information, students must be able to choose the best medium. Consequently, they must understand how to use a wide range of media, from speeches to paper reports, from electronic presentations—such as video and multimedia reports—to Web sites.

8 Evaluate Results

Finally, students need to judge the success of their projects, whether to recognize new needs (thus restarting the cycle) or to identify new information to apply to their next task.

Incorporating Technology

Incorporating both technology and group skills into the classroom may seem a tall order. However, a few steps in the right direction are sufficient to begin, and soon technology literacy gains a momentum of its own.

Use Technology

Much of technology literacy is simply becoming comfortable with technology. Many electronic devices and programs have too many features for any one person to master. Instead, users learn what they need to get started, and they explore other functions later. In other words, the best way to become comfortable with new technologies is a hands-on approach.

As you explore technologies, look for ways to incorporate them into your life. For example, make it a point to use e-mail whenever possible for your communications. Make an online search engine your first choice for finding information. Seek out other resources online to make your work and personal life easier.

Use Technology in Class

As you get comfortable with these technologies, model technology literacy for your students. Share a printout of information you found on the Internet. Then make sure to plan Internet access as part of the research time for student projects. Establishing and maintaining e-mail communication between teacher and students can be a great way to keep a response journal. To gain familiarity with multimedia presentations, start by creating one of your own to use in class. In doing so, you model the appropriate role of technology as a medium for the content you wish to convey.

Include Technology in Assignments

Construct assignments that require students to use technology for themselves. Certainly the first step is to have them use a word processor for writing papers. From there, have them work with fonts, formats, and imported graphics. Make certain they are familiar with Web browsers. Then have them capture images from Web pages to incorporate into their papers—remembering to credit the sources. Familiarize them with an e-mail program; then have them submit an assignment as an e-mail attachment.

Use computer programs to make written and oral comments on student papers and invite students to respond to one another's writing in this way.

A multimedia project can serve as a follow-up to an oral report. (See *Write for College* pages 459–463 for details.) Eventually, incorporate task-management software into projects as well.

Build Professional Relationships

Teachers and computer professionals alike work best in an environment of mutual support. Cross-curricular projects serve as a natural arena for partnerships. Many teachers are developing contacts with other teachers across the Internet, allowing their classes to communicate with one another as well. Add an international dimension to this communication and to all classroom learning by forming partnerships with educators and classrooms in other countries.

Resources on the Web

For more information, explore the ISTE (International Society for Technology in Education) home page <www.iste.org>. This Web site contains many teacher resources.

Trait-Based Writing **Activities**

Implementing the Writing Activities

The writing activities can be implemented in a number of different ways to meet the students' needs. As noted below, they can work hand in hand with the forms of writing, serve as self-contained units for general instruction, or accommodate individuals who want or need enrichment work.

Integration into the Writing Units

Every effort should be made to integrate the writing activities with the forms-of-writing units. (Working on various traits of good writing, writing skills, and strategies always makes more sense within the context of the composing process.) The chapter-by-chapter notes cross-reference the related writing activities in this guide.

Classroom Instruction

Specific writing activities can be used as the starting point or focus of instruction. Teachers who feel the entire class would benefit by working on a particular trait could implement an appropriate activity to meet this need. For instance, finding a focus for a writing assignment and composing a thesis statement are tasks that address the trait of ideas.

Mini-Units

Teachers may decide to implement *mini-units* of related activities for classroom instruction. If, for example, students need to hone their revising skills and strategies, a teacher could implement several trait-based activities suited to revising.

Small-Group Work

When members of a writing group share a particular concern about their writing, teachers can direct them to an appropriate activity for small-group work.

Individual Learning

The activities can also be implemented on an individual basis to help specific students refine their writing skills.

Instructor/Student Conferences

During one-on-one writing conferences, teachers may use an activity to illustrate a particular writing skill or strategy.

Ideas: Searching and Selecting

Read: Read and reflect on the following quotations from a variety of famous writers about the process of writing.

"A really good writing class or workshop can give us some shadow of what musicians have all the time—the excitement of a group working together, so that each member outdoes himself."

—Ursula K. LeGuin

"Writing is the only thing that, when I do it, I don't feel I should be doing something else."

—Gloria Steinem

"To write about people you have to know people, to write about bloodhounds you have to know bloodhounds, to write about the Loch Ness monster you have to find out about it."

—James Thurber

" . . . as soon as you connect with your true subject you will write."

—Joyce Carol Oates

"Easy writing makes hard reading."

—Ernest Hemingway

"The real writing takes place between the first miserable, crude draft and the finished thing."

—Gloria Naylor

"You always feel when you look it straight in the eye that you could have put more into it, could have let yourself go and dug harder."

—Emily Carr

React: Select one of the quotations that matches up well with your own writing experience. Explain the connection in a freely written exploratory draft on your own paper.

Extend

Write your own pithy statement about writing to be posted in a writing center. Review "One Writer's Process" (pages 1–14) in the handbook if you're having trouble coming up with ideas.

Ideas: Discovering Interesting Subjects

"Writing is easy," said the well-known sportswriter Red Smith. "All you have to do is sit down at a typewriter and open a vein."

Right now, let's assume that you have been asked to "open a vein." Maybe your instructor has said, "You'll have 10 minutes for freewriting." Freewriting is also known as **impromptu writing, writing bursts,** or **stop 'n' write**.

Whatever the name, the problem is the same: how to get started, go hard, and present a polished piece of writing. Nobody can give you rules for what is supposed to be a free and creative process. However, you can learn to write better at high speed if you will learn how to talk to yourself as you write.

Listen: For this exercise you don't need to mumble or move your lips. Instead, activate the quiet voice inside your head that whispers encouragement to you as you're going along, a voice that improves your attitude, increases your energy, raises your ambition, and broadens your interest. Listen to some of the words a writer's brain might whisper:

get going

try it

faster, faster

use shorthand

what's it all about?

let go of yourself

what else?

what's the difference?

what comes next?

so what?

prove it

don't erase

show it

why?

how do I feel?

do some more

what do I think?

Write: Read these over and over until they start echoing in your brain. Now, start writing about a general topic of your own choosing. Let that little voice inside drive you on. Never talk back to it!

NOTE: The kind of freewriting you'll be doing here is good for finding potential writing subjects as well as for shaping your initial ideas about a subject already in hand. *However,* it is not as good for writing an essay answer on a test or turning in a quick diagnostic essay that shows your new teacher what an excellent writer you are. Formal impromptu writing calls for more discipline.

Ideas: Searching and Shaping Subjects

Read: If you have a topic, use the writing method called "cubing" to search for more of what you already know. You can use the six sides of a cube to remind you of six ways to explore a topic. Here is how you might "cube" a report about the TV coverage of a major sporting event.

Side 1: Describe It Write at top speed about the sights and sounds (and other senses) that you connect with the TV broadcast. Describe it so that a reader feels he or she has been there.

A camera was mounted right on the woman's skis during her slalom run. The edges of her skis hissed as they cut through the ice crystals. The snow sprayed the camera lens, making brilliant circular rainbows . . .

Side 2: Compare It Write a comparison between the telecast and something comparable to it: for example, a related personal experience or another channel's coverage of the same event.

Because of the camera angle at snow level, it registered every bump and whoosh. Watching this broadcast reminded me of my best ski run. The wind passing my ears made me think I was flying. My skis on edge, I zipped happily through turn after turn . . .

Side 3: Associate It Write about something that in some way you connect with the telecast. Maybe it reminds you of an afternoon nap or a carnival sideshow or a really bad play.

The telecast was like a daydream when the mind swirls with wild images but somebody keeps breaking in talking and spoiling the mood. The announcers thought their jokes merited more airtime than the skiing, but I wanted to stay caught up in the dream . . .

Side 4: Analyze It Write about the different identifiable parts of the telecast.

The broadcast had four or five layers. The obvious commercial layer broke in every few minutes. Then the chitchat layer was the announcers talking about themselves, mostly . . .

Side 5: Apply It Write about what the telecast is good for, how it could be used, and so on.

Parts of this broadcast would work for a ski school, showing fine points of balance and shock-absorber knees. In a journalism class, parts of the broadcast could be used to analyze the faults of a typical sports broadcast . . .

Side 6: Argue for or Against It Make a pro or con case for the telecast to change it or to leave it the same. Argue for its style of presentation, argue against its length, or whatever.

I contend that sports broadcasters should monitor the ratio between talk and sports action footage. For me, the ideal would be five minutes of footage per minute of talk. Talk about what the athlete is doing and why, not on who went to what college and such.

Cubing should generate some new ideas to channel into your writing.

Write: Freewrite about an appealing topic for 5 to 8 minutes. Then search for more ideas about your topic by cubing it. Or take an editorial or an essay you have already written and cube that for new ideas. Underline any thoughts you especially like in your freewriting and cubing.

Ideas: Experimenting with Form

After a caterpillar has spent time in its chrysalis, it is transformed into a butterfly. Transformations occur in writing, too, when a writer takes the substance from one piece of writing and recasts it in a new form. You can use transformations to develop new drafts of your work, especially in the early stages of exploring. Read on to learn how these transformations work.

Read: Read the following "base text," a general paragraph from a first draft. Then study the sample transformations listed below to see how transformations could add dimension to your writing.

Discovered and named years ago, Pluto was removed from the list of planets recently. From the beginning, astronomers argued whether or not Pluto should be called a planet. After comparing Pluto with standards for planet status, scientists felt the decision was correct.

Transformation 1: Ideas List

planets—discovery—astronomers—asteroids—moons—comets—gravity—solar system

Transformation 2: Sentence Fragments

Finding and naming Pluto. Arguments about planet's status. Defining planets. Unpopular decision. Solar system now at eight planets. Some asteroids bigger than Pluto. Little-known world.

Transformation 3: Questions

Is Pluto a planet? If Pluto is a planet, shouldn't asteroids larger than Pluto be planets? What is a planet? Who determines what a planet is? Will people accept this decision? Why is it important to define what constitutes a planet?

Transformation 4: Prepositional Phrases

For 75 years. In our solar system. With three newly devised criteria. For true planet status. From the list of planets. By hundreds of astronomers. After comparing Pluto. In 1930.

Reflect: Each one of these transformations brings out something new. The list brings out related topics. The fragments generate specific facts. The questions and prepositional phrases suggest layers of detail and additional research possibilities. Each transformation offers new slants on the topic.

Write: Choose a short piece of your own writing, something that you would like to develop further. Write as many different transformations of it as time and interest permit. In addition to the four types above, consider the list of transformations below. Make up some of your own as well.

- Describe sounds.
- Write in exclamations!
- Describe colors.
- Turn it into a poem.
- Write it as a play script.
- List possible titles.
- Turn the topic into a character.
- Write for a different audience.
- Create headlines.
- Turn it into a news item.

Ideas: Supporting Your Points

If you state an important idea in writing, your reader will know what you think. But if you back up your statement with solid facts and figures, your reader may also begin to believe that what you think is true. For that reason, experienced writers stay alert for quotations, anecdotes, details, and provable facts that they can use to support their ideas.

Read: Here are some quotations, anecdotes, details, and provable facts that a writer might store away in her or his memory, hoping someday to use them in writing.

Quotations:

1. "I have a dream that one day on the red hills of Georgia the sons of former slaves and the sons of former slave owners will be able to sit down together at the table of brotherhood." (Martin Luther King, Jr.)
2. "You cannot shake hands with a clenched fist." (Indira Gandhi)

Anecdotes:

1. When IBM introduced its PC in 1981, critics complained that no one would ever need more than a 64K memory.
2. A research assistant once excitedly told Justus von Liebig, a famous German scientist, that a universal solvent had been discovered. Liebig asked the assistant to explain what a universal solvent was. The assistant somewhat incredulously replied, "One that dissolves all substances." Liebig then asked him, "Where are you planning to keep this solvent?"

Details and Provable Facts:

1. Flowing 4,160 miles from Lake Victoria to the Mediterranean Sea, the Nile is the longest river in the world.
2. By 2010, marketers estimate that $1.5 billion will be spent for advertising received by cell phones.

Reflect: In your writing, which should come first—your thoughts or the support you borrow from an authority? Use common sense: If your ideas spring from the words of an authority, place the borrowed material first and follow with your commentary. If you borrow material to support an idea of your own, place your idea first.

Write: Practice incorporating borrowed material into your writing. Write a short paragraph that uses one of the bits of information above to reinforce something you have to say.

INSIDE INFO Generally, offering plenty of support for your ideas is desirable. However, if you supply too much support and not enough personal statement or commentary, your own voice may be drowned out. Remember that support must support *something,* which is your own line of thought.

Ideas: Improving Openings

What can fishhooks teach you about writing? Consider the fishhook. Why does it work? It's got a curve to make it catch, a point to make it sink in, and a barb to make it stick. Oh yes, and there's the bait. Many writers speak of the need for a "hook" in their writing. The reader is the fish they want to catch. The subject is the bait. The angle of approach is that curving hook. The surprise in the opening is the point that sinks in. And that idea left open or that hint of things to come is the barb that won't let the "hook" slip out.

Read: Here are the opening lines from two published essays. As you read these openings, see if you can spot the hook and barb in each one. (Share your thoughts.)

Crowds stand around all day long and criticize that bridge, and find fault with it, and tell with unlimited frankness how it ought to have been planned, and how they would have built it had the city granted them the 14,000 it cost. It is really refreshing to hang around these and listen to them. A foreigner would come to the conclusion that all America was composed of inspired professional bridge builders.

—Mark Twain, "The Broadway Bridge"

(*Hint:* Can you tell that this opening pokes fun using sarcasm?)

In government circles it's called the "NIMBY problem." Whether the proposal is for AIDS clinics, halfway houses for prison parolees or dumps for toxic and nuclear waste, it is usually met by the opposition of citizens' groups who shout NIMBY—"not in my backyard!"

—Ted Peters, "The Waste-Disposal Crisis"

(*Hint:* What is your emotional response immediately after you read the final phrase?)

Reflect: How do you think the writers go from these openings to the next paragraphs? In many cases, there is some kind of turn—a *but,* or *yet,* or *nevertheless,* or *still.* (The writer does that when she or he knows the "hook" is set, and it's time to start reeling in the fish.)

Write: Here is a chance to practice writing "hooks" for three different kinds of essays: personal, subject (expository), and reflective.

1. **Personal** Write an opening sentence or two with a "hook" about an aspect of your life that you think might be fascinating to a reader.

2. **Subject** Write a "hook" opening to an essay in which you communicate some specialized knowledge you already possess.

3. **Reflective** Write a "hook" opening to an essay in which you propose how to correct the number one irritant in your life. (Be sure you have a proper audience in mind.)

Ideas: Improving Focus

Sometimes the meaning of an essay needs to be communicated in one crucial paragraph. That calls for a paragraph that has . . .

- a clearly stated main idea,
- details supporting that main idea, and
- an order that clarifies the relationship between the details and the main idea.

Read & React: One of the three passages below focuses on the topic of the California condor. The other two miss the mark. Choose the one that you think is a focused paragraph. (Be prepared to discuss the reasons for your choice.)

NOTE: Look for the passage that is focused and clear, that contains a topic sentence and effective supporting detail.

______ **1.** The California condor was near extinction when efforts were started to save the species. Conservationists, state departments of natural resources, and the federal government were all involved in this noble effort. These groups acted because too many other animals have disappeared forever such as the passenger pigeon. The last passenger pigeon died in 1913. Thanks to hard work, the California condor's numbers are increasing. Today, the birds can be seen soaring, and sometimes roosting, near the south rim of the Grand Canyon not far from the visitor center. The center is open all year and tells the story of the reintroduction of this magnificent bird. Park rangers give presentations about the California condor near the place where the birds are often seen.

______ **2.** Many animal species have been saved from extinction thanks to the dedicated efforts of conservationists. The California condor is one example and it is making a dramatic comeback from near extinction. Researchers took eggs out of nests and carefully raised the young to make sure the population would grow. The success of the program can be seen along the south rim of the Grand Canyon near the visitor center. There the striking black and white markings of the condor and its 9-foot wingspan delight thousands of bird-watchers.

______ **3.** In 1987, fearing the extinction of the California condor, the U.S. Fish and Wildlife Service captured all 27 wild birds. Thus began one of the most intense captive breeding programs in history to save the largest bird in North America. With a 9.5-foot wingspan and standing 45-55 inches tall, the California condor is a striking bird symbolic of the remote country in which it lives. In preparation for the birds' future release in the wild, Service agents secured additional lands to protect the limited Sespe Condor sanctuary in southern California. By carefully monitoring the captive birds and removing eggs from nests thus forcing the birds to lay more eggs (often called double clutching or even triple clutching), the agency was able to steadily increase the condors' numbers. Today, 290 birds soar the skies of Arizona, California, and Baja, Mexico.

Extend

Locate the crucial paragraph in one of your own essays. Does it have a clearly stated main idea, sufficient supporting detail, and a sense of order? Discuss the paragraph with a classmate.

Organization: Finding a Form

One way to generate a text is to make it *imitate* your subject. How can your writing "imitate" your subject? Well, inspect the following paragraph about the blasting of a cliff face in a mining operation.

> **Controlling the spinning drill bit that bites deeply into the rock, a miner punches holes at strategic spots along the cliff face of the ore-bearing rock. Then a slurry of explosive splashes into each hole, priming a powerful pump. Gingerly placing the blasting caps, connecting the wires running from all over the cliff, and hooking up the electronic switch, miners prepare for the violent action to come. A last check, and all quickly run for cover. Yelling "Fire in the hole," the foreman punches the control button. The cliff face dissolves, heaves up, flies forward, collapsing in a dusty jumble of broken rock. Mangled, sailing chunks crash to the ground. Then the air is still.**

Did you notice that the cliff blasting happens in the way the sentences happen? The sentences and words are at first methodical, but then mimic the explosion demolishing the cliff. Does that give you an idea for how to add this dimension to your writing?

Imitate: For practice, write a paragraph describing a tornado in a way that conveys this type of weather phenomenon. In other words, try to make your writing imitate your subject.

A Tornado

Before you write, briefly consider the pattern of a tornado: from calm to crescendo to climax to decrescendo to calm once again. Try to reflect that pattern in the shape and tone of your description:

Extend

Have somebody else react to your writing and offer some suggestions. Then put your new knowledge to work by writing an entirely different essay in which you take advantage of the possibilities of imitative form.

Organization: Devising a Writing Plan

Mitchell Ivers, in *The Random House Guide to Good Writing,* identifies a six-step process that, if applied and practiced, will help turn uncertain writers into more confident and persuasive essayists. (Remember that the essay is the basic form of writing practiced in most school settings.)

React: Put Ivers' process into action by completing the following plan. Do your work on your own paper. (Share your work upon completion.)

1. Choose a subject about which you have a strong opinion. (Refer to "Topics" in the handbook index for ideas.)
2. Write a thesis statement, identifying what you would like to explain or prove about the subject. (Generally speaking, a dominant feeling or attitude about the subject is expressed in the thesis statement.)
3. Identify at least one important counterargument to your thesis. (That is, admit to a possible weakness in your way of thinking, or point out that there is another way to look at your subject.)
4. List five or six points in support of your thesis. (If you can't think of five or six, list as many as you can.)
5. Identify your most persuasive argument or point. (Put a star next to the strongest point you have listed in #4.)
6. Come to some conclusion about your argument. (Decide what it is you have proved or determined through your planning.)

Write: The next step is to put your plan into action by writing a first draft of your essay. Develop your writing freely, starting with your thesis statement and then incorporating other ideas from your plan. A *suggestion:* Deal with the counterargument early on and save your most persuasive argument for the knockout punch near the end of your essay. (Continue working with your essay if you like how it is shaping up.)

Organization: Limiting Your Topic

The focus of a piece of writing may be plainly stated near the beginning, postponed until later, or not stated at all. How can a person tell what the focus of a piece of writing is? And how can you create a clearer focus in your next piece of writing? Start with this general formula. A focus is the specific combination of the following elements:

1. a central subject
2. a specific aspect of the subject
3. an idea or a feeling about the specific subject

For the writing to be clearly focused, all of these elements should be present, although they may not need to be directly stated. (**NOTE:** Compare this formula with the formula for a topic sentence found in your handbook. See "Topic sentence" in the index.)

Read & React: Read over the beginnings of the student essays below. Try to identify the different elements that make up the focus in each passage.

Pandemonium. Players high-fiving. Fans cheering. Students singing. The scoreboard flashing the score. Randolph High had finally defeated its longtime rival in the championship game of a hard-fought soccer season.

Our physical education teacher, Mr. Selmer, wants to whip us into shape. He says we are part of a generation that has sat too long and walked too little. He plans to show us how to properly use all the equipment in the workout room and promises we will see results. With a serious look in his eyes, he tells us, "I want you not only to live to see your grandkids but also to be able to keep up with them."

In our social studies class, group research is the way we learn. When our teacher wants us to explore the issues of the day, she is not satisfied with dull speeches or bland presentations. She is not interested in biased reports. With every issue, a group of students represents each side. To gather information, we rely on the Internet, the library, and interviews. We are challenged to make our contributions stimulating and worthwhile. Remarkably, Ms. Brock never expects us to echo her viewpoint. At the same time, no group escapes a well-deserved critique for poor organization or half-hearted research.

Reflect: Which paragraph seems most clearly focused? Which one has the most implicit (unstated) focus? Which one states its focus most plainly?

Organization: Logical Organization

There are two distinct ways to arrange the details in your writing: *inductively* and *deductively*. Watch how two different paragraphs can be developed from the same idea. Here's the sentence that will serve as the main idea for each paragraph:

The summer and fall of 2005 will be remembered as a season of never-ending storms.

The first paragraph is arranged inductively. In other words, the statements begin with specific details that eventually guide the reader toward the main idea.

For months, intensifying low-pressure systems marched across the Atlantic and terrorized millions in the Caribbean and in the United States. Hurricane experts tracked the storms, and televised reporters, buffeted by the winds, brought the extent of the devastation into the nation's living rooms. The Gulf states were all threatened and hit hard. There were 27 named storms of which 15 were hurricanes. Of the seven major hurricanes, four reached category 5 status. Seven of the hurricanes made landfall causing more than $100 billion in damage and 1,300 deaths. The most well-known hurricane, Katrina, ravaged New Orleans and nearby communities. Since record keeping began in 1851, never had there been so many storms in a single season. The summer and fall of 2005 will be remembered as a season of never-ending storms.

The second paragraph is arranged deductively. In other words, the main idea comes first, followed by specific details that serve as illustrations, proofs, or explanations.

The summer and fall of 2005 will be remembered as a season of never-ending storms. For months, intensifying low-pressure systems marched across the Atlantic and terrorized millions in the Caribbean and in the United States. Hurricane experts tracked the storms, and televised reporters, buffeted by the winds, brought the extent of the devastation into the nation's living rooms. The Gulf states were all threatened and hit hard. There were 27 named storms of which 15 were hurricanes. Of the seven major hurricanes, four reached category 5 status. Seven of the hurricanes made landfall causing more than $100 billion in damage and 1,300 deaths. The most well-known hurricane, Katrina, ravaged New Orleans and nearby communities. Since record keeping began in 1851, never had there been so many storms in a single season.

Write: Write a paragraph about an issue at your school or in your community. Decide whether inductive or deductive organization is called for and use that method consistently.

Extend

Find an article in a newspaper or magazine that is clearly inductive or deductive. Bring it in for a class discussion. Be able to point out the features of the article that make it an example of one or the other methods of organization. Why might each organization pattern be used? When? To what effect?

Voice: Finding Voice

The voice in any piece of writing is the person you hear "speaking" to you from the words on the page. Voice has five basic aspects, which can be mapped on the "Style Matrix."

1. **Purpose:** The purpose describes what the writer is trying to do.

informative	**enlightening**	**persuasive**
entertaining	**polemical**	**inspiring**

2. **Tone:** The tone reveals the writer's opinion of the topic.

enthusiastic	**flippant**	**playful**
solemn	**humorous**	**bored**

3. **Attitude:** The attitude shows the writer's opinion of the reader.

respectful	**combative**	**didactic**
condescending	**chummy**	**adoring**

4. **Personality:** The personality shows who the writer is (or is pretending to be).

sensitive	**kindly**	**neurotic**
lonely	**imaginative**	**naïve**

5. **Language Use:** The use of language demonstrates the writer's skill.

homespun	**stuffy**	**staccato**
direct	**baroque**	**poetic**

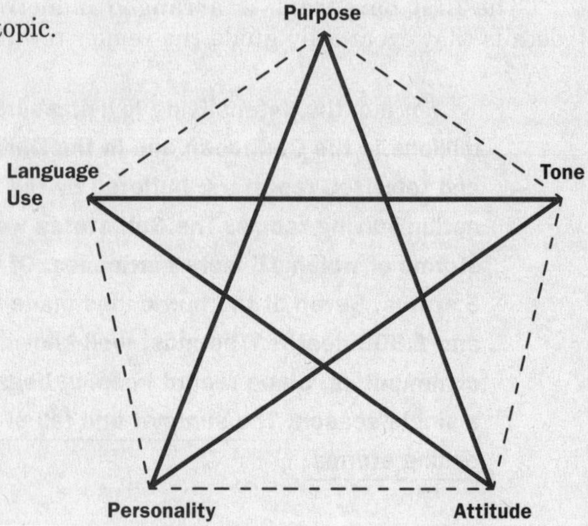

Read: Here is a paragraph from a professional essay. Read it, noting the purpose, tone, attitude, personality, and language use.

As a child, I often wondered where my sound tracks were. In movies, the sound track always sympathized with the hero: Luke Skywalker stood on a ridge and watched the twin suns set over his desolate planet of Tatooine, and violins and cellos swelled with a theme full of longing. I stood on the edge of Cady Marsh Ditch in my subdivision and watched the fetid water roll away toward the horizon and felt the same longing, but there were no strings for me, no trumpets, not even a bassoon. Sherlock Holmes stepped around a shadowy corner and saw with horror a dead man in an alley, and trombones blatted his shock and dread. I sat at a desk in Mrs. El Naggar's plane and solid geometry class as she handed out a pop quiz, but my shock and dread were met with only dead silence. I wanted the world to feel what I felt, to care about what happened to me. I wanted to be the hero. That's why I decided to become a filmmaker—so that I could make the movies in my head and hire an orchestra to sympathize.

React: How would you describe the voice of the writer in this paragraph? Select adjectives to describe the purpose, tone, attitude, personality, and language use. Explain your answers.

Voice: Unifying Tone

If a piece of your writing needs expanding and clarifying, how are you going to come up with the necessary details? One way is to invent an appropriate central metaphor and then s-t-r-e-t-c-h it. See "Writing Metaphorically", page 117 in your handbook, for an explanation of how extending an appropriate comparison can unify a piece of writing.

■ Here is a short paragraph that could use some enrichment:

> **Monarch butterflies gather in the spring and the fall to migrate. Even scientists who study the migrations marvel at what these delicate insects do. The brightly flashing orange and black wings signal a grand tour of determination.**

■ One way to expand and clarify this paragraph metaphorically is to work with the idea of the "tour." Notice all the words and phrases in the revised paragraph below that are associated with a tour, or travel. Embedding an idea like this throughout a paragraph is known as using a hidden metaphor.

> **Directed by instinct, monarch butterflies gather in the spring and the fall to migrate distances once thought reserved for birds. Even scientists who study the migrations marvel that these delicate insects make the trek from Mexico to the northern United States and back again. Brightly flashing orange and black wings move over ever-changing scenery seeming to delight in the adventure, while pausing at enticing rest stops for food and water. However, instinct doesn't let them stay in one place for long. Determined to keep the schedule that has been followed for thousands of years, the monarchs rise and join together in huge numbers to continue the journey.**

Rewrite: Read the paragraph below and then rewrite it, expanding on the metaphor by using words and phrases that depict a tree as "home."

> **People think of trees as many things. Homeowners think of them as beauty or shade, loggers think of them as timber, and children think of them as fortresses. But for many animals, a tree is a home.**

NOTE: Stretching a metaphor works well as a special effect, and, on occasion, the buried metaphor will tie together the elements of an entire essay. If this technique is overused, however, it will draw attention to itself and sound artificial.

Extend

Find a paragraph or short essay that you've previously written that could be improved if developed around a central metaphor. Revise it accordingly and share your results.

Voice: Achieving Ecomony

Read: Most writers can delete more unnecessary words and phrases from their writing than they think. For example, all of the words in parentheses in the following paragraph can be removed or simplified:

At the basketball game (that was played) last night between St. Thomas College and its archrival, Horton College, (the players who were considered the best on each team) (were injured) (in the course of the action). Marty Grunwald, (who plays for) St. Thomas, (received an injury to) her shoulder (when she collided) (without warning) with an opposing player (from Horton). (Regrettably,) (the force of the collision was responsible for) dislocating (her) right (shoulder). (Likewise, in a surprising coincidence), Cassie Ribero from Horton (also suffered a dislocated right shoulder) (in an accidental collision). (The loss of their top players was a disappointment to both teams). [104 words]

When all of the useless words are removed, the thought can be fully expressed in one smooth-reading sentence:

At last night's college basketball game between archrivals St. Thomas and Horton, Marty Grunwald and Cassie Ribero, team leaders for their respective schools, both dislocated their right shoulders in collisions with opposing players. [33 words]

Rewrite: With a partner, study the following paragraph (129 words) adapted from an article about the next generation of aircraft fighters. Then cut or simplify all of the words and phrases that are unnecessary. Rewrite the paragraph on your own paper. Compare your results with other teams.

The next goal in military aircraft is a fighter jet plane that will reach an incredible, unbelievably fast Mach 7, which is seven times the speed of sound. Besides having to develop materials that can always handle, on a regular basis, the scorching heat generated by air molecules passing over the plane's skin because the plane is flying so fast, scientists must perfect the use of the scramjet to push the aircraft to faster and faster and faster speeds and extremely higher ceilings than ever achieved before up to this time. Aircraft designers, the people who will dream up the next plane, have to think about the limits of materials, the laws of physics, and tons of other matters to take this plane from the drafting table to reality.

Voice: Improving Diction

The **connotation** of a word is what it suggests or implies beyond its literal meaning. Careless writers sometimes lose sight of connotation and its effect on communication. They end up suggesting things they never intended. When you refine your writing, check the connotation of your words so that your message is exact.

Read & React: For each blank in the paragraph below, choose the word that best fits the meaning and feeling being communicated. (**NOTE:** Several words will work in each instance, but you must choose the one that best conveys the writer's disapproving tone.)

Too many times I have picked up the evening newspaper to see a photograph of a very ....1.......... -looking person splashed all over the front page. Usually, this person has just gone through a ....2.......... experience, like a car accident, a fire, or a shooting. You would think newspapers would use a little more ....3.......... and not choose such pictures to ....4.......... the front page of their papers. The people have suffered a misfortune to begin with, and then to have their grief ....5.......... for everyone to see all seems very wrong. It ....6.......... their tragedy unnecessarily and makes it even more unlikely they will soon forget what has happened. They will be reminded over and over again by neighbors, friends, coworkers, and ....7.......... just how "terrible" and "awful" and "frightening" all of this must have been. They will be forced to ....8.......... an event weeks and months and perhaps years after it would otherwise have faded in their memory. This is the power of the press—at its worst.

1. .... (unhappy, miserable, distressed, tortured)
2. .... (disagreeable, traumatic, bad, difficult)
3. .... (discretion, intelligence, sensitivity, compassion)
4. .... (brighten, appear on, emblazon, decorate)
5. .... (shown, reproduced, advertised, broadcast)
6. .... (inflates, builds up, supplements, exaggerates)
7. .... (pals, well-wishers, troubled people, acquaintances)
8. .... (relive, recall, remember, recollect)

Voice: Evaluating Style

Evaluating means assessing the value or worth of something. The best way to evaluate a writer's style is to ask yourself questions based on the five aspects of voice.

1. **Purpose:** What is the writer trying to accomplish? Does the writer succeed or fail? Why?

2. **Tone:** What is the writer's opinion of the topic? Does this opinion give the writing energy and freshness? Does the writer provide concrete details? Is the piece coherent?

3. **Attitude:** What is the writer's opinion of the reader? Does this opinion help the writer achieve the purpose? Why?

4. **Personality:** What does the writer seem like? Does the writer seem sincere? Does the personality of the writer strengthen or weaken the writing?

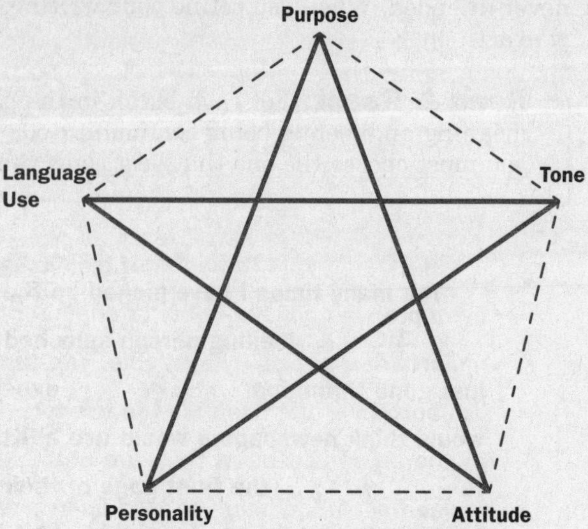

5. **Language Use:** Is the writing formal, informal, or conversational? Is the writing direct or indirect? Ornate or plain? Poetic or prosaic? How do the language choices of the writer strengthen or weaken the writing?

Read: Here is a paragraph by a professional writer. Read it, paying attention to purpose, tone, attitude, personality, and language use.

Sound is life. Have you noticed that? We all fear things that go bump in the night because things that go bump are alive. We look at a photograph, a painting, a sculpture, and we see an image of life, but if we hear breath in the thing, if it speaks to us—then suddenly it is alive. "Annie, can you hear me?" we're taught to say as we kneel above that poor resuscitation dummy in health class, and when she doesn't answer, we tilt her head back and give her the kiss of life—just as we would do for a person who is not breathing. But you don't resuscitate a person who says, "Why, I can hear you just fine." And if Resuscitation Annie says such a thing—well, everyone runs screaming from the room and the National Guard arrives and the scientists cut her up to find out how plastic spoke. Mannequins don't speak, you see; nor do dead men. That's because sound is life, and silence is the grave.

Reflect: Ask yourself the questions above about the paragraph you just read. Then use your answers to write a paragraph that evaluates the writer's style.

Word Choice: Active vs. Passive Verbs

If your writing lacks energy and enthusiasm, it may be because you are falling into the trap of using passive verbs instead of active ones. In a sentence with a passive verb, the subject is acted upon rather than acting, as in this example: The United States Constitution was signed by George Washington and James Madison in 1789. Here is a sentence with an active verb: Both George Washington and James Madison signed the United States Constitution in 1789.

Read: The following passive-voice passage would benefit from the use of a variety of active verbs.

In recent years, the idea of building a tunnel from the United States to Europe has been proposed by a number of engineers and businesspeople. Most technology for such an undertaking is already available. The tunnel would not be built along the ocean floor because the bottom of the ocean is too uneven and, in places, too deep. The tunnel would be crushed by the enormous water pressure at such depths. Instead, the tunnel would be anchored to the ocean floor while being buoyed up by the surrounding water. The tunnel would be designed in such a way that it would actually float several hundred feet below the surface. An ultrahigh-speed train would be used to carry passengers and freight from one continent to the other in about an hour. Scientists have been asked by researchers if such a train could travel 5,000 miles per hour. One day, if the problems can be overcome and the money for such a project raised, such an incredible idea may become a reality through the efforts of governments, scientists, and technicians. People could be transported from shore to shore before they finish reading the morning paper.

Rewrite: Edit this entire passage for word choice. Change from passive to active voice as appropriate and make any other word-choice revisions that would improve this paragraph.

Write: Write a paragraph on a topic of your choice. Use a sportswriter approach to word choice to see how dynamic you can make your writing.

Word Choice: Using Adverb Clauses

When you're a little child, ideas typically come to your mind one at a time:

I want to swim.

When you grow older, ideas may come in groups of two or three or more. And, as you speak or write, your mind is capable of sorting them in order of importance and linking them, putting some into main clauses and others into subordinate (or lesser) clauses, like this:

If the weather is warm and sunny, I want to swim in Chub Lake near Waters, Michigan. (This sentence begins with a subordinate adverb clause, which modifies the verb in the main clause.)

Adverb clauses can be identified by the special function they serve and the distinctive words that introduce them:

- Some show the "time" of an idea. They begin with introductory words (called subordinating conjunctions) such as *before, after, when, until, since,* and *while.*
- Some show "reasons why." They begin with *because* and *since.*
- Some show "purpose" or "result." They begin with *that, so that,* and *in order that.*
- Some show "conditions." They begin with *if, unless, although, as long as,* and *even though.*

Read: Here is a short paragraph without any adverb clauses in it.

The Louisiana Purchase nearly doubled the size of the country. President Thomas Jefferson wanted to dispatch an expedition into the region. He also hoped to find a quick passage to the Pacific. Lewis and Clark accepted the president's plan to explore the new territory.

React: On your own paper, rewrite the short paragraph, using adverb clauses effectively. Do this by turning the sentences below into adverb clauses and combining them with the main clauses of the paragraph. For each adverb clause, use a subordinating conjunction that shows the relationship mentioned in parentheses.

- Most of the new land was unexplored. *(condition)*
- President Jefferson needed to acquire information about this land. *(purpose)*
- A quick passage to the Pacific would mean an end to dangerous travel around the tip of South America to reach the western coast. *(reason)*
- Lewis and Clark started their journey in 1804. *(time)*

Extend

Now try rewriting the paragraph, turning the original sentences into adverb clauses and including the four additional clauses as needed. (For a smooth-reading paragraph, you may change the wording slightly.)

Word Choice: Clarity

Would you like an easy and effective strategy for fixing problems with wording? All you have to do is use the 3 C's of editing.

Editing Code:

CUT [brackets] If you find a part that's unnecessary or off the topic, put brackets around it. If you decide that section is really unneeded, cut it!

CLARIFY ~~~~~~ If you see something confusing, unclear, or incomplete in your writing, put a wavy line under that section. You should rethink it, reword it, explain it, or add detail to it.

CONDENSE (parentheses) If you come across a section of your writing that is wordy or overexplained, put a set of parentheses around it. (Refer to "Wordiness," "Deadwood, in sentences," and "Flowery language" in the handbook index for help.)

Read & React: Read the following paragraph to see how one student edited what he had written about the book *Bury My Heart at Wounded Knee.* Then rewrite the paragraph.

Bury My Heart at Wounded Knee by Dee Brown tells [with a great deal of angst] of the struggle of the Native American ever since the arrival of people from other continents and places. The newcomers to North America talked about private property and owning the land. This [unique and strange] idea clashed with the Indians' understanding and led to one fractured treaty after another. Ultimately, war determined which side would emerge as (the caretakers of a vast, fertile land stretching from the Atlantic to the Pacific). The site of Wounded Knee and what happened there signaled the (demise, in fact the very destruction,) of an era for the Native Americans.

Extend

Compare your revision of the above paragraph with a classmate's. What do you agree and disagree on? Now read and revise the following paragraph about wolves in the Yellowstone ecosystem. Once you mark what should be cut, clarified, or condensed, rewrite the paragraph.

At one time, the administrators of Yellowstone National Park believed beyond a shadow of doubt that wolves were the ultimate enemy. Helpless, beautiful, stately elk and other animals suffered from the terrible predation of wolf packs. Then more studies showed the error of the original assumption. Since the reintroduction of the wolf, scientists have discovered, much to their amazement, how valuable the wolf is to the entire ecosystem of the park. For example, because the wolves keep elk on the move, the huge ungulates no longer overgraze and overbrowse the marvelous plants and trees on the riverbanks.

Word Choice: Relative Clauses

One way to show which idea in a sentence is more important is to use an adjective clause for the less important idea. An adjective clause modifies, or describes, a noun or a pronoun.

Adjective clauses are usually introduced by the **relative pronouns:** *who, whom, whose, which, that.* Such clauses are called "relative clauses." *Who, whom,* and *whose* are used to refer to people. *Which* refers to nonliving objects or to animals. *That* may refer to people, nonliving objects, or animals. An adjective clause can also be introduced with the words *when* and *where.*

Combine: Combine the following simple sentences into complex sentences. An asterisk (*) is printed after the more important idea in the first groups of simple sentences. Place the less important idea in an adjective clause. You decide which of the two ideas is more important in the remaining groups.

1. The whale shark is the largest fish in the world.

   It is found in the warmer areas of the Atlantic, Pacific, and Indian Oceans.

   The whale shark, which is found in the warmer areas of the Atlantic, Pacific, and Indian Oceans, is the largest fish in the world.

NOTE: An adjective clause may be **nonrestrictive** (set off by commas because it is not required to identify the noun or pronoun, but merely supplies extra information) or **restrictive** (not set off by commas because it is required to identify the noun or pronoun).

2. Dr. Andrew Smith examined the first recorded whale shark specimen in 1828.*

   He was a military surgeon with the British army.

3. The fishermen harpooned the shark.

   The fishermen had noticed its unusual gray coloration with white spots.*

4. The dried skin is preserved in the Museum d'Histoire Naturelle in Paris.*

   Dr. Smith originally purchased the dried skin for $30.

5. In 1868, a young Irish naturalist studied the whale sharks in the Seychelle Islands.*

   He had heard the natives speak of a monstrous fish called the "Chagrin."

6. He saw several specimens.

   The specimens exceeded 50 feet in length.

7. Many men reported sharks measuring nearly 70 feet in length.

   These men had always been considered trustworthy.

8. The only other exceptionally large fish is the basking shark.

   It compares in size with the whale shark.

Word Choice: Economy

React: Make the following sentences more concise by eliminating *deadwood, redundancy,* and other wordiness. For clear definitions of each of these terms, consult the handbook index. Place parentheses around any unnecessary words or phrases that you find.

1. The former tenant (who had lived in the apartment before we moved in) painted all the walls (with a coat of) pink (paint).
2. The length of the average basketball court is normally 90 feet long.
3. The main reason he didn't pass the test is because he didn't study carefully or look over his class notes.
4. There are six students who volunteered on their own to clean up after the homecoming dance is over.
5. The mountain climber was unable to descend down the mountain by himself and needed the help of another climber to assist him.
6. The fragile vase, which would surely break if mishandled, was shipped "Special Handling" so that it would be handled with care.
7. The canceled game has been rescheduled for 8:00 p.m. tomorrow evening.
8. A cell phone can be carried anywhere and is especially handy for jogging, biking, and other outdoor activities.
9. As a general rule, he usually spends about one hour of his time each day reading.
10. Needless to say, wordiness is a writing problem that should be eliminated from all writing, which goes without saying.
11. The complex financial problem, which was not easy to understand, had caused the team to move to another city where the money issue was not such a big problem as it had been before.

NOTE: Compare your answers with a partner's. In each case, see who was able to remove the most words without changing the basic sense of the sentence.

Fluency: Adding Energy and Originality

Have you ever finished a piece of writing, then read over your work, and finally, with profound critical insight, blurted out the word "blah"? Almost every writer has experienced such a moment. Some proceed to throw their work away. But that isn't necessary. Creating fluency in your writing may require more than a cosmetic addition of transitions and a conscious effort to vary your sentences. It may demand a deeper consideration of all the traits. Here are six questions to help you review your writing. You may catch opportunities you missed the first time around:

1. Is your topic stale?
2. Is your purpose unclear?
3. Is your voice unnatural or fake?
4. Is your organization predictable?
5. Is your focus foggy?
6. Do your sentences fall into a rut?

Notice, also, that these six are in descending order of importance. In other words, if your topic **(1)** is stale, don't worry yet about your organization **(4)** or your sentence structure **(6)**. If you change your topic, all of the next five aspects of your writing will change as well.

Read & React: Here's a challenge. Read the following paragraph, which most readers would consider boring, and examine each of the six aspects mentioned above until you've found the one that is most responsible for making this writing boring. Compare your reactions with someone else's. Then read the commentary below the paragraph.

(1) In today's society, there is much advertising to be found. (2) There are interesting ads in magazines, and there are commercials on TV about every 5 to 10 minutes or so. (3) Some people think the ads are better than the programs, and I kind of agree with them. (4) Maybe that's why there are so many ads, because people like them. (5) Someday maybe TV will be all ads and no programs. (6) Would that be good?

Commentary:

Working up from the bottom of the list, notice that the **sentences** are in a rut. Almost all have uninteresting subjects and verbs, and too many clauses start with "there is" or "there are." The lack of **focus** is evident. Every sentence seems to have equal weight; therefore, none has special weight. In addition, the writer has poorly organized the paragraph using vast generalizations, observations about what "some people" think, and a half-hearted question addressed to the reader. Moreover, the **voice** is tired, impersonal, and bored with its own subject. It has a short attention span. Worse yet, the writer's **purpose** is weak and indefinite. The writer seems to be trying to get through an assignment. Finally, the writer's **topic** is too big, too ordinary, to be of interest to a reader.

Write: Pretend the paragraph about advertising was your own first draft. Now that you've reviewed it and seen its problems, write a thorough revision about some aspect of advertising. Make your revision better than the original in all six areas; but this time, start improving from the **top** of the list (your topic) down.

Fluency: Parallel Structure

Parallel structure is the balanced arrangement of sentence elements that are equal in importance. Similar ideas arranged in a similar way can add a sense of rhythm and balance to your writing style that makes it more appealing to your reader. (Refer to your handbook for more information on parallel structure.)

Revise: Look at the sentences below. Each one contains two ideas or items (underlined) that are equal in importance but not expressed in equal or parallel form. Revise each sentence by substituting a parallel expression for one of those that is underlined.

1. Swimming is a great exercise for strengthening your heart and one that increases your lung power.

   Swimming is a great exercise for strengthening your heart and increasing your lung power.

2. Swim for 10 minutes, dividing the time between the breaststroke, the crawl, and doing the backstroke, and you will have had a good workout.

3. Swimming improves the mobility of major joints and strength to the muscles.

4. There is a myth that swimming in freezing water is beneficial and you will enjoy it.

5. At best, plunging into cold water may give you a kick; at worst, you may have a heart attack.

6. Some people get less exercise at the pool than they intend; they talk to friends, tread water, and are hanging onto the side while watching others.

7. Practice will result in a smooth swimming style, and your breathing pattern will be efficient.

8. A steady ten-minute swim is a good workout, while swimming furiously for three minutes is not.

Complete: Complete each of the following sentences by adding a word, phrase, or clause that is parallel to the underlined portion of the sentence. (Each addition must be sensible as well as parallel.)

1. Sitting in the middle of the dorm room were a suitcase, a box of books, and ....

2. He hopes to get a job on campus either working in the library or ....

3. On Saturday we want to attend the football game, go out for pizza, and ....

4. This time should really be spent planning for the future, not ....

5. We drove all morning to get to the taco stand, and we drove all afternoon ....

Fluency: Complex Sentences

Read: As you revise, you may want to combine some of your short simple sentences into more mature, efficient sentences. To join two ideas that are not equal in importance, you may use a **complex sentence** (one independent clause and one or more dependent clauses). The more important idea (main idea) is placed in the independent clause; the less important idea is placed in the dependent clause, also known as a subordinate clause.

An adverb clause is one kind of subordinate clause. It generally modifies a verb in the main clause of the sentence. To use adverb clauses effectively, become familiar with the subordinating conjunctions that introduce them.

Subordinating Conjunctions Used to Introduce Adverb Clauses

Showing time:	*before after when until since while*
Showing a reason why:	*because since*
Showing a purpose or result:	*so that so that in order that*
Showing a condition:	*whereas if unless though although as long as while*

Combine: Combine each set of simple sentences into a complex sentence by placing the less important idea in an adverb clause. An asterisk (*) marks the more important idea in the first few sets. After each of your complex sentences, tell what your adverb clause shows.

1. Eagles will usually kill animals lighter than themselves.
   Some fast-moving species have been known to attack much heavier prey.*
   Although eagles will usually kill animals lighter than themselves, some fast-moving species have been known to attack much heavier prey. (condition)

2. The writhing, talon-pierced carp weighed 13 pounds.
   The sea eagle flew low and was almost pulled underwater by its prey.*

3. The young eagle is heavier than its parents by as much as one pound.* It leaves the nest.

4. The hunters looked up toward the mountain crest.
   They saw a golden eagle descending with a mule deer fawn in its talons.*

5. Arthur Bowland once persuaded a Verreaux's eagle to snatch a 20-pound pack while in flight.
   He could test the bird's supposed tremendous strength.

6. Scientific tests for muscularity and power will not be a true guide for the species.
   They are done with wild, not captive, eagles.

7. Eagles can kill prey four times their own size.
   They ordinarily cannot carry a load weighing much more than six pounds.

Fluency: Creating Connections

Transitional words between sentences and paragraphs reassure and steer the reader along, giving writing a more pleasing flow. Let's see how a professional writer uses transitional words and phrases to link ideas . . . and smooth out the writing.

Read: Here is a passage from an article on allergies. (The effective transitions between sentences and paragraphs have been capitalized.) You can learn about transitions simply by noticing them and thinking about how they work.

Acute attacks of asthma occur when the bronchial tubes become partly blocked. FOR VARIOUS REASONS, the lungs become overstimulated by exercise, viral infections, allergens, or pollutants. The body RESPONDS TO THIS STIMULUS by activating various defense cells in the immune system. THEIR MOBILIZATION causes the airways to swell. AT THE SAME TIME, the muscles surrounding the airways contract, cutting off airflow. WHEN THAT HAPPENS, asthmatics may inhale a corticosteriod substance to stop the muscle spasm and reopen their airways.

IF REPEATED ATTACKS OCCUR, HOWEVER, the lungs do not return to normal. This constant STATE OF INFLAMMATION damages the bronchial walls and creates scar tissue. AS A RESULT, the airways can no longer clear the mucus that forms deep in the lungs. The ENSUING BUILDUP reduces the flow of air and sets the stage for the next asthma attack.

Respond: Write thoughtful answers to the following questions. Afterward, share your answers with a classmate.

1. Where do most of the transitional words appear in the sentences? Do you see a good reason for this pattern?

2. What makes the phrase "responds to this stimulus" transitional? Consider the previous sentence.

3. To what words in the previous sentence do the words "their mobilization" refer to?

4. From what you can observe about transitions in these two paragraphs, write two of your own personal "rules for transition."

NOTE: You'll find a complete list of transitions in your handbook. (Refer to "Transitions, Useful linking" in the index.)

Extend

Apply what you've learned about transitions in a two-paragrap
about the effects of something new (3-D television, stricter colle
requirements, and so on) on you and your peers. Explain your use
to a classmate.

Fluency: Crafting Sentences

Readers want to know what a sentence is about from its very start. Then they want to know where the idea is going. When they move on, readers look to see if the next sentence is about the same thing, or if it changes course entirely. Sensitive writers give their readers clues about such things by using *repeated subjects, pronouns, synonyms,* and *transitional words or phrases*.

If you want to help your readers follow your line of thinking, remember these points:

- Shove toward the LEFT—that is, toward the beginning of your sentence—key words that name your topic and any transitional words or phrases that link your sentence to the sentence before it.
- Shove toward the RIGHT—that is, toward the end of your sentence—any words or phrases you want to emphasize because they are new, surprising, or important.
- When you move on to the next sentence, try to echo one of the key words in the previous sentence. (Usually, echoing the SUBJECT of the previous sentence will keep you on course.)

Note how the subject is echoed in the following two sentences:

In our culture, CARS loom as large and lethal toys. THEY tempt young drivers to play in dangerous ways.

React: Find a magazine article or a piece of your own writing to analyze in terms of its direction and flow. Focus your attention on two or three longer, consecutive paragraphs. Consider the following questions in your analysis.

- Does the writer echo a key word from a previous sentence when she or he moves on to a new thought? *(Underline examples.)*
- Does the writer use specific transitional words or phrases? *(Circle examples.)*
- What is the overall effectiveness of the piece? Does it clearly and smoothly move from one point to the next? *(Explain.)*
- What else might the writer do to enable the flow of ideas?
- Has the article reinforced or changed your feelings about the construction of effective writing?

Extend

Write freely about a past experience or phase in your life (as a team member, as an employee, as a newcomer). Afterward, analyze the direction and flow of your writing. Does it follow the "familiar first, new next" formula? Does it contain specific transitional words or phrases? Are key words echoed from sentence to sentence? Consider how to improve this initial writing.

Conventions: Sentence Fragments

From elementary school onward, students are taught to avoid writing sentence fragments. However, published writing often contains intentional fragments for dramatic effect.

Read: The paragraph below includes some "accidental" fragments (italicized words).

- **Both pleasant and unpleasant situations can cause stress. *Any incident that places a demand on you to readjust or change.* The reaction of the physical body to stress is the same. *Whether the stressor is pleasant or unpleasant.* One can be free of stress. *But only after death.***

Read & React: Determine the stylistic purpose of each of these "deliberate" fragments.

- **Everyone in the family, including the youngest children, speak German. *Fluently.***
- **Mrs. Stokes: Weezie, come get your lunch, girl.**
  Weezie: *No time. Lots of homework.*

Edit: In this paragraph, underline the deliberate fragments but *edit* (correct) the accidental ones.

Time for recreation to ease the mind. Physical exercise to relieve physical and mental tension. Having a job that you enjoy, that you feel well-equipped to perform, and that others appreciate. These are a few of the keys to managing stress. However, recreation, physical exercise, and work are stressors in themselves. Dr. Hans Selye, a physician from Montreal, Canada, who did some of the earliest research on stress in the 1950s, said that the reaction of the body to stress is the same. Whether the stressor is pleasant or unpleasant. Generally speaking, stress makes life more interesting. A person free from stress only when he or she dies. However, a type of stress called "distress" is potentially harmful (Engel). Distress can be caused by a daily job. That is immensely unpleasant, so exchange a distressing job for a more satisfying one. If that is not possible, one should talk over the pressures of work. With someone who is trusted and respected. One must try to accept what cannot be changed. Everyone ought to plan time. For exercise and rest (Stress).

Extend

In a short paragraph, deliberately use a few fragments for s

Conventions: Sentence Errors

React: Carefully review the following paragraph, correcting the sentence errors as you go along. (You will find examples of sentence fragments, comma splices, and run-on sentences.) Cross out incorrect punctuation marks and add punctuation and capital letters as needed. (Refer to "Sentence, Writing effectively" in the handbook index for help.)

As a small child, he had eaten jelly doughnuts for breakfast. Now, however, at an obese and rather easily winded 29. He had switched over to granola and skim milk. Along with his new eating habits, his looks had also begun to change. He wore his hair a bit longer in back and thinner on top and his shoes were designed to reduce lower back pain. He thought about this as he sat gazing out at the backyard where the neighbor kid with the nose ring was mowing the lawn. Maybe his younger brother Kevin was right in his appraisal, maybe he had become old-fashioned and far, far out of step. The brothers had just gone out with their parents the night before, a monthly ritual. Kevin had walked into the restaurant and had scanned his brother's clothes and posture, in addition, he had even seemed to scan his brother's thoughts, with slow-mounting amusement, Kevin had said, "You look so . . . granola." Unable to disguise his obvious embarrassment, the older brother picked up a menu and boldly ordered a chef's salad.

Extend

As you probably know, professional writers occasionally break the rules in their work. A writer might, for example, purposely use a series of sentence fragments or express a long, rambling idea. Try breaking or stretching the rules yourself in one of your upcoming pieces of writing, but do so carefully and electively, with a clear purpose and desired effect in mind.

Conventions: Consistency

Read & React: Study the guidelines for subject-verb agreement in your handbook. In the exercise below, underline the subject and circle the correct verb choice in parentheses.

1. Half of the dorms on campus *(is, are)* coed dorms.
2. Most of the students *(is, are)* upperclassmen.
3. The science faculty *(present, presents)* a lab orientation session every year.
4. Some of the students *(is, are)* commuting to school every day by bus, taxi, or subway.
5. The school calendar *(include, includes)*, among other items, a list of activities for the week.
6. Health for Life is one of the new classes that *(is, are)* being offered this semester.
7. None of the freshmen *(realize, realizes)* that one of the gymnasiums is located underground.
8. All of the school organizations *(is, are)* looking for new members among the incoming freshmen.
9. This is one of the books that *(is, are)* required for the AP English course.
10. Mathematics *(is, are)* a requirement for almost any field of study.
11. The cause of the bad grade *(was, were)* poor study habits.
12. Of the tests that *(is, are)* used for evaluating college applicants, the ACT and SAT are used most frequently.
13. Some of the students *(request, requests)* a specific instructor for each course they take.
14. Business is one of the majors that *(is, are)* always popular.
15. The reason for the long lines on registration day *(was, were)* the inefficient system the school used.
16. Some of the students attending college today *(is, are)* required to attend all classes.
17. Any of the students missing classes *(is, are)* required to report the reason for the absence.
18. Statistics *(is, are)* not as difficult as calculus for most people.
19. The room and time slot that *(was, were)* assigned to this class have been changed.
20. The increased enrollment for the class *(was, were)* the reason for these changes.

Conventions: Pronoun-Antecedent Agreement

Read & React: Study the rules in your handbook concerning agreement of pronouns and antecedents. Then underline the correct pronoun in parentheses and circle its antecedent in each of the following sentences.

1. For the job hunter to get the best possible job, *(he or she, they)* needs to have two or three job offers from which to choose.
2. Everyone looking for a job should be aware of the different methods of searching available to *(her or him, them)*.
3. Every job hunter owes it to *(himself or herself, themselves)* to become acquainted with all phases of the job-hunting process.
4. Both Ashley and her friend, Shelli, use newspaper ads for local job leads that *(she, they)* then follow up with a phone call and a letter or an e-mail message.
5. Neither Ashley nor Shelli expects to find the perfect job on *(her, their)* first attempt.
6. Sometimes job hunters try to make *(her or his, their)* availability known by placing ads about themselves and *(her or his, their)* job skills in newspapers or on job-search Web sites.
7. Most colleges have especially good placement services because *(they, it)* understand that finding a good job is one reason *(their, its)* students came to college in the first place.
8. Some colleges offer *(its, their)* students a complete job placement service, including placement help years after the students have graduated.
9. The private employment agency charges *(its, their)* customer only when *(he or she, they)* get(s) a job.
10. Whe... employers use an executive search firm, *(she or he, they)* want the firm to hire people ...mployed by other companies.
11. ...ver and the job hunter can send *(his or her, their)* listings to a clearinghouse.
12. ...vous during *(her or his, their)* first job interview.
13. ...nor those being interviewed want *(his or her, their)* interview(s) to

Conventions: Pronoun References

A pronoun is like the jacket you leave on a seat at a concert to show that the seat is saved. The jacket is not the person; it stands in place of the person. In the same way, a pronoun is not a noun; it stands in place of a noun, which is referred to as the pronoun's "antecedent."

A pronoun works well when the reader can tell exactly which word is its antecedent. In the following sentence, the pronoun "it" does not work well.

As she edged her car toward the drive-up window, it made a strange rattling sound.
(Does "it" refer to the car or to the window?)

This is an example of **indefinite pronoun reference.** The pronoun could be referring to either of two words in the sentence. To correct the error, replace the indefinite pronoun with a noun. (Rephrasing the sentence is also acceptable.) Here are two ways to correct the sample sentence:

As she edged her car toward the drive-up window, the car made a strange rattling sound.

As she edged toward the drive-up window, her car made a strange rattling sound.

Challenge: Each of the following sentences has an indefinite pronoun in it. Correct each sentence so its meaning is clear.

1. The team moved the wrestling mat off the gym floor so that it could be cleaned.

2. When Tara entered her program into the computer, it completely froze up.

3. Alina asked her mother if she could carry one of the boxes for her.

4. The senator let the MC know that his microphone wasn't working.

5. Check the newly installed switches for wiring errors so that the instructor can inspect them.

6. Shortly after the car had been given a final coat of paint, it began to run.

Extend

Write three sentences of your own that contain indefinite pr
Exchange your work with a classmate and correct each other

Conventions: Dangling Modifiers

Read: What is wrong with the following sentence?

After finishing her routine on the parallel bars, the judge gave Juanita the winning score.

It sounds as if the judge herself finished the routine, instead of Juanita. To correct the mistake, we could change the opening phrase or the main clause:

After Juanita finished her routine on the parallel bars, the judge gave her the winning score.

After finishing her routine on the parallel bars, Juanita was given the winning score by the judge.

When a modifying phrase at the opening of a sentence does not describe the subject of the sentence, it is called a *dangling modifier*. Dangling modifiers destroy the logic of a writer's statement.

Handbook Helper: Look up "Modifiers, Dangling" in the index of your handbook. Then look up "Verbal." There you will find a description of three types of verbals: participles, infinitives, and gerunds. These three types of verbals are often found in dangling modifiers. Learn to recognize them and to understand how to use them correctly as modifiers. That will make fixing or editing dangling modifiers easier.

Directions: Correct the following sentences by rewording either the modifying opening phrase or the main clause. If the sentence is already correct, place a C on the line.

1. Using a computer to help diagnose engine problems, the car was repaired by our mechanic.

Using a computer to help diagnose engine problems, our mechanic repaired the car.

2. While playing the piano, our dog began to howl at me.

3. After writing spontaneously for half an hour, our teacher said we should gather in small groups to discuss our drafts.

ing the horizon, we spotted a faint plume of smoke.

e bargain, the grocer and the supplier shook hands.

the bobcat made Thurgood tremble with fear.

w's branches back and forth, we huddled in the doorway to watch the wind.

ing for phrase modifiers that are incorrectly "hanging out." They will

weaken the overall effect of your work.

Conventions: Commas

Read & Insert: Read and study the handbook rules on using commas. Then insert commas where they are needed in the sentences below. Circle each comma you insert. Some sentences may not need commas.

1. Yesterday in health class, we learned the Heimlich maneuver, a method of clearing a choking person's blocked airway.
2. The Heimlich maneuver not artificial respiration is used to save a choking victim.
3. Unless you act to save him or her a victim of food choking will die of strangulation in four minutes.
4. When using the Heimlich maneuver you exert pressure that pushes the diaphragm up compresses the air in the lungs and expels the object blocking the airway.
5. A friend of mine who had apparently paid attention to her first-aid class saved the life of a choking victim.
6. The victim who had been eating steak was forever grateful that my friend had learned the Heimlich maneuver.
7. That is why it is important for everyone to know how to perform this maneuver or to get quick professional help.
8. Whenever you think a situation is life threatening don't hesitate to call an ambulance or the rescue squad.
9. After calling for emergency help be prepared to state your name the injured person's name the address or place where the injured person is located and a brief description of what happened.
10. This is necessary so that the emergency personnel know exactly what they have to do when they arrive.
11. Remember that your objective to help save a life can be better accomplished when you remai calm and follow suggested procedures.

Extend

Commas are used to separate a vocative from the rest of the
know what that means? If not, find out by referring to your h

Conventions: Colons

Review & Insert: Review the colon rules in your handbook. Then insert colons where they are needed below. (Some sentences may not need a colon.) Circle the punctuation marks you add.

1. Rob has sent for information about the universities in these states: Wisconsin, Illinois, California, and Florida.

2. Dear Registrar

   Please send me your latest catalog. I am also interested in . . .

3. One question is very important to anyone seeking a college education How much is it going to cost?

4. Rob made his decision after carefully considering the information about tuition, housing, programs, and financial aid.

5. Here is another important two-part question for prospective college students to ask Will I receive a quality education, and will the degree I earn be recognized as valid in the career area I have chosen?

6. My father had important advice he never tired of repeating "These days, you've got to get a good education."

7. In college, Rob plans to take courses in several subjects history, English, geography, chemistry, and math.

8. Students soon learn that you sometimes have to leave a noisy dormitory in search of two important ingredients for productive studying peace and quiet.

9. It is [illegible] wonder that during final exam time the college libraries are filled with students doing one th[illegible]dying.

10. All th[illegible]ered, the first year of college can be exciting, challenging, and fun.

[illegible] identify and learn one colon rule in the handbook that wasn't covered in this [illegible]

Conventions: Commas and Semicolons

Insert: Place commas and semicolons where they are needed in the paragraphs below. Circle punctuation marks you add. (Refer to your handbook for more information about the rules for using commas and semicolons.)

One of the most remarkable and brilliant scientists of our time is 50-year-old Stephen Hawking—physics professor, author, and theorist. His studies concerning the nature of the universe and black holes have advanced our understanding of space. More importantly Dr. Hawking has done more than any other physicist in describing and detailing his life's work in language understood by the average person. In short he has brought the outer limits of the universe "down to earth."

These accomplishments alone merit our praise and respect that Dr. Hawking has accomplished them despite disabling personal setbacks is almost incomprehensible. In 1962 when he was only 20 years old Stephen Hawking learned he had amyotrophic lateral sclerosis or ALS. ALS gradually destroys the nerves and muscles needed for moving. Doctors told him that he would probably die before he finished his doctoral degree however Stephen didn't let their prognosis stop him. With the support of fellow Cambridge student Jane Wilde whom he later married he continued his studies and received his Ph.D.

Stephen Hawking's work on black holes and the nature of the universe was published in a book entitled *A Brief History of Time: From the Big Bang to Black Holes*. The book was written for people who do not have a scientific background. It is a remarkable book. What makes it even more remarkable is that it was written by a man unable to move his arms and hands to write unable to speak and unable to communicate normally. The book is a testament to one person's determination to succeed to be heard and to overcome personal tragedy.

Extend

A semicolon is used to separate groups of words that already c
Provide an example sentence illustrating this rule. Then refer t
to check your work.

Conventions: Usage

Select: As you carefully read through the following sentences, underline the correct word in each set of parentheses. (Refer to "Usage, mixed pairs" in the handbook index for help.)

1. Elisha attended the *(annual, perennial)* career fair at the local college.

2. She and her classmates had to *(accept, except) (their, there, they're)* invitations four weeks in advance in order to attend the fair.

3. *(Already, All ready)* the *(amount, number)* of people attending was *(all together, altogether)* too many.

4. Even though the *(sight, site)* of the fair was a large auditorium, *(their, there)* was hardly room for all those who came.

5. Elisha found she had no *(personal, personnel)* interest in one workshop leader's topic, "Let computers make *(your, you're)* career choice."

6. *(Among, Between)* the speakers at the fair were some very eminent members of the business community.

7. Still, *(there, their, they're)* were *(fewer, less)* speakers *(than, then)* Elisha anticipated.

8. At one point, Elisha had to *(chose, choose) (between, among)* visiting a college recruiter and a vocational counselor.

9. The vocational counselor presented her material *(good, well)*, *(accept, except)* for those few times she was *(to, too, two) (quiet, quite)*.

10. The [illegible]ooths of the college representatives were set up *(beside, besides)* the vocational [illegible]tives' booths.

11. [illegible]*her)* down were the booths of the two-year and specialty schools.

12. The [illegible]*ontinual)* activity and loud talking created a county-fair atmosphere; still, [illegible]*nent, complement)* the organizers on a job well done.

Conventions: Proofreading Review

Correct: Proofread the essay below. Draw a line through any errors you find in capitalization, numbers, abbreviations, punctuation, spelling, and usage. Write the correction above each error. Add (and circle) punctuation as necessary. (*Hint:* Numbers are used frequently in this piece. Refer to the rules on "Numbers" in your handbook.)

About 450 miles off the coast of Newfoundland in 12,500 feet of water, scientists discovered the remains of the great ocean liner the S S Titanic. The seventy-three year search for the Titanic, which went down in what is considered the worlds' greatest sea disaster was a challengeing one. It concluded finally in September 1985. Because of this discovary interest in this legendary ship became stronger then ever.

In part this interest may be due to the titanics reputation. When it was first launched in 1912, the british steamer was the largest ship in the world. An incredible 882 ft. long and 175 ft. high, The Titanic was comparable to 4 city blocks in length and 11 stories in hieght. It was proclaimed the most expensive most luxurious ship ever built. It was said to be "unsinkable".

The later claim was the result of special features. The Titanic was equiped with a double bottom and the hull was divided into 16 separate watertight compartments. These added features, it was felt, would make the Titanic unsinkable.

Despite its reputation, the mighty Titanic did sink; and on its maiden voyage too. Carrying approximatly 2200 passengers and over $420,000 worth of cargo, the Titanic set sail from England in April, 1912, bound for New York. Just a few days out of port, however on the night of April 14 the Titanic collided with an iceberg in the north atlantic, damaging several hull plates along its starboard side. The mighty "floating palace" sunk in a matter of 2 1/2 hours, taking with it all of its cargo and the lives of 1522 of its passengers.

Answer Key

Answer keys are supplied only for activities calling for specific answers. For the remaining activities, the answers may vary.

187 Ideas: Improving Focus

Read & React:

Paragraph 3

Extend: (Answers will vary.)

190 Organization: Limiting Your Topic

Read & React:

Paragraph 1: central subject—championship victory
specific aspect—defeating a longtime rival
idea or feeling about the subject—pandemonium, excitement of high-fiving, cheering, singing, flashing score

Paragraph 2: central subject—exercise
specific aspect—out-of-shape students
idea or feeling about the subject—to live long and active lives

Paragraph 3: central subject—group research for learning
specific aspect—presenting all sides of an issue
idea or feeling about the subject—challenged to think for ourselves

Reflect:

clearly focused paragraph—1
implicit focus—3
plainly stated focus—2

192 Voice: Finding a Voice

React: (Answers will vary.)

1. Purpose: The paragraph is entertaining but also enlightening. The purpose is to make the reader smile but also to think.
2. Tone: The paragraph is humorous and sarcastic, and a little sad.
3. Attitude: The writer is confessing something to the reader. The writer sounds like a complaining friend looking for sympathy.
4. Personality: The writer is sensitive, imaginative, and whimsical.
5. Language Use: The writer equates music and emotion, sound tracks and empathy. The paragraph contrasts movies with real life and carries the theme of escape.

Voic… …ieving Economy

…s will vary.)

…ilitary aircraft is a fighter that will reach an incredible Mach 7, which is …of sound, or nearly 5,000 miles per hour. Besides having to develop …rly handle the incredible heat generated by air molecules passing …ists must perfect the use of the scramjet to push the aircraft …her ceilings than any current generation fighter can achieve. …the laws of physics to make this vision a reality.

195 Voice: Improving Diction

Read & React: (Answers will vary.)

1. distressed or tortured
2. traumatic or disagreeable
3. discretion or sensitivity
4. emblazon
5. broadcast or advertised
6. inflates or exaggerates
7. acquaintances or well-wishers
8. relive

196 Voice: Evaluating Style

Reflect: (Answers will vary.)

The writer of this paragraph has an infectious style, as if ideas were exploding into his or her head and words were stumbling from his or her mouth. The sentences seem breathless, dropping conjunctions out of series, piling clause on clause, using dashes as if they were little hiccups. The writer seems eager to share a sudden realization—"Have you noticed that?"—to make the reader say hmm. Use of the pronoun "we," present tense verbs, and frenetic language makes the ideas immediate and compelling. These style choices and numerous concrete details help the writer succeed in sharing this idea.

197 Word Choice: Active vs. Passive Verbs

Rewrite: (Answers will vary.)

In recent years, a number of engineers and businesspeople have proposed building a tunnel from the United States to Europe. Most technology for such an undertaking is already available. Workers would not build the tunnel along the ocean floor because the bottom of the ocean is too uneven and, in places, too deep. Besides, the enormous water pressure would crush the tunnel at such depths. Instead, the builders would anchor the tunnel to the ocean floor, and the tunnel would actually float several hundred feet below the surface. An ultrahigh-speed train would carry passengers and freight goods from one continent to another in about an hour. Researchers have asked scientists if such a train could travel 5,000 miles per hour. One day, after overcoming problems and raising the money for such a project, governments, scientists, and technicians may make such an idea a reality. People will quickly travel from shore to shore before they finish reading the morning paper.

198 Word Choice: Using Adverb Clauses

React: (Answers will vary.)

Because most of the new land of the Louisiana Purchase was unexplored, President Thomas Jefferson wanted to dispatch an expedition into the region so that he could acquire information about it. He also hoped to find a quick passage to the Pacific because this would mean an end to dangerous travel around the tip of South America to reach the western coast. Before Lewis and Clark started their journey in 1804, they accepted the president's plan to explore the new territory.

Extend: (Answers will vary.)

Most of the new land of the Louisiana Purchase was unexplored. Unless President Thomas Jefferson dispatched an expedition into the region, he would not acquire the information that he needed about this land. Also, if he could find a quick passage t Pacific, it would mean an end to dangerous travel around the tip of South Americ the western coast. After Lewis and Clark accepted the president's plan to explo territory, they started their journey in 1804.

199 Word Choice: Clarity

Extend: (Answers will vary.)

At one time, the administrators of Yellowstone National Park believed [beyond a shadow of doubt] that wolves were the [ultimate] enemy. [Helpless, beautiful, stately] elk and other animals suffered from the terrible predation of wolf packs. Then more studies showed the error of the original assumption. Since the reintroduction of the wolf, scientists have discovered, (much to their amazement,) how valuable the wolf is to the entire ecosystem in the park. For example, because the wolves (keep elk on the move, the huge ungulates no longer overgraze and overbrowse) the [marvelous] plants and trees on the riverbanks.

At one time, the administrators of Yellowstone National Park believed that wolves were the enemy. Elk and other animals suffered from the constant harassment of the wolf packs. Too many animals were killed causing herd numbers to fall. Then more studies showed the error of the original assumption. Since the reintroduction of the wolf, scientists have discovered how valuable the wolf is to the entire ecosystem in the park. For example, because of pressure from the wolves, the elk keep moving and no longer overgraze. As a result, riverbank plants and trees are flourishing.

200 Word Choice: Relative Clauses

Combine: (Answers will vary.)

2. Dr. Andrew Smith, who was a military surgeon with the British army, examined the first recorded whale shark specimen in 1828.
3. The fishermen who harpooned the shark had noticed its unusual gray coloration with white spots.
4. The dried skin, which Dr. Smith originally purchased for $30, is preserved in the Museum d'Histoire Naturelle in Paris.
5. In 1868, a young Irish naturalist studied the whale sharks in the Seychelle Islands where he heard the natives speak of a monstrous fish called the "Chagrin."
6. He saw several specimens that exceeded 50 feet in length.
7. Many men who had always been considered trustworthy reported sharks measuring nearly 70 feet in length.
8. The only other exceptionally large fish that compares in size with the whale shark is the basking shark.

201 Word Choice: Economy

React: (Answers will vary.)

2. ...ormally) (long)
3. ... main reason) (is) (or look over his class notes)
4. ... are) (who) (on their own) (is over)
5. ... in) (down) (by himself) (to assist him)
6. ...ld surely break if mishandled,) (so that it would be handled with care)
7. ... (evening)
8. ... anywhere and)

... time)

... (writing) (which goes without saying)

... to understand,) (where the money issue was not such a big

... before)

203 Fluency: Parallel Structure

Revise:

2. and the backstroke
3. strengthens the muscles
4. enjoyable
5. it may give you a heart attack
6. hang onto the side
7. an efficient breathing pattern
8. a furious three-minute swim

(Possible Answers)

1. a lamp
2. cutting grass around the dorms
3. watch a movie
4. thinking about the past
5. to reach Canada

204 Fluency: Complex Sentences

Combine: (Answers will vary.)

2. The sea eagle flew low and was almost pulled underwater by its prey because the writhing, talon-pierced carp weighed 13 pounds. (reason why)
3. The young eagle is heavier than its parents by as much as one pound when it leaves the nest. (time)
4. When the hunters looked up toward the mountain crest, they saw a golden eagle descending with a mule deer fawn in its talons. (time)
5. Arthur Bowland once persuaded a Verreaux's eagle to snatch a 20-pound pack while in flight so that he could test the bird's supposed tremendous strength. (purpose)
6. Scientific tests for muscularity and power will not be a true guide for the species unless they are done with wild, not captive, eagles. (condition)
7. Although eagles can kill prey four times their own size, they ordinarily can't carry a load weighing more than six pounds. (condition)

207 Conventions: Sentence Fragments

Edit: (Corrections will vary.)

Deliberate: Time for recreation . . ., Physical exercise . . . , Having a job . . .

Accidental:

1. Dr. Hans Selye . . . 1950s said that . . . unpleasant.
2. A person is . . . dies.
3. If that is . . . with someone who . . . respected.
4. . . . to plan time for exercise and rest (Stress).

208 Conventions: Sentence Errors

React: (Answers will vary.)

(1) . . . winded 29, he . . . . (2) . . . on top, and his shoes . . . .
(3) . . . his appraisal; maybe he . . . . (4) . . . and posture. In addition, he . . .
(5) brother's thoughts. (6) With slow-mounting . . . .

209 Conventions: Consistency

Read & React:

2. most are
3. faculty presents
4. Some are
5. calendar includes
6. that are
7. None realize
8. All are
9. that are
10. Mathematics is
11. cause was
12. that are
13. Some request
14. that are
15. reason was
16. some are
17. any are
18. statistics is
19. that were
20. enrollment was

210 Conventions: Pronoun-Antecedent Agreement

Read & React:

2. Everyone her or him
3. job hunter himself or herself
4. Ashley, friend they
5. Ashley, Shelli her
6. job hunters their their
7. colleges they their
8. colleges their
9. agency its customer he or she
10. employers they
11. employer, job hunter their
12. everyone her or his
13. interviewer, those their

211 Conventions: Pronoun References

Challenge: (Answers will vary.)

1. So that the wrestling mat could be cleaned, the team moved it off the gym floor. (or) The team moved the wrestling mat off the gym floor so the floor could be cleaned. (or) . . . so the mat could be cleaned.
2. When Tara entered her program into the computer, the computer completely froze up.
3. Alina asked if she could carry one of the boxes for her mother. (or) Alina asked her mother to carry one of the boxes for her.
4. Because the senator's microphone wasn't working, he let the MC know. (or) The senator's microphone wasn't working, so he let the MC know.
5. So that the instructor can inspect the newly installed switches, check them for wiring errors.
6. The paint began to run shortly after the car had been given a final coat.

212 Conventions: Dangling Modifiers

Directions: (Answers will vary.)

2. While I played the piano, . . .
3. After we wrote spontaneously for half an hour, . . .
4. C
5. C
6. Afraid to look at the bobcat, Thurgood trembled with fear.
7. As the wind whipped the willow's branches back and forth, we huddled in the doorway to watch.

213 Conventions: Commas

Read & Insert:

2. maneuver, not artificial respiration, is . . .
3. or her, a victim . . .
4. maneuver, you . . . up, compresses . . . lungs, and . . .
5. mine, who . . . class, saved . . .
6. victim, who . . . steak, was . . .
7. C
8. threatening, don't . . .
9. help, be . . . name, the . . . name, the . . . located, and . . .
10. C
11. objective, . . . life, can . . .

214 Conventions: Colons

Review & Insert:

2. Registrar:
3. education:
4. C
5. ask:
6. repeating:
7. subjects:
8. studying:
9. thing:
10. C

215 Conventions: Commas and Semicolons

Insert:

line 3 importantly, Dr. . . .
line 5 short, he . . .
line 7 respect; that . . .
line 8 1962, . . .
line 9 old, Stephen . . . sclerosis, . . .
line 11 degree; . . . however, Stephen
line 12 Wilde, whom . . .
line 13 married, he . . .
line 18 write, unable . . . speak, and . . .
line 19 succeed, to . . . heard, and . . .

216 Conventions: Usage

Select:

2. accept their
3. Already number altogether
4. site there
5. personal your
6. Among
7. there fewer than
8. choose between
9. well except too quiet
10. beside
11. Farther
12. continuous compliment

217 Conventions: Proofreading Review

About 450 miles off the coast of Newfoundland in 12,500 feet of water, scientists discovered the remains of the great ocean liner the S.S. Titanic. The ~~seventy-three year~~ 73-year search for the Titanic, which went down in what is considered the world's greatest sea disaster, was a ~~challengeing~~ challenging one. It concluded, finally, in September 1985. Because of this ~~discovary~~ discovery, interest in this legendary ship became stronger ~~then~~ than ever.

In part, this interest may be due to the Titanic's reputation. When it was first launched in 1912, the British steamer was the largest ship in the world. An incredible 882 feet long and 175 feet high, the Titanic was comparable to four city blocks in length and 11 stories in ~~hieght~~ height. It was proclaimed the most expensive, most luxurious ship ever built. It was said to be "unsinkable."

The ~~later~~ latter claim was the result of special features. The Titanic was ~~equiped~~ equipped with a double bottom, and the hull was divided into 16 separate, watertight compartments. These added features, it was felt, would make the Titanic unsinkable.

Despite its reputation, the mighty Titanic did sink, and on its maiden voyage, too. Carrying ~~approximatly~~ approximately 2,200 passengers and over $420,000 worth of cargo, the Titanic set sail from England in April 1912, bound for New York. Just a few days out of port, however, on the night of April 14, the Titanic collided with an iceberg in the North Atlantic, damaging several hull plates along its starboard side. The mighty "floating palace" sunk in a matter of 2 1/2 hours, taking with it all of its cargo and the lives of 1,522 of its passengers.

Minilesson Answer Key

If You Had to . . . (page 245)

John, where Jim had used just "had," had used "had had"; "had had" had had the teacher's approval.

In Praise of the Phrase (page 246)

1. studying a map
   to study a map
   studying a map

   Studying a map is interesting.
   I like to study a map.
   Studying a map, we planned our trip.

2. taking a vacation
   to take a vacation
   taking a vacation

   Taking a vacation is fun.
   I like to take a vacation.
   Taking a vacation, the family relaxed.

Minilessons

The following pages contain more than 90 minilessons that you can use with the *Write for College* handbook. The topics of the minilessons are presented in the same order that they are addressed in the handbook.

Using the Minilessons

Minilesson can transform any classroom into an active learning environment. (We define a minilesson as instruction that lasts about 10 minutes and covers a single idea or a basic concept.) Minilessons can include the entire class, be individualized, or be done in cooperative learning groups.

Implementation

Minilessons work very well in the writing workshop classroom. Perhaps one group of students needs to know how to punctuate works-cited entries in research papers. Another group of students may need practice combining sentences.

The minilessons that follow are referenced in the chapter-by-chapter teacher's notes on pages 8–120 in this guide. They may serve as discussion starters, workshop-skill exercises, or follow-up, end-of-class, or extension activities. They focus on important concepts covered in *Write for College* and address a variety of writing, reading, thinking, and learning skills.

The Process of Writing

Words of Wisdom — Why Write?

- Read the quotation "Writing allows you to penetrate your life and learn to trust your own mind."
- Think about what this quotation means; then write your own quotation about writing.

Any Questions? — One Writer's Process

- Review "Prewriting" on pages 2–5 in the chapter "One Writer's Process."
- Look closely at the cluster on page 2.
- Use it to generate and list as many additional questions about the cluster's subject as you can. If possible, brainstorm with a partner.

Sizing Up the Situation — Traits of Writing

- Choose any piece of sample writing in *Write for College*.
- Write an evaluation of the piece, telling how well the writer used the six traits of effective writing (ideas, organization, voice, word choice, fluency, and conventions). Give examples from the piece to support your evaluation.

Great-Ideas Exchange — Traits of Writing

- Explore what makes a topic a great idea by working with a partner. Take turns suggesting ideas you feel would make interesting research topics.
- Alternate suggestions. After you propose a topic, have your partner rate it personally on a scale of 1 (not interesting) to 10 (fascinating).
- Continue until you each receive at least one 10 rating for one of your topic ideas.

Work the System

Traits of Writing

- Study the types of paragraph arrangements (see pages 80–87) in *Write for College.*
- Write down a specific topic that would be appropriate for each pattern of organization.
- Select your favorite topic. Then write a paragraph modeling that pattern of organization.
- Share your work with a partner or the class. Discuss the effectiveness of your choice.

Making Connections

Traits of Writing

- Review the list of subordinating conjunctions on page 578 in the "Proofreader's Guide."
- Write five sentences, each one including a different subordinating conjunction.
- Use the conjunctions to create either complex or compound-complex sentences.
- Exchange your work with a partner and check each other's sentences for clarity, accuracy, and fluency.

A Deal for You

Traits of Writing

- Write a simple description of a used vehicle of your choice.
- Put yourself in the shoes of a salesperson on the lot. Then carefully write your sales pitch for each of the following customers:

  teenage boy   **family with three young children**

  retired couple   **customer of your choice**

- Reflect on how the changing audience affected your word choice, tone, and all the other aspects of your writing voice.

Bigger Not Always Better

Traits of Writing

- Find a paragraph that uses a high-level vocabulary, technical terms, or jargon in a textbook or scholarly journal. Your teacher may supply this text.
- Rewrite the text in simple language, using vocabulary that would communicate effectively with an audience of high school students.
- Discuss the resulting versions. How does simpler language make the text better? What is lost, if anything, in simplifying the text?

One Red Pen

A Guide to Prewriting

- Turn to "Selecting a Topic" on page 22 in *Write for College.*
- Read "Listing."
- Pretend you've found a list on a scrap of paper in the school library.
- Write the list so that a reader knows it was written by a high school student researching a topic. (Ask a classmate to guess the research topic from the "lost list" you write.)

What I Found

A Guide to Prewriting

- Turn to “Selecting a Topic” on page 22 in *Write for College.*
- Read about the technique of clustering.
- Form a cluster based on the assignment of writing a detailed description of something that you find in the room where you are now sitting.
- Explore one of the ideas in the cluster by freewriting for 3 to 4 minutes.

Shaping a Topic

A Guide to Prewriting

- Read about the 5 W’s of writing on pages 25–26 in *Write for College.* Then open one of your textbooks to any page and jot down the first main idea or heading that catches your eye.
- Write about this idea by answering the 5 W’s of writing.
- Share the results of your work with a writing partner.

Tracking Down the Thesis

A Guide to Prewriting

- Read “Forming a Thesis Statement” on page 30 in *Write for College.*
- Write a thesis statement for each of the following pieces of writing: “Isn’t It Romantic?” on page 206; “The Humors Theory” on page 208; “Let There Be Art” on page 55; and “Eye to Eye” on page 237.
- You may find that you can copy some thesis statements word for word from the samples; you may need to construct some thesis statements yourself, using information in the texts.

The Shape of Things to Come

A Guide to Prewriting

- Quickly read the sample writings that begin on pages 177, 192, and 196–197 in *Write for College.*
- For each piece of writing, choose one type of graphic organizer shown on pages 27–28 that would have been a good prewriting tool.
- Write a sentence explaining why you chose each organizer.

For Example

A Guide to Drafting

- Read “Developing the Middle” on page 34–35 in *Write for College* to learn about ways to support a thesis.
- Choose three methods of support and search through some of the writing samples in your handbook to find good examples of each.
- Write a sentence or two explaining why each text you chose is a good example.

Sparking Interest

A Guide to Drafting

- Read about opening or lead paragraphs on page 32 in *Write for College.*
- Then select an essay or a narrative from your writing folder.
- Write a new opening paragraph following one of the suggestions in the handbook.

Best Foot Forward — A Guide to Revising

- Choose three cliches from the list on page 124 in *Write for College.*
- Think of original ways to phrase them.
- Use your new expressions in three sentences.

Field Trip — A Guide to Revising

- Read the narrative paragraph on page 81 in *Write for College.*
- Think about what changes you would suggest to the writer to improve the paragraph.
- Respond to the writing, using the response sheet on page 159 (in TG) to guide your response.

Mock Trial — A Guide to Revising

- In a small group, pick a piece of sample writing from the handbook to respond to. One group member will pretend to be the writer of the piece. The rest of you will respond to his or her work.
- Use the peer response sheet on page 159 (in TG).
- When you finish, let the "author" critique the responders. Were you too personal? Too negative? Too hesitant to offer constructive criticism? Too vague?

Delete — A Guide to Editing

- See the editing and proofreading marks on the inside back cover of *Write for College.*
- With a partner, exchange papers you wrote earlier this year for any of your classes.
- Edit your partner's paper, using the proofreading marks wherever possible.
- Add a written comment that conveys your personal response to your partner's paper as a whole.

Stand-Ins — A Guide to Editing

- Study the section on pronouns on pages 563–566 in the "Proofreader's Guide."
- Look over the first paragraph or two in a paper you've recently completed.
- List each pronoun on a piece of paper. Next to it, list its antecedent. (If there is no clear antecedent, check whether the pronoun is used accurately.)

Ready to Launch — A Guide to Publishing

- Get out the piece of your writing that you like best.
- Review the chapter "A Guide to Publishing" on pages 57–61 in *Write for College.*
- Use the information to help you find one publication (printed or online) that sounds like a good place to publish your favorite piece.
- Prepare and submit your work.

The Basic Elements

Sincere Flattery — Making Sentences Work

- Read about modeling sentences on page 73 in *Write for College.*
- Then find a sentence in your favorite book or story that you think is especially powerful.
- Model it at least twice.

All Arranged — Making Sentences Work

- Read about the different sentence arrangements on page 585 in the "Proofreader's Guide."
- Write one sentence describing something you have done in the past week.
- Decide which sentence arrangement your sentence uses.
- Rewrite the sentence two times, arranging it differently each time so that you end up with one example of each arrangement.
- Think about which sentence you like best, and why.

Going in Style — Making Sentences Work

- Study loose, balanced, periodic, and cumulative sentences on page 585 in the "Proofreader's Guide."
- Choose an interesting article from a major newsmagazine such as *Time, Newsweek,* or *U.S. News and World Report.*
- Count the occurrences of each type of sentence (loose, periodic, and so on) in the article.
- Decide if one type dominates in the writer's style.
- Write an original sentence for each example you recorded, imitating its structure.
- Share your work.

Complex Authors — Making Sentences Work

- Study simple, compound, complex, and compound-complex sentences on pages 584–585 in the "Proofreader's Guide."
- Choose an article from a magazine of your choice.
- Choose one column (or one page) of copy from the article.
- Underline examples of each of the four types of sentences. Use a different colored marker or pencil for each type (red for simple, blue for compound, green for complex, and yellow for compound-complex).
- Share your discoveries with a writing partner.

Like They Always Say — Making Sentences Work

- "To err is human, but don't over do it." The writer began with a well-known expression but ended by going in an unexpected direction. Below are some more well-known sayings.
- Complete each saying in an unexpected way that makes a statement about sentences or about writing in general. Make your sentences complete and clear.
  - The best things in life are . . .
  - One picture is worth . . .
  - The more things change . . .

On Topic — Developing Strong Paragraphs

- Turn to the sample essay on pages 240–241 in *Write for College.*
- With a partner, find the topic sentence in each paragraph of the essay.
- Discuss the reasons for your choices.
- If you are unsure of any choice, ask another classmate or your teacher for input.

Too Many Pets — Developing Strong Paragraphs

- Turn to page 81 in *Write for College.*
- Read carefully the persuasive paragraph on neutering pets.
- Draw a line down the middle of a blank sheet of paper.
- In the left column, list the paragraph's major reasons for neutering pets.
- In the right column, write a solid objection to each of the reasons in the left column.
- Write your reaction to the weight of the support and evidence presented.

Paragraph Roundup — Developing Strong Paragraphs

- Find seven different methods of arranging details in a paragraph on pages 84–87 in *Write for College.* Working with a partner, find another example of each method.
- Search textbooks, newspapers, magazines, and other sources.
- Write down where you found each paragraph; cut it out, or make a copy of it, if possible.
- Discuss with your writing partner the details that exhibit each paragraph's organization.

While You Were Out — Mastering the Academic Essay

- Select a traditional essay you have written for science, history, or another academic class.
- Study your writing by comparing its approach to the original approach essay, (*Write for College* pages 104–109).
- Rewrite your essay maintaining the topic and supporting details while developing a creative perspective.

Writer's Resource

Time for a Makeover
Understanding Style in Writing

- Read over some pieces you have written.
- Find one or two pieces that reflect your style, and analyze them for purposefulness, clarity, and sincerity. Use "Key Stylistic Reminders" on page 112 in *Write for College* as your guide.

A Slice of Life
Understanding Style in Writing

- Read about anecdotes on page 120 in *Write for College.*
- Think of an incident that had a lasting impact on you.
- Write an anecdote about it.
- Then write one sentence that tells how this anecdote could be used in your writing.

Take Action!
Understanding Style in Writing

- Read about passive style on page 123 in *Write for College.*
- Then review a piece of writing that you have just completed or are presently working on.
- Check each of your sentences to see if it is written in the passive or active voice.
- Decide if you want to change any passive verbs to active ones.

Getting a Kick out of This
Understanding Style in Writing

- Review active voice and passive voice on page 572 in the "Proofreader's Guide."
- Choose a sport that involves hitting or kicking a ball.
- Write a paragraph describing a moment of intense action in that sport from the point of view of one of the players; use verbs in the active voice.
- Rewrite the paragraph, describing the same action from the point of view of the ball; use verbs in the passive voice.

Looking Good
Designing Your Writing

- After you read the chapter "Designing Your Writing," turn to page 192 and read the sample process essay.
- List at least three things you could do on a computer to create a clear, easy-to-follow design for this essay. Be specific; explain your ideas and how they would contribute to an effective design.
- If possible, type the essay into a computer and make the changes you have suggested.

Making Connections

Writing Terms and Techniques

- Read the definition of *metaphor* on page 117 in *Write for College.*
- Then rewrite each of the following statements using original metaphors:

  The test was hard.

  Fresh orange juice is great.
- Share the results of your work with a writing partner.

Categories of Forms

Writing Terms and Techniques

- With a partner, list the many different kinds of writing you've done in the past year (letter to your cousin, grocery list, book report, e-mail, and so on). Then study the survey of writing forms on page 141 in *Write for College.*
- Reorganize your list by categorizing your writing according to the different headings in the survey.

A Young Audience

Writing Terms and Techniques

- Choose a cause and effect topic.
- Write a simple explanation of the causes as if you were writing a book for young children.

Inductive Reasoning

Writing Terms and Techniques

- Read about inductive reasoning and deductive reasoning on page 86 in *Write for College.*
- Write an inductive paragraph about a topic of your choice.
- Then develop a deductive paragraph for the same topic.
- Discuss the results.

C'est La Vie

Writing Terms and Techniques

- Find a foreign word or phrase in the glossary on pages 139–140 in *Write for College.*
- Write a sentence that uses the word or phrase and suggests its meaning through context.
- Share your sentence with a partner, a small group, or the class.
- Have the listener(s) (without consulting the glossary) try to define the foreign word or phrase.

The Forms of Writing

What a Day — Reminiscence

- One's sense of smell often triggers memories of special moments.
- Think about an odor that evokes an experience (for example, baking bread).
- Recall what you were doing during that time.
- Write so a reader can join in the sensations of the memory.

Going Through a Phase — Personal Writing

- Freewrite about an important phase in your life.
- Consider the following questions as you write: *What is there about this phase that makes it important to me? How has this phase changed me? Is the change positive?*
- Keep your freewriting in a notebook as a source of future writing ideas.

After high school, then what . . . — College-Entrance Essay

- List goals you have for your life and choose one that's important to you.
- Focusing on that goal, jot down phrases that express its importance.
- Create an outline for an essay, exploring how a college education will help you achieve your goal.

The Key Elements — Summary Report

- Choose a topic currently of interest to archaeologists (Who built Stonehenge? Did Atlantis exist?) or another group of scientists.
- Read about the topic and take notes on the writer's views or research.
- Write a summary report of your findings.

The Right Source — Compiled Report

- Choose a controversial subject (Bermuda Triangle, life on other planets).
- Gather information using the library and the Internet.
- Compare the information from the two sources.
- What differences do you see? How would those differences affect a compiled report? How can you tell whether a source is trustworthy?

Searching for Information — Interview Report

- Interview a classmate about a personal accomplishment or an unusual experience.
- Take notes throughout the interview.
- Share what you have learned about your classmate in an interview report.

Eyewitness Accounts — Observation Report

- Stage a skit involving lots of talking and action (perhaps a student debating a test point with a teacher).
- Then have students write detailed observation reports about what happened.
- Afterward, have students share and compare their observations.

Learning About Yourself — Personal Research Report

- Research a topic of personal interest (your heritage, a medical issue, a community situation, and so on).
- Write a thesis statement for a report on your topic.

The Way It Works — Analysis of a Process

- Explain a process (remove a splinter, change the oil in a vehicle, make an omelet).
- Name the steps from beginning to end.
- Design a storyboard that illustrates the process so that you can picture each step you would need to write about in an analysis.

Apples and Oranges — Essay of Comparison

- People say you shouldn't compare apples to oranges. That may be true for very different ideas, actions, or objects, but you can actually compare apples to oranges.
- Draw a Venn diagram showing the two fruits' similarities and differences.

Classified Information — Essay of Classification

- Think about how you spent your time last summer. Order your activities into five classifications (for example, work, entertainment, and so on).
- Under each heading, estimate what percentage of your time a category represents.
- Draw a bar graph based on the information. This graphic could serve as the basis for an essay of classification on the subject.

Beyond Dictionary Meaning — Essay of Definition

- Choose a word often used as slang, such as "cool," "ripped," or "bad."
- Consider how the slang word differs from its traditional usage.
- Then freewrite for an essay of definition about that word.

Cause or Effect? — Cause-Effect Essay

- Choose a local situation involving water pollution, if possible; otherwise, outline a hypothetical situation.
- Then make a T-chart showing the causes and the effects of water pollution.

One Solution to the Problem

Problem-Solution Essay

- Identify a problem in your life, your school, or your community that needs to be resolved.
- List reasons for the problem.
- Write a thesis statement in which you offer one workable solution to the problem.

Restaurant Review

Essay of Evaluation

- Review the forms of adjectives on page 575 in the "Proofreader's Guide."
- Write for 5 to 10 minutes about your best or worst dining experience.
- Exchange papers with a classmate and circle examples of superlative adjectives in each other's work.

From My Perspective

Personal Commentary

- Focus on a social issue (friendship, popularity, kindness).
- Freewrite about your topic.
- Then, based on your freewriting, write a personal anecdote that could serve as an opening to an essay on your topic.

That's Debatable

Essay of Argumentation

- Brainstorm a list of current debate topics at your school.
- List your reasons for and against the issues in two columns.
- Respond to these two questions: *What exactly is the position I wish to promote and support? How strongly do I feel about it?*
- Choose the topic about which you have the strongest feelings and the most facts to support your position.
- Write an informed statement for your position. (See page 244 in *Write for College.*)

Standing Strong

Position Paper

- Take a stand on an issue you feel strongly about or on the question "Should students be allowed to graduate from high school in three years?"
- Consider how you would, or would not, support your stand.
- Develop a body paragraph (your most or least compelling reason) for a position paper on your topic.

Touched by Words

Personal Response

- Choose a classic play you have read *(Hamlet, Cherry Orchard).*
- Explain how you identify with a character in the play.
- Write an opening paragraph for a personal response based on your insights. Be sure to include a strong thesis statement.

A Book Review — Writing a Book Review

- List some of your favorite books or current books you have read.
- Think of a common element that two of the books share (for example, they describe events that lead to a tragic outcome or talk about how the main character must decide whether a best friend is a true friend).
- Create an outline for an essay comparing the common elements of the two works.

Never judge a book by its movie. — Writing a Limited Literary Analysis

- Pretend you are a famous writer whose book (adventure, romance, science fiction, mystery, historical fiction, and so on) has recently been made into a movie.
- Choose an event, a character, or a setting from "your" book that would be portrayed differently on-screen.
- Write a short analysis for your audience that explains the change.

It all comes down to . . . — Writing an Extended Literary Analysis

- Select a poem or read "Sonnet 18" on page 406 in *Write for College.*
- Try to describe in one word (action, hope, fear) what element drives the poem.
- Write a brief analysis explaining what the poem means in light of that element.

Under the Microscope — Writing an Extended Literary Analysis

- Consider two fables, two classic children's stories, or two tall tales ("Fox and Grapes," "Dog and Bone"/ "Goldilocks and the Three Bears," "Jack and the Bean Stalk"/ "Paul Bunyan," "Pecos Bill").
- Select two characters, events, settings, or other aspects of the stories that could be compared in an extended literary analysis.
- Establish a thesis and have fun developing an in-depth literary analysis.

The World's Greatest Job — Business Writing

- Read the sample letter of application on page 305 in *Write for College.*
- Suppose there is an opening for the position of substitute teacher for your class.
- Suppose all the others in your class are applying for the job.
- Write a letter of application so convincing that you are certain to get the job.

Class Kudos — Special Forms of Workplace Writing

- Read the guidelines and the sample e-mail message on pages 314–315 in *Write for College.*
- Write a short e-mail message to your teacher that explains what you like about the class.
- Check your writing for correctness before sending it.
- Wait for a reply.

The Research Center

Stellar Minds
Writing the Research Paper

- Study "Prewriting: Selecting a Topic" on pages 22–24 in *Write for College.*
- Choose one of these famous astronomers:

Ptolemy	**Copernicus**	**Galileo**
Isaac Newton	**Tycho Brahe**	**Johannes Kepler**
William Herschel	**Edmund Halley**	**Carl Sagan**

- Look up the astronomer you've chosen in an all-purpose encyclopedia or in an encyclopedia of astronomy.
- Note the following in the encyclopedia article, if they are available: an introductory outline, headlines, illustrations, questions for discussion, topics for cross-reference, a bibliography for further reading.
- Write down a good question about your topic that you would like to explore.

Card Games
Writing the Research Paper

- Read "Prewriting: Searching for Information" on pages 322–323 of *Write for College*; pay attention to "Taking Notes."
- Read a featured essay at the end of a recent issue of *Time* or *Newsweek.*
- On one note card, paraphrase the paragraph that best reveals the thesis of the essay.
- On another card, quote directly the most memorable sentence in the essay.
- On a third card, comment personally in response to what you've read.

One Strike, You're Out
Writing Responsibly

- Read the comments on the meaning of plagiarism on pages 328–329 in *Write for College.*
- Suppose you were in a debate on the topic "Resolved: Students who plagiarize on a paper should automatically fail the unit."
- Take one side or the other (pro or con) in the debate and write a paragraph, trying to persuade the other side of your view.
- Add one fact from a published source that is not common knowledge about the side you have chosen to support.

In Your Own Words
Writing Responsibly

- Read the guidelines for writing paraphrases on pages 330–331 in *Write for College.*
- Choose a short speech or document that was created in the 1700s or 1800s. (Possible authors include Susan B. Anthony, Frederick Douglass, Patrick Henry, Abraham Lincoln, and Tecumseh.)
- Write a paraphrase of the whole (or part of the) speech or document. Write one full page.
- Cite the source.

And I Quote — Writing Responsibly

- Read about "Writing Paraphrases" on pages 330–331 in *Write for College*.
- Find a short article in a magazine about a topic you are studying in science or history.
- Write a short paraphrase of the article, include a quotation from the article, and be sure to cite the source.

Amusing Ourselves to Death — Writing Responsibly

- Read "Using Quoted Material" on page 332 in *Write for College*.
- Read the following passage until you understand it:

> **Whereas television taught the magazines [like *People* and *US*] that news is nothing but entertainment, the magazines have taught television that nothing but entertainment is news. Television programs, such as *Entertainment Tonight*, turn information about entertainers and celebrities into "serious" cultural content, so that the circle begins to close: Both the form and content of news become entertainment.**
>
> (Neil Postman, *Amusing Ourselves to Death*, 112)

- Rewrite the passage using ellipses (. . .) to reduce it to less than half of its original length so that only the essential ideas remain. (In shortening the passage, do not distort its meaning.)

Laurel, According to Hardy — Documentation Styles

- Study the section "Model In-text Citations" on pages 334–337 in *Write for College*. (Focus on the instructions for "A Work Referred to in Another Work" on page 336.)
- Read this information: The artist Paul Klee told his students once that "art is exactitude winged by intuition." William Zinsser quotes Klee's comment on page 55 of his book *Writing to Learn*. Zinsser says he likes Klee's comment as a definition of good writing.
- Write a sentence about Zinsser in which you quote Klee's words, and cite them parenthetically as a quotation from an indirect source.

From the Horse's Mouth — Using the Internet

- Read about primary and secondary sources on page 394 in *Write for College*.
- List some pros and cons of primary and secondary sources. (What advantages and disadvantages does each kind of source have?) How are these types of sources affected by the Internet?
- If possible, compare your lists with those made by classmates.

Speaking Out — Using the Internet

- Do this minilesson with a partner.
- Choose a topic that students are talking about—movies, sports, fashion, music videos—or any other issue that interests you.
- Create a survey designed to gather facts and opinions about the issue. Use a blog to generate responses.

Says Who? — Using the Internet

- Do this minilesson in a small group.
- Talk about exactly how you would evaluate information using the eight questions on pages 394–395 in *Write for College*. For example, how would you find out if the information was current? Where in the information source would you look for clues? What questions would you ask yourself?
- Discuss six of the questions in this way.
- Take notes on good ideas you can use in the future.

Grammar, Dahling — Using the Library

- Read about the dictionary on page 390 in *Write for College*. Reread the paragraph on "Etymology."
- Look up the etymology of the word *grammar* in a dictionary.
- Look up the etymology of the word *glamour*.
- Write a paragraph in answer to the question, "What do *grammar* and *glamour* have in common?"

Mochaloco — Using the Library

- Study the information about using a dictionary on pages 390–391 in *Write for College*.
- Use your imagination to think up a new beverage—a coffee concoction, a fruit or vegetable juice blend, and so on.
- Make up a name for your beverage.
- Write a dictionary entry for your creation, including all the types of information listed on page 391.
- Share your entry with classmates.

Croak/Cash In/Kick the Bucket — Using the Library

- Read about the thesaurus on page 389 in *Write for College*.
- Choose one of the following pairs of words: *live, die/give, take/build, destroy.*
- Look up both words in a thesaurus and study the words listed under each.
- Write a paragraph explaining the differences you notice between the positive vocabulary words and the negative ones.

The Tools of Learning

SQ3R — Critical Reading

- Read about PQ4R on pages 403–405 in *Write for College.*
- List three pluses for this reading strategy.
- List one potential drawback.
- Discuss PQ4R with your classmates, using your lists as a guide.

In the News — Critical Listening and Note Taking

- Review "Critical Listening and Note Taking" on pages 410–420 in *Write for College.*
- Have a partner read a short news story from a newspaper.
- Listen carefully and write down the *who, when, where, what, why,* and *how* of the story.
- If you don't get them all the first time, ask your partner to read the story again.
- Trade roles; have your partner listen while you read.

Fact Check — Critical Listening and Note Taking

- Review the handbook chapter on listening and note-taking skills (pages 410–420).
- Use the sample essays in your handbook's section "Persuasive Essays" to help you practice listening for fact and opinion.
- Have a partner read an essay while you listen and jot down facts and opinions you hear.
- Then review your notes with your partner to see how you did. Did you note all the important facts and opinions? Did you classify facts and opinions correctly?
- Trade roles so that your partner can practice listening.

yr spcl dctnry — Critical Listening and Note Taking

- Study the guide to creating a shorthand system on page 418 in *Write for College.*
- Start your own shorthand dictionary, either an all-inclusive one or separate shorthand glossaries for each subject.
- Use a loose-leaf notebook and begin with one page for each letter.
- Think about terms that come up often in topics you are studying.
- Write down each term and your special shorthand for it.

Captain's Log — Writing to Learn

- Read the information about learning logs on pages 422–423 in *Write for College.*
- Write a learning-log entry for a topic you are currently studying in one of your classes.

Dramatic Scenarios

Writing to Learn

- Explain "Dramatic Scenarios" on page 138 in this guide to the class.
- Choose a class that interests you.
- Choose a famous person in that field (Mozart, Einstein, Napoleon, Plato, and so on).
- Read about that person in an encyclopedia, a book, or a trustworthy online source.
- Choose an important moment in that person's life.
- Imagine and then write this person's thoughts at that crucial moment.

Why? Why? Why?

Writing to Learn

- Write a sentence stating what you think would be an ideal summer job.
- On the next line, write the word *Why?*
- On the next line, answer the question *Why?* in a complete sentence.
- On the next line, write *Why?* again and answer in a complete sentence.
- Keep on going this way until you can't write anymore.
- Or . . . if the summer job question leads nowhere, try this one: State what you would buy first if you won the lottery tomorrow.

Medical Terminology 101

Building a College-Sized Vocabulary

- Medical terms sound big and impressive, but they are fairly easy to learn since they're built from a relatively small number of prefixes, suffixes, and roots.
- Below is a list of frequently used suffixes. With a partner or small group, brainstorm and list medical terms you have heard that end with these suffixes.

-ectomy (removal)	**-oma (tumor)**	**-plasty (reconstruction)**
-emia (blood)	**-osis (condition, disease)**	**-scopy (visual examination)**
-itis (inflammation)	**-otomy (incision of)**	

- Write down what you think each word means.
- Look up the words in a dictionary to check their spellings and meanings.

Getting to the Root

Building a College-Sized Vocabulary

- Turn to the lists of prefixes, suffixes, and roots on pages 435–444 in *Write for College*.
- Write a reasonable-sounding one-sentence definition for each of the following make-believe words, after consulting the handbook lists.

amphidictive	**micromorphosteroid**	**similcalorizoic**
perfractacardiology	**retrojectophobia**	**philidiocapticule**

- Put together your own words and challenge the class to write a definition for each.

Vocabulary Pro — Building a College-Sized Vocabulary

- Turn to the lists of prefixes, suffixes, and roots on pages 435–444 in *Write for College*.
- List the following words on a piece of paper. Skip a line between each word.

  contradict   defect   postscript   recede   neologism

- Draw a line between the word parts in each word.
- Write a definition using the lists of prefixes, suffixes, and roots as your guide.
- Check your work using a dictionary.

Being Narrow Minded — Speaking Effectively

- Write down a general subject that interests you.
- Narrow the subject three times in three ways to focus on a specific topic for (1) an informative speech, (2) a persuasive speech, and (3) a demonstration speech.

Oh, Captain, My Captain — Speaking Effectively

- In the chapter "Speaking Effectively," turn to the box presenting symbols for marking interpretation on page 450.
- Suppose you are expected to read a report you have written.
- Mark the text with appropriate symbols for an expressive reading.
- Read the report to a partner in class, following your own markings for expression.
- Discuss your reading with your partner and revise your markings accordingly.

Speaking Up — Speaking Effectively

- Study the chapter on speaking effectively on pages 445–458 in *Write for College*.
- Choose one of the writing samples in your handbook that you think would make a good speech.
- Write a paragraph telling why this piece lends itself to spoken presentation. Also list what visual aids you would add to make this a strong speech.

More Power! — Multimedia Reports

- Read Albert Einstein's quotation, "Computers are incredibly fast, accurate, and stupid; humans are incredibly slow, inaccurate and brilliant; together they are powerful beyond imagination."
- Write a paragraph explaining how this quotation applies to the writing you do in school. In what ways are you and a computer a more powerful writing force than you alone?

The Testing Center

Ready, Set, Go! — Writing On Demand

- Study the material on pages 489–494 in *Write for College.*
- Read the sample essay on page 486.
- Use the STRAP to analyze the essay.
- Write a response essay.
- How long did it take you?

Exploring the Unknown — Answering Document-Based Questions

- Read the February 4, 1805, entries in the Lewis and Clark journals. lewisandclarkjournals.unl.edu/index.html
- Study the map of the exploration and note the location of Mandan, North Dakota. www.nationalgeographic.com/lewisandclark (Go to journey log number 5.)
- Examine the photo of a Mandan earthen lodge covered in snow, found on the interactive journey number 5, image 7 on the National Geographic Web site.
- Look at the collage that leads the section called "The Corps." www.lewis-clark.org
- Choose one of the following questions and write an opening paragraph for an essay. Be sure to include a thesis statement.
  1. What would the crew of the Lewis and Clark Expedition have to do to survive a winter in North Dakota?
  2. How important would cooperation be on a journey such as this? Explain.
  3. What key items would be needed for the journey?

Key Questions — Taking Entrance Exams

- Do this minilesson with a partner. Together, read the key words and sample essay-test questions on pages 467 and 472 in *Write for College*.
- For each key word, write another sample question based on information you are studying in your classes.
- Then rephrase each question as a topic sentence.

Testing Yourself — Taking Advanced Placement* Exams

- Turn to the chapter "Taking Advanced Placement* Exams" on pages 495–507 in *Write for College*. Focus especially on the information related to essay tests.
- Find an interesting paragraph in one of your textbooks (other than English).
- Read over the paragraph several times.
- Write an essay-test question to which the paragraph you chose would be an excellent answer.

Proofreader's Guide

If You Had to . . . — Punctuation Review

- Scan the rules for commas, semicolons, and quotation marks on pages 511–516 and 523 in the "Proofreader's Guide."
- Try to punctuate the following sentence so that it makes perfect sense, using two commas, one semicolon, and three sets of quotation marks:
- John where Jim had used just had had used had had had had had had the teacher's approval.
  (See page 224 in this guide for the answer.)

Test Case — Capitalization Review

- Review the rules for capitalization on pages 529–531 in the "Proofreader's Guide."
- Work with a partner and choose a topic you have just studied in science class.
- Write a paragraph, using a variety of words that should be capitalized; lowercase these words as a test for your partner.
- Exchange paragraphs and correct each other's work.

Right Word Rap — Using the Right Word Review

- Review "Using the Right Word" on pages 551–560 in the "Proofreader's Guide."
- Create a memory strategy or technique to help you remember how to use one or more of the commonly mixed pairs of words listed in this section.
- Share your strategies with a classmate.

Ladders of Concrete — Nouns

- Some nouns are general, some are more specific, and some are highly specific. You can form a "ladder of specificity" by putting words in increasing order of concreteness. For example, mammal—biped—human—male—scientist—Bill Nye.
- Build "ladders of specificity" starting from these general terms:

  machine **motion** **group** **material**

- Write a short paragraph using mostly words from the general end of the "ladder."
- Write the same paragraph, replacing the general words with your specific ones.

Above and Beyond — Prepositions

- Read about prepositions on page 577 in the "Proofreader's Guide."
- Write about the antics of a fast-moving, very persistent fly at a picnic. Keep writing until you have used at least 20 different prepositions.
- Then exchange your writing with a partner, and underline all the prepositions you find.

Language Review — Parts of Speech Review

- Find the "Parts of Speech Quick Guide" on page 579 in the "Proofreader's Guide."
- Write these words (the parts of speech) across the top of a piece of paper.
- Then record your favorite sentence from anywhere in *Write for College.*
- Identify how each word is used in the sentence. (Is the first word a noun?)
- Exchange your sentence with a writing partner and check each other's work.

In Praise of the Phrase — Gerund, Infinitive, and Participial Phrases

- Study the definitions of *gerund, infinitive,* and *participle* on page 569 in the "Proofreader's Guide" and the information about these verbal phrases on page 582.
- Read the following short sentences:

  1. I study a map. **2.** We take a vacation.
- Convert each short sentence into first, a gerund phrase; second, an infinitive phrase; and third, a participial phrase.
- Then write a complete sentence for each phrase you have made. (See page 224 in this guide for the answer.)

Adding This to That — Verbs, Direct and Indirect Objects

- Learn about transitive verbs, direct objects, and indirect objects on pages 567–568 in the "Proofreader's Guide."
- Make up five weird sentences using your own combinations from the following lists:

Verbs	Indirect Objects	Direct Objects
passed	beetle	microphone
gave	kazoo	pizza
sent	hockey stick	note
awarded	mirror	sardine

Advanced Language Review — Parts of Speech

- Write an example of each term below in a short paragraph. Try it without checking the handbook.
- Then exchange papers with a classmate and label each example you find.
- Check your work using the "Parts of Speech" section beginning on page 561 of *Write for College.*

abstract noun	**infinitive**	**participle**
gerund	**intransitive verb**	**pronoun and its antecedent**

Additional Resources

These sources offer helpful information on the following topics.

Assessment

Anderson, Carl. *Assessing Writers.* Portsmouth, NH: Heinemann, 2005.

Black, Laurel, Donald Daiker, Jeffrey Sommers, and Gail Stygall, eds. *New Directions in Portfolio Assessment: Reflective Practice, Critical Theory and Large Scale Scoring.* Portsmouth, NH: Boynton/Cook, 1994.

Elbow, Peter. "Ranking, Evaluating, and Linking: Sorting Out Three Forms of Judgment." *College English* 55 (1993): 187–206.

Gere, Anne Ruggles, Leila Christenbury, and Kelly Sassi. *Writing on Demand.* Portsmouth, NH: Heinemann, 2005

Hillocks, George, Jr. *The Testing Trap: How State Writing Assessments Control Learning.* New York: Teachers College Press, 2002.

Marzano, R. J. *Transforming Classroom Grading.* ASCD, 2000.

White, Edward. *Teaching and Assessing Writing.* 2nd ed. Portland, ME: Calendar Island Publishers, 1998.

Wiggins, Grant. *Assessing Student Performance: Exploring the Purpose and Limits of Testing.* San Francisco: Jossey-Bass, 1993.

Creative Writing

Eco, Umberto. *Six Walks in the Fictional Woods.* Cambridge, MA: Harvard, 1994.

Lynn, Steven. *Texts and Contexts: Writing About Literature with Critical Theory.* 3rd ed. New York: Longman, 2001.

Wallace, Robert. *Writing Poems.* 5th ed. New York: Longman, 2000.

Welty, Eudora. *One Writer's Beginnings.* Cambridge, MA: Harvard, 1984.

Grammar and Style

Flood, James, et al., eds. *Handbook of Research on Teaching the English Language Arts.* 2nd ed. Mahwah, NJ: L. Erlbaum Associates, 2003.

Hickey, Dona J. *Developing a Written Voice.* Palo Alto, CA: Mayfield, 1993.

Noguchi, Rei R. *Grammar and the Teaching of Writing: Limits and Possibilities.* Urbana, IL: NCTE, 1991.

Williams, Joseph M. *Style: Ten Lessons in Clarity and Grace.* New York: HarperCollins, 1994.

Pedagogical Strategies

Ballenger, Bruce. *The Curious Researcher: A Guide to Writing Research Papers.* 5th ed. Pearson/Longman, 2006.

Burke, Jim. *Writing Reminders.* Portsmouth, NH: Heinemann, 2003.

Duffy, Donna Killian, and Janet Wright Jones. *Teaching Within the Rhythms of the Semester.* San Francisco: Jossey-Bass, 1995.

Elbow, Peter. *Writing Without Teachers.* 2nd ed. Oxford University Press, Inc., 1998.

Jones, Elizabeth A. *Goals Inventories: Writing, Speech Communication, and Critical Thinking.* University Park, PA: National Center for Postsecondary Teaching, Learning, and Assessment, 1994.

Kadel, Stephanie, and Julia A. Keechner. *Collaborative Learning: A Sourcebook for Higher Education.* Vol. 2. University Park, PA: National Center for Postsecondary Teaching, Learning, and Assessment, 1994.

Kirby, Dan, Dawn Lattakirby, and Tom Liner. *Inside Out.* 3rd ed. Portsmouth, NH: Heinemann, 2004.

Meyers, Chet, and Thomas B. Jones. *Promoting Active Learning: Strategies for the College Classroom.* San Francisco: Jossey-Bass, 1993.

Writing Across the Curriculum

Fulwiler, Toby, and Art Young, eds. *Programs That Work.* Portsmouth, NH: Heinemann/Boynton/Cook, 1990.

Howard, Rebecca, and Sandra Jamieson. *The Bedford Guide to Teaching Writing in the Disciplines.* Boston, MA: Bedford Books, 1995.

McLeod, Susan, ed. *Strengthening Programs in Writing Across the Curriculum.* San Francisco: Jossey-Bass, 1988. (Available online)

Thaiss, Christopher. *The Harcourt Brace Guide to Writing Across the Curriculum.* New York: Harcourt Brace, 1997.

Walvoord, Barbara, et al., eds. *In the Long Run: A Study of Faculty in Three WAC Programs.* Urbana, IL: NCTE, 1997.

Professional Bibliography

We recommend the following titles for teachers.

Active Voice: A Writing Program Across the Curriculum
James Moffett

Activities for an Interactive Classroom
Jeffrey N. Golub

Authentic Assessment for English Language Learners: Practical Approaches for Teachers
J. Michael O'Malley and Lorraine Valdez Pierce

Blending Genre, Altering Style: Writing Multigenre Papers
Tom Romano

Classroom Instruction that Works: Research-Based Strategies for Increasing Student Achievement
R. J. Marzano, D. J. Pickering, and J. E. Pollock

Creating Writers Through 6-Trait Writing Assessment and Instruction, 4th Edition
Vicki Spandel

Developing Minds: A Resource Book for Teaching Thinking (3rd Edition)
Arthur L. Costa, editor

A Fresh Look at Writing
Donald H. Graves

Grammar Alive!
Brock Haussamen

Grammar and the Teaching of Writing: Limits and Possibilities
Rei R. Noguchi

Great Films and How to Teach Them
William V. Costanzo

Inside Writing: How to Teach the Details of Craft
Penny Kittle and Donald H. Graves

Investigate Nonfiction
Donald Graves

Learning by Teaching
Donald Murray

Mind Matters: Teaching for Thinking
Dan Kirby and Carol Kuykendall

New Literacies in Action: Teaching and Learning in Multiple Media
William Kist

The Online Classroom
Eileen Cotton

On Writing Well, 25th Anniversary: The Classic Guide to Writing Nonfiction
William Zinsser

Reading Without Nonsense
Frank Smith

School Smarts: The Four Cs of Academic Success
Jim Burke

Student-Centered Classroom Assessment
Richard J. Stiggins

Teaching the Argument in Writing
Richard Fulkerson

Teaching Grammar in Context
Constance Weaver

When Learners Evaluate
Jane Hansen

Writing Reminders
Jim Burke

Writing to Be Read
Ken Macrorie

Writing to Learn
William Zinsser

Writing with Power: Techniques for Mastering the Writing Process
Peter Elbow

Index